THE FARM

THE FARM

Growing up in Abilene, Kansas, in the 1940s and 1950s

Mark J. Curran

Order this book online at www.trafford.com
or email orders@trafford.com

Most Trafford titles are also available at major online book retailers.

© Copyright 2010 Mark J. Curran.

All rights reserved. No part of this publication may be reproduced, stored in a retrieval system,
or transmitted, in any form or by any means, electronic, mechanical, photocopying, recording,
or otherwise, without the written prior permission of the author.

The views expressed in this work are solely those of the author and do not necessarily
reflect the views of the publisher, and the publisher hereby disclaims any responsibility for them.

Printed in the United States of America.

ISBN: 978-1-4269-4557-1 (sc)
ISBN: 978-1-4269-4558-8 (e)

Library of Congress Control Number: 2010914866

*Our mission is to efficiently provide the world's finest, most comprehensive book publishing
service, enabling every author to experience success. To find out how to publish your book,
your way, and have it available worldwide, visit us online at www.trafford.com*

Trafford rev. 10/12/2010

 www.trafford.com

North America & international
toll-free: 1 888 232 4444 (USA & Canada)
phone: 250 383 6864 ♦ fax: 812 355 4082

For those that lived on the farm,

Dad--Joseph Cornelius Curran

Mom--Nellie Marie Curran

James Curran--my oldest brother

Jo Anne Curran (Whitehair)--my sister

Tom Curran--my other brother

For school friends from the Class of 1959

And, for anyone who may read this book and may have grown up on a family farm and had similar experiences

Table of Contents

PART ONE--"THE FARM"

1. The Original Introduction	1
2. Prologue To "The Farm"--"Memories From The Farm"	3
3. Neal And Nellie [Neal]	9
4. Nell	17
5. The Farm House	23
6. Modern Applicances In The Farm House	34
7. Food And How We Got It	36
8. Wheat Harvest And Fieldwork On The Farm	41
9. Chores	51
10. Accidents	55
11. Flowers And Birds	58
12. Pets On The Farm And 4-H Animals	60
13. 4-H Days	66
14. Cars And Memories	70
15. Dad, Horses And The Palominos	74
16. Fears For Mom And Dad	76
17. The Flood Of '51	78
18. Hard Times	80
19. The School Bus At The End Of The Farm Lane	88
20. Buddies, Sports And Games On The Farm	90
21. Mike Kippenberger And Sunday Afternoons	94
22. Games And Hunting	97
23. Pretend Games	102
24. Music And The Family	106
25. The Movies And Old Abilene	113
26. Radio And Early Television In The 1940s And 1950s	117
27. Growing Up Catholic	122
28. Staying In Touch With The Relatives	132
29 The Last Visits With Mom And Dad	136

PART TWO. SCHOOL DAYS AND GROWING UP IN ABILENE, KANSAS, IN THE 1940S AND 1950S

Preface — 147

I. GROWING UP: GRADE SCHOOL AT GARFIELD SCHOOL — 149

Kindergarten. 1946. Age 5. — 149
First Grade. 1947. Age 6. — 150
Second Grade. 1948. Age 7. — 150
Third Grade. 1949. Age 8. — 150
Fourth Grade. 1950. Age 9. — 152
Fifth Grade. 1951. Age 10. — 153
Sixth Grade. 1952. Age 11. — 157

II. ABILENE JUNIOR HIGH SCHOOL DAYS — 160

Seventh Grade. 1953. Age 12. — 160

    Sports And Other Times In Junior High — 161
    More Athletics And Junior High — 164

Eighth Grade. 1954. Age 13. — 164

    The County Tournament--Basketball — 165
    4-H Basketball — 165
    Christmas Time, All The Candy And Santa Claus! — 166
    The First Dance. — 166
    Summertime Baseball—Junior High Days — 167
    A Big Event At The Time—Ike For President! — 170
    About The Same Time, The Dickinson Country Free Fair And Rodeo — 170
    Other Events At The Rodeo Grounds — 171
    The Fair Alongside The Rodeo — 171

III. ABILENE PUBLIC HIGH SCHOOL 1955-1959 — 173

    High School Football. — 173
    High School Basketball. — 173
    Running Track In High School. — 176
    A Change In Direction — 177

A Moment Of The Times--Captain Video To Sputnik To Werner Von Braun And The Man On The Moon	179
Speech And Debate At Abilene High School	180
Music, Everett Smith And Seeds For The Future.	182
Boys' And Girls' State.	183
But I Digress; To Love, Laughter And Disappointment	184
Dating In High School–An Innocent And Perhaps Typical Story	184
Student Council And The Final Days	186
ABOUT THE AUTHOR	189

The book "The Farm" is not in the form of a novel nor is it necessarily chronological. Sections 1-29 however will follow the "memories" as recorded by the author. Part One is the essence of the narrative; Part Two is an addendum written years later to reflect the life of a schoolboy in Kansas in what I like to call the "Age of Innocence," that is, the 1940s and 1950s. Many readers will agree with me.

LIST OF ILLUSTRATIONS

THE FARM

1. Mark looking to the southwest, wheat field and grain elevator in the distance
2, Mark, the lane, latter days
3. The old farm house, west side, 1940s
4. Neal and Nellie, telling their story, the 1970s
5. Neal's family, 1918, he on the left
6. Dad in Merchant Marine uniform, 1918
7. Neal out west, the motorcycle trip, 1925
8. Combining wheat, eastern Washington
9. Granddad Kelley's new car, Mom
10. Mom and the sod house, eastern Colorado
11. The country school, Mom's class
12. Mom a young lady in Colorado, 1930s
13. Mom, the early days on the farm in Abilene
14. The old farm house from the front porch, 1940s
15. The farm house with new asbestos siding, Jo Anne's days
16. Mark looking to the southeast, alfalfa field, later days
17. Mark on the old Ford tractor
18. Mark inspecting a restored Ford tractor at county fair
19. Brother Jim and Ginger the dog who had a Catholic funeral
20. Mark in 4-H T-shirt leaning on the Chevy
21. Sheep in the barnyard on 4-H Project Day
22. Jo Anne, Mark and the old Buick on a snowy day
23. The old 1940s Plymouth, Chevy, Mark and the cat
24. Dad, Keah and the horse barn, 1970s
25. Mark and Tom on a happy day
26. Mom, Dad, Sarah and Joe Kippenberger playing cards in the old farm house
27. Tom and Mark's snowman
28. Mark in Elks' All-Star baseball uniform
29. St. Andrew's Catholic Church, Abilene
30. Tom's first communion
31. Dad and Mom in the house on Rogers St. in Abilene
32. Mom and large flower, the garden in Abilene
33. Mom, the Irises, the garden in Abilene

34. Dad, onions in the vegetable garden at the farm
35. Nell, Neal at the vegetable farm on he farm
36. Dad inspecting trees at the pond
37. Mark and a full pond, the 1970s
38. The final picture of the family at the farm
39. The final family picture, 1979

SCHOOL DAYS

40. Mark dressed for first day at school, age 5
41. Mark in new school clothes, later years
42. Mark, 6th grade class, Garfield, School, Mr. Horst
43. Team picture, 7th grade football
44. Team picture, 8th grade football
45. The 8th grade play: "Auggie Evans, Private Eye"
46. Team picture, 8th grade basketball
47. Team picture, freshman basketball
48. Mark, "Mercury," and others at Latin Banquet
49. Mark playing "Malagueña" at the Spanish Banquet
50. Mark at the podium, debate class at Abilene High School
51. State Champions in Debate, 1959
52. Boys and Girls State students, AHS, 1959
53. Mark's graduation picture, 1959
54. The class of 1959, 50th year reunion picture, 2009

1. THE ORIGINAL INTRODUCTION

I have thought for some time about beginning to write about growing up on the farm near Abilene, Kansas, but I must admit I am not totally comfortable with the idea. Both the reasons for writing and the form it should take need to be clarified. I have this feeling that my intentions could be mistaken, and that all this could be judged as the result of an inflated ego. That is really not the case. I have no illusions about the importance of my memories and feelings of growing up for others, particularly others than my immediate family or friends from those days. When it comes down to it, the main reason to write is to leave a record of a way of life I personally cherish and want to relive through the writing. It is a view of a way of life that I believe has value and which may, at least to some extent, be of a very small minority of people in this country (there were less than five million people on family farms in the United States in 1988). This is what I think now, after some 47 years on this planet and writing from another place.

I would very much like for these pages to be kept by our only daughter Katie as a memory and treasure from her Dad. I also believe that my sister Jo Anne and her family and my deceased brother Tom's first wife Valerie and their two children Kevin and Kyle would appreciate them, and their children after, if not now, later on. Although not a part of Keah's life prior to our marriage, the farm was an early memory of our marriage since we regularly visited Mom and Dad in Abilene and made forays out to the farm. So this is for her too.

If anyone else sees these pages, the account will probably be a curiosity piece for them. I have read works of literature based on biography or autobiography, thinking particularly about José Lins do Rego's "Menino de Engenho" ("Plantation Boy") from Northeast Brazil. Lins do Rego was successful in taking his childhood memories and "recreating them," thus creating fiction. I do not have the gift of fiction, nor do I aim to do anything so high and mighty. But down deep, I strongly believe that my childhood was unique in many ways, growing up in the wheat belt of central Kansas on a family farm with Catholic traditions and small town customs, and will become more unique as time goes on. So, for my daughter Katie, for my wife Keah, for my sister Jo Anne and her family, and other family members and friends I have mentioned, I hope these pages have meaning. For persons who did not know me, should you read them, enjoy yourselves, but note that this account is mainly a desire to remember the past and relive it.

2. PROLOGUE TO "THE FARM"--"MEMORIES FROM THE FARM"

This was the handwritten note at the top of the page:

"Dear Mom and Dad, I wrote this in 1971. I can think of no better time to give it to you than now."

The short essay "Memories from the Farm" was a Christmas present to my parents during a time when I didn't have much money to spend, but also when I thought this might mean more. I had no idea how much. Mom told me years later that as they read it in the house on Rogers Street in Abilene they both cried. It was to become the seed for "The Farm" which I started many years later, writing notes of memories as I sat in a Coleman tent on the acre in Colorado with a Smith-Corona Electric typewriter on an aluminum camp table, and a Coleman lantern hanging above me for light and warmth, and gradually writing the short "chapters" of "The Farm" over the years as I recalled and cherished the memories.

"MEMORIES FROM THE FARM" (THE ORIGINAL TEXT TO MOM AND DAD)

It's been fifteen or twenty years now, but wherever you begin, it's not going to happen again. It will never be the same for us. And I have a feeling it will never be the same for my people and my generation. So I write this not so much as to have it stand as a monument to those days, but to force myself to remember them, to cherish them. I think something beautiful has passed and I doubt if it will ever be the same again.

I remember you could go out the back door of the farmhouse, north across the yard and through the gate in the fence beside the chicken house, then through the windbreak which used to be empty ground and into the pasture. The grove of trees beyond the windbreak isn't there anymore, for that matter most of it is gone now. Things you don't figure will ever be gone. Then you realize what has happened. But they were funny trees, with funny bark. They had long black pods with smooth shiny seeds. We called it "the coffee bean tree." You went through the grove, and then there was only buffalo grass, thick, and it smelled good. Then you walked a quarter of a mile up the gradual slope to the bare spot on the low hill. You were tired by now and a little thirsty. So you sat down to rest and looked back ...

Mark, looking to the southwest, wheat field and grain elevator in the distance

It was to my mind the prettiest view in the entire valley, summer or winter. The people in town kept their airplanes up here on the hill during the '51 flood. The valley was almost totally covered with Smokey Hill muddy river water then. But now you could see the green fields, dark green alfalfa down by the highway, corn that hadn't tasseled out yet next to it, and in nearby fields, the wheat beginning to turn. You could hear the trucks coming along old U.S. Highway 40 almost before you saw them. Hear the hum of the tires. And you knew a lot of the cars that went by, farmers down the road, the M.D. everyone thought was uppity and not really a farmer, whose farm had the pretty white rail fence facing the road and thoroughbreds behind the fence. The farm across the highway was pretty, completely flat with good soil. Beyond it the railroad tracks. The trains that came through there! They caused more than one fire at harvest time that was before the diesels. You heard them at night, with a cool east-southeast breeze and the wail of that whistle. Good dreams.

To the southwest of the hill was the gradual slope in the pasture, then the farmhouse, farm buildings and barnyard, a bit south from that yet was the farm across the highway with the Leckron's dairy on it, beyond that the outline of the city hospital, and the good buddy's place and town. I used to cut across the fields on Sunday afternoons to the Kippenbergers for ball games and talk and home grown popcorn. Later on I rode a bike on the highway up the hill and by the hospital. You could make out the buildings on the edge of town pretty well, but most clear were the grain elevator and the alfalfa mill.

So the view was nice, as nice as any around in the central Kansas flatlands. But looking down that hill gave me the feeling you hear about, thinking this is mine. Even if it wasn't, it felt good to know my Daddy owned it. You could look down and see the windbreak with the cedars, walnut and other trees that were all planted from scratch and watered with carried buckets of water by my Dad. Along with them the low chicken house with the tin roof, the two-story granary to its right, then the silo and corral. Beyond the silo was the great old barn with the old-fashioned loft and all that goes with it. The water tank for the livestock and the hog house were on the other side of the barn. But the house was best, a two-story frame with an attic and basement. Asbestos on the sides when the hundred year old boards began to go, but with the great front porch where you could sit on a summer evening and watch the activity down the road and hear the trains coming.

At the top of the hill there were two lone trees and what we called the dump. That was where we took the unburnable trash, old fence wire, about anything we didn't need up ended up there. It made the best place for a rabbit to hide, and consequently we headed there first when hunting cottontails or jack rabbits. From the two trees, practically the only ones in the entire north 80 which was all pasture, you could see to the north, the county road marking the north end of the section and the 80. At least what used to be the north 80. In the late 1950s the government took twenty acres in the name of progress to build the interstate. It's a nice interstate, but the view, the farm and especially the water drainage down into our pasture and pond have never been the same since. It was great fun watching all the big earthmoving equipment, the caterpillars and graders when they were building it. And I learned a lot about eminent domain. And progress.

The east part of the north 80, the part being developed now by my restless seventy-seven year old Dad, was rough pasture. It used to have a good stand of brome and was baled more than once but now it has gone to weeds. That is where Dad is selling the lots, where he built the barn to board the horses for the kids in town, where he started another windbreak, where the kids from town park at night and dump their beer cans, where they open the gate and let the horses out in a cold January so a seventy-seven year old man and his wife and his son home from college can freeze their butts off chasing the horses back in during subzero weather. So they wouldn't get out on the interstate and be run over by a progressive truck.

But the best part, the part that's left, lies in between the east 80 and the top of the hill with the dump and rabbits. We call it the pond. It isn't really a pond since there isn't any water in it most of the time, not since the highway came through. But once it was the best of all possible ponds with huge umbrella shaped shade trees, many birds about, lots of water, enough for my Dad to stock some small bass and channel cats, and huge mosquitoes. But mainly it was trees. Trees planted by the hands of my father and watered by hand with buckets and barrels of water he brought one by one from the well about one hundred yards away. All kinds of trees, trees I don't even know the name of. But mainly black walnut trees. For walnut fudge of course, and to feed the squirrels.

The pond was a player for awhile in local history, especially when you hear about swimming, overnight camping out and later on some notorious beer blasts. I had the entire freshman football team out for a bon fire with hot dogs and a fair amount of Coors donated by my brother Jim from the pool hall. The pond was one of my favorite places to go. When I was a little guy, it was inhabited by Iriquois Indians and later on by other types of varmits and sidewinders. They didn't last long when challenged by the 22single-shot.

To the south of the pond, all the way back down to old Highway 40 was the plowed land where most of the work took place. I covered most of it myself on a little Ford tractor, not by my own will, but covered it just the same. I can remember what was planted where, how it did, how it was rotated, where the muddy spots were during the plowing, where the rocky spot up on the hill was. I had favorite fields, generally the ones near the highway so I could see friends go by on their way into town. I remember the planes and police the day of the great Enterprise bank robbery. More local history.

At the end of the circle I'm trying to make was the lane leading from the old highway up to the house, barnyard and corral. The lane had an alfalfa field on one side and another small field in brome grass to the west. My first excursions into that latter field are foggy notions of brome grass as tall as me, huge sunflowers in the corners and the small forest of trees down by the highway. Ronald Rice's huge Chevy sign, the farm jungle gym, was planted in that corner as though it were to produce in the spring. There were times when I went slashing through that jungle of sunflowers and weeds with my machete and the wilds of Africa and South America were part of Dickinson County.

Mark, the lane, latter days.

The lane was about one hundred yards long, give or take a few, straight and true all the way up to the house. I traveled it at least twice a day for nine months a year during the school year and once the rest of the year to get the paper and mail, all together for close to fifteen years. It had three trees; two of them were old and noble cottonwoods. You could always hear the leaves whir in the wind. The third was a dinky one, not worth much except to break the monotony of the walk. From the front porch of the old farmhouse you could see clearly all the way down the lane and the mailbox at the end of it. The paper came all the way from Kansas City; the mail, the school bus from the Abilene Public Schools and the Easter Bunny candy eggs in season provided the reasons for being of that road and my memories. Best of all about the lane was the walk on a cool summery evening. Birds along the way, beetles in the ruts (we blew them up with firecrackers on the 4th of July), gophers and the mounds along the alfalfa field on the right, and especially the view of the yard of the old house at its end.

The old farm house, west side, 1940s

The house completes the half section, a story in itself. From the plains came the rocks of its foundation and its look of permanence. I thought it would last forever. It didn't. Only the yellowed pictures and faded memories are left. Mostly my Mother and Dad's memories.

3. NEAL AND NELLIE [Neal]

Neal and Nellie telling their story, the 1970s

The following are notes taken from a conversation with Mom and Dad at our home in Tempe, Arizona, during the winter of 1977. When possible I'm quoting them, otherwise am paraphrasing what they said. They skipped around chronologically, and sometimes I might have not gotten the facts straight, but it's the best I could do two years later when writing this down. Dad's part is more anecdotal while Mom basically recalls growing up and life until they married. Both talk up to the period when they moved out to the farm in 1942. What later will become "The Farm" begins approximately in the mid to late 1940s. With Mom and Dad, Tom, and now Jim gone, only Jo Anne can pick up the early and mid 1940s. But my memories have to come second to these original anecdotes from Dad and Mom.

NEAL

"We lived on the north bank of the south fork of the Nemeha River (Southeast Nebraska). The house itself was thirty to forty feet from the river bank." Dad told of standing on the edge of the river bank and talking to a man across the river and that the very next day that portion of the bank had dropped in. He told of an old Quackenbush rifle which shot bullets with shot. Told of shooting rats at night in the kitchen!

He digressed to tell of my brother Tom who while very tiny sat in a box in the basement of the farm house that had a litter of puppies in it and got the fleas that the puppies were carrying.

Dad said he was eleven years old when his own dad died and when they moved down to Kansas. He told of growing up with an old yellow shepherd pup called "Don." He told of the kids taking the dog out and getting from five to ten rabbits at a time for eating. The method was for the kids to jump up and down on a brush pile and scare out the rabbits which the dog would then run down. The dog went with them on the trip to Kansas and eventually became deaf and blind and died at about eighteen or nineteen years of age.

Up home on the original homestead in Kansas, Uncle Bryan's place while Mark grew up there was a cistern with a wooden cover which was left open. The same dog jumped in and Dad pulled it out with a rope, the dog barking the whole time. A good watchdog, he said. It seems that Leda Tryell fell into the same cistern when she was a baby. Dad's sister Amy jumped in and pulled her out.

In Nebraska Dad's people lived on three separate farms. The school district was given land to support itself, and Dad's aunt who was a domestic owned some of this land. Dad's dad rented the place from her.

Dad was born in 1893. It was the spring of 1898 when they all moved to a second farm, this one north of Dawson, Nebraska. They lived there for two years. This farm was rented from a certain Mr. Ryan. In 2004 Keah and I visited the old Catholic cemetery at Dawson and there were many, many tombstones with the name Ryan on them. The entire cemetery seemed to be Irish. Later on they would move to the south fork of the Nemeha to a farm of one hundred and fifty acres.

They used horses to farm, Cleveland Bays, about 1300 pounds each. The mare was called "Grey Bird" and another called "Black Bird." They got twelve colts from Grey Bird and brought her to Kansas. Dad said he was eleven when they came to Kansas. They also had milk cows, a few hogs, chickens and raised wheat and corn. They had four work horses and always had colts each year. Each horse was worth from one hundred to one hundred and thirty dollars. The stallion was called "Charley," a deep bay.

Dad's sisters Maggie and Liddie and Dad were all born on the aunt's place up in Nebraska. Amy and Mark on the two-year farm in 1898. The landlord of the second farm, Mr. Ryan, had a drugstore in Dawson.

At that time the house was wood frame. Rural free delivery went in at about that time, coming out of Dawson. They had no phone, but there were a few in the county. About one of ten to fifteen families had a phone. When Dad's father died, Dad rode on horseback to a neighbor's house to call the doctor, this during a cold February. When the snowstorms were bad, you could walk over the fence rows.

They also had brood sows and turkeys. They generally had about fifty turkeys in the Fall. They would keep from eight to twelve hens and a gobbler. The hens would hide their nests from people, but in the fall the hen would come in with six to ten little ones. The turkeys would fly up into the trees and roost at night. There was a hay stack in a meadow, and they would drive the turkeys from the stack and they would then fly into the barnyard. Dad told how they would put feed in the granary, the turkeys would come in to eat, and they would shut the door and catch them. They had a grain wagon with a big box. They would put slats on it and haul the turkeys to town that way. They got eleven to fourteen cents a pound. Also sold chicken eggs in town, at three cents a dozen.

(Dad really got tickled here; he could hardly talk when he told this story.) There was a fat lady in the neighborhood who must have weighed about three hundred pounds, name was Lola. Had a sister named Maud who probably weighed about two hundred pounds. They came over and wanted to buy a turkey, and Dad's dad sold them a year-old gobbler that weighed twenty-six pounds. Lola had a horse and buggy. She sold picture frames and delivered them over the county. Somehow or other Dad's father was always trying to get Lola to tell how much she weighed or find it out. He got her to drive the buggy up on a scale, supposedly to weigh the turkey. She would never get up on the scale but would always walk around it. One time Lola came to see them and cracked a board on the front porch and fell through it and fainted. (Dad heehawed here.)

Dad's granddad smoked a pipe and had a white, bushy beard. Dad's dad was forty-three years old when he died of cancer of the stomach or ulcers. He was never a well man. They tried three times to build him up so they could operate on him. He left insurance money, and it was with that that Dad's mother bought the land in Kansas at Buckeye northeast of Abilene. She brought originally eighty acres with a small house for $2,800. Now in 1977 it's worth three hundred dollars per acre.

Mark J. Curran

Dad's family, 1918, he on the left.

The family moved down to Kansas in an immigrant car (a box car) loaded at Dawson, Nebraska, in the spring of 1906. "We took three horses, one cow and machinery, a binder and a plow." The people went to Sabetha where they got on a passenger train. "Mom had a food basket." They took the train from there to Marysville. There they got on a "hog train" to Manhattan, this train having one passenger car. There they changed to the Union Pacific to get as far as Detroit, Kansas, five miles east of Abilene. Uncle Bill (Dad's brother) met the train with five or six teams and wagons to haul the machinery out to the homestead. Dad and the family went up to the new farm in a spring wagon, a carriage without a top, pulled by two horses.

The old house on the farm at Buckeye had three rooms aside from the kitchen: one room upstairs where the women slept, one down where the men slept, and a dining room. They had a wood stove and burned hedge wood which had to be enclosed because it sparked. They used corn cobs for kindling to start the stove. It heated the dining room and kitchen. They slept on feather tick (goose down) with straw tick or clean corn husks under that. There were no mattresses. Dad recalled here that in his grandfather's house in Nebraska they would awaken with snow on the blankets in the morning, saying "You had to have bedclothes." Mom interjected here that she lived in a sod house when teaching in eastern Colorado.

Eight years later, with the money from milk cows, they bought the eighty acres south of them. They had had six head of red shorthorns to start out. They had hogs, a couple of sows. Generally had calves to sell. They would bucket feed them and in the Fall they would weigh from four hundred to five hundred pounds and would sell for sixty to seventy dollars apiece.

The new eighty-acres were bought for about $3,000. They borrowed money from the bank to do it. "Uncle Bill bought a third eighty next to the second." They raised horses, as many as thirty head at a time. Had two six-horse teams. Rented the quarter of land across the road to the east, this in 1913. Now there was a total of four 80s in all. In 1918 when World War I broke out, they had three six-horse teams. The boys worked for shares, not wages. At this time Bryan, another of Dad's brothers, bought the first mules for the farm; they were tougher and worked better than the horses. Back in 1917 Dad had started to do some farming for himself, thirty acres of corn.

Dad in Merchant Marine uniform, 1918

After returning from the service, the Merchant Marine, in 1919 (Dad used to tell stories of sleeping in hammocks in the ship, of a time when he was up in the crow's nest and during a storm it was almost horizontal to the water), Dad and others helped build a new house on the original eighty, the one that we all knew as Bryan and Marie's while growing up in the 1940s and 1950s. Dad moved at this time and rented the Roupe place (Gefeller's now, a farm about one mile east of the one I grew up on, located a few miles south of the old homestead on old Highway 40) and lived on it until 1925. This is the place next to Ward Barber's as we grew up.

Neal out west, the motorcycle trip, 925

1925 AND THE MOTORCYCLE TRIP OUT WEST. This is the story Dad would tell so often, and Mom would just get up and go into the other room because she had heard it so often and knew it by memory by now. Dad picked fruit, helped a truck farmer outside of Denver, worked at a huge dairy in Oregon and drove a huge team, 36 horses if I am not mistaken, combining wheat in eastern Washington State. As he told these stories, they came to take on an epic tone, and you could tell he loved the freedom of it all, the adventure of being "on the road" in the twenties. But there seemed to be more and more milk cows milked each morning, more and more horses on the combine team as he told and retold, and I listened to the stories. Keah heard some of them herself when we visited Mom and Dad on Rogers street in the early 1970s.

Combining wheat, eastern Washington

On the 1925 trip there were no paved roads at all. Somewhere, lost now, I have seen pictures of Dad in a spiffy Irish-type hat, and high laced leather boots, well polished, at about this time. In the Fall of 1926 Dad arrived back home at the home place. His brothers Bryan and Leo had both married and were gone, so Dad ran the farm, the original home place. It consisted of five eighties. They raised some cattle, had Holsteins for milking and sold the calves. They bought Holstein bull calves from the orphanage herd and heifer calves at sales. By 1934, the depression years, they had some 75 to 80 head. They kept 22 calves or yearlings. In 1933 they had hogs, sold about 65 head of fat hogs twice a year. They were sold in Kansas City for $2.85 a hundred, about three cents a pound. (As I wrote this in 1975, hogs were selling at 65 dollars a hundred pounds.) Dad said they would raise a hog, sell it, and buy a cow. They sold cattle in 1935 for about $275 a head.

In May, 1935, when Dad married Mom (a bit of that story is told by Mom later), he bought the cream station on the south side of Abilene. He did not want to live with his mother on the farm, so he bought the cream station from his brother Leo. Dad's brother Bryan had moved back to the original farm at Buckeye at that time and lived with their mom, my grandma. I can barely remember her, so maybe my image of her comes just from the picture of her, a very heavy farm lady. Dad bought five acres of ground in northeast Abilene, just on the edge of the city limits (this is all being developed for housing in the1970s). The earliest pictures of Mark are from the yard of that house when I was a tiny baby, curly hair and being held by brother Jim. The cream station prospered.

In 1942, Mom's brother, Leo Cusick, was discouraged with farming and wanted to move to Chapman or Herington, small, relatively near-by farm towns. The farm belonged to Minnie Kelly, Mom's mom; Kelly being her second marriage, the first was to Cusick, and Mom's brother Leo. They had inherited it from Mr.Kelly in 1930.

Dad kept the creamery until 1944 or 1945. There is an old photo showing me in bib overalls coming out of the screened door of the creamery, crying, and brother Tom is outside with a smirk on his face. I can't remember what Tom did, but I was mad! Dad said the creamery made him $300 a month clear in those days, a respectable income at the time. But federal programs were initiated and with the price of grain and feed up, the price of eggs and cream went down, so the farmers stopped raising so many chickens and dairy cattle. (I don't understand the logic of this today, but it was one of Dad's favorite themes: the government's sticking its nose into something working well and lousing it up. Another was the "millers." They were the root of all evil.)

For the days on the farm from 1941-1959 see the rest of "The Farm.

Dad sold the farm in 1962. He had paid $22,000 for a half-section back in 1942 and sold 240 acres for $54,000 in 1962. The federal highway had taken 20 acres for $125 dollars per acre a few years earlier, some $3000. Dad said that the price at the time was unjust, too low, since on either side of him the government had paid $150, but it was not worth it to fight it since it could have taken three to four years in the courts. He would have lost the use of the money and the pasture during that time.

This was the end of Dad's reminiscing that day. As I look at it now I have regrets that I did not get him to tell more. I heard stories of the 1925 trip several times myself, more frequently as Dad grew older and reminisced during visits to Arizona in the winters during the 1970s, this when I was older, more mature and more interested in all this. I also recall the stories about the time in the merchant marine told out in Arizona and also in Abilene. I regret we do not have those stories on tape or more facts about them, but I am glad we have the little we do now, results of just one afternoon when I put a tape recorder in the living room and cajoled Dad into talking.

4. NELL

Mom was born in Solomon, Kansas, in 1900, on a farm one mile west and south of town. The farm had 160 acres. Her parents were Michael Cusick and Minnie Enright. Michael had been married before, thus Mom had two half-brothers, Leo and Bill. Her father Michael died of typhoid fever in 1905, so her Mom, Minnie Cusick, and her two boys, Mom's half brothers, farmed the land.

A certain John Kelly lived just up the road, and Minnie eventually married him, her second marriage, in November of 1908. They then bought a farm near Kipp, Kansas, fifteen miles southwest of Solomon. I saw that farmhouse with Mom and Dad while on a drive, some years back. John and Minnie had no honeymoon trip. Mom remembered spending that time, John and Minnie's honeymoon, at the Enright house in Solomon. Her uncle John Enright lived there at the time.

Mom went to school in Kipp, Kansas, a one-room country school. They lived by a creek and always went ice skating in the winter. They rode to school in the "hack," a wagon with seats and a canvas covering so you could roll it up in nice weather. Mom's chores were to sweep the floor in the house and help clean it on Saturdays. She liked to be outside. Another chore was to pick up corncobs and hedge wood for the fire.

She went to school in Kipp until a sophomore in high school, then to Sacred Heart Academy in Salina, Kansas. She boarded in Salina from Monday to Friday and rode the train from Salina to Kipp on weekends, a 22 cent fare. She would go to the movies once or twice a week in Salina for ten to fifteen cents. She stayed with the Sullivans in their boarding house. They were "misers" and gave her principally oatmeal and coffee for food. They tried to make her eat the oatmeal with coffee instead of milk. She did not get enough to eat. A new boarder came in that year, and Mom moved with her and her daughter to a different boarding house, but now with plenty to eat. She went home on weekends, riding the caboose of freight trains. Later on she boarded with Mrs. Taylor in Salina. Mom told of a roommate, Mary Brungardt of Hays, who never took a bath, but was a "good girl." They often went to the movies together in 1916-1917.

During her senior year at Sacred Heart Mom lived with Mrs.Wilburs on the east side of Iron Avenue in Salina. She walked to school and came home at noon for lunch. She studied German at Kipp and Latin at Sacred Heart with some tough Catholic sisters. She studied piano all four years; her final recital was a big event. Three girls were playing at the same time at one piano. She graduated 5th in a class of 17. There were no extra-curricular activities in those days.

Grandpa Kelley's new car, Mom

Mom told of a friend, Helen Schwartzman, who had a car; they went on rides, a big event for Mom in 1917-1918.

Mom and the sod house in eastern Colorado

The Farm

After graduation, Mom returned to the farm at Kipp, not sure if she wanted to teach or not. In the fall she decided to go ahead and try it. In 1918 she rode out West on the train, accompanied by Mr. Kelly as far as Colby. Then on to Kanorado near the Colorado line. Some people named Cody met her there and took her to a relative's house which was 18 miles from Kanorado into Colorado. The house was part sod, part wooden frame. They went to mass in Ray, Colorado, 25 miles to the northwest, an overnight trip. At first she earned 60 to 65 dollars per month, later on was to earn $125. She paid twenty dollars per month room and board.

Her school was two miles from the farmhouse where she boarded. She walked or rode a horse to school. In winters she used a "wagon-box sled," a bobsled with runners front and back. She recalled a little boy student who brought her an orange each day to class. There was no water at the school; they had to go a quarter-mile for water. Mom's duties were to make the fire in the morning at the school in the coal stove. She recalled that her students were good ones, although very poor. She recalled a poor family that lived on parched corn, a browned corn, "like popcorn but not popped." She taught eight grades in the school. Boys were there part-time and worked on farms the rest of the time. I remember of Dad speaking of his schooling, a very similar situation. He studied through the eighth grade in the school house northeast of the house at Buckeye. He left school because he was needed on the farm. Mom said that the last day of school was always celebrated with a big dinner and a special program. This was between 1920 and 1923.

The country school, Mom's class.

Mom, a young, lady in Colorado, 1930s

In her third year after graduating from Sacred Heart she returned "home" to teach in a country school eight miles north of Solomon, in Grandma Enright's school district. She taught there for two and one-half years, suffering once from appendicitis. Then she returned to the same place as before in Colorado to teach, now in 1924. At this time she married Phelps, and my half-brother Jim was born at Cameron, Missouri, east of St. Joseph. He was one and one-half when Mom left Phelps, came home and "that settled that." All I ever recall Mom ever saying of this was that Phelps was not a good man, was in fact a bad man "who had deceived her badly," thus her decision to leave him. Jim has since said that our Dad is the only father he has ever known. But I have a vague recollection of Jim, in his cups one night in Kansas City, telling me of trying to look up his father many years later, this without any success.

Mom later taught for one year, in 1929, in Woodbine, Kansas, southeast of Abilene. She did not like it, having to board in a filthy place with bad food; she talked of the insects in the biscuit dough. She was very lonesome at this time; Jim was living on the farm (where I grew up) at Abilene. Note that the farm belonged then to Mr. Kelly, Mom's mother's second husband. Kelly had bought this farm in 1924 and had moved the family there from Kipp, Kansas. Mom said one of the main reasons for the move was the activities of the Ku Klux Klan which was very active around Kipp and was opposed to the Catholics. A man named Tobers sold the half-section (the farm one mile east of Abilene where I grew up) to Mr. Kelley in 1924 or 1925 for some $35,000. Kelley had sold his place at Kipp for $16,000.

At this time Uncle Bill Cusick, Mom's brother, was in business college and worked for United Trust in Abilene. He later moved to Kansas City and then to Grand Island, Nebraska, where I remember visiting him, his wife Helen, and my cousins Billy and Jana. Uncle Bill turned out to be the black sheep; I think he actually got caught for embezzlement and served some time; I remember when he worked for a Schlitz distributorship and was into beer breaks. I think Billy, Tom's age, died, but Jana a bit younger than me was always a dolly and I understand married an M.D. and life has turned out all right.

During the time in Woodbine, Mom boarded during the week and would come home to the farm east of Abilene on weekends, riding as far as Chapman on Friday nights. Her brother Leo (my Uncle Leo of Salina and then Colorado Springs days) would pick her up there and bring her to the farm at Abilene.

Mom moved once again and taught school for three years at Sandburn School, a country school three miles east of Detroit and one mile north. She lived on the farm at Abilene during this time and drove a Studebaker back and forth, from 1930 to 1933.

She told of one summer when she, her Mom Minnie, and her son Jim went to Boulder, Colorado where Mom attended summer school. They drove in the Studebaker and stayed overnight at Uncle Walter Wright's house in Kanorado, Kansas. The car broke down in a little town in western Kansas and delayed them, so later that day they got tired and pulled into a farm lane to sleep. A thief came in the night and said "I want your gas." He was a veteran on a veteran's march to Washington, D.C. during the depression days.

Then she taught at Kapp School, the school on Buckeye Road two miles north of Highway 40, the building Uncle Bryan bought later on and moved up to his farm, this in 1934 and 1935.

She met Dad at church in Abilene. They had known each other in recent years around Abilene. Mom's step-dad (Kelly) knew Dad because both of them had taken the 4th Degree in the Knights of Columbus together. Mom and Dad were married on May 28, 1935, at St. Andrews's by the then parish priest, now Monsignor Roach. They went to Kansas City for their honeymoon, but there was rain and floods on the wedding day. They had planned a trip to the Ozarks, but it was too wet to go. They lived at first in an apartment in Abilene, then on to the house on Brady Street in northeast Abilene, and finally to the farm in 1942.

Mom, the early days on the farm in Abilene

That was the end of the talk that afternoon in the 1970s in Keah and my house on Palmcroft Dr. in Tempe, AZ., a Sunday afternoon I think. I had put a tape recorder on a table in the living room and coaxed Mom and Dad to talk about old times. How I wish I had done it more often! I just remembered; a few years before, I had given a tape recorder to Dad and told him it would be fun if he would just turn it on once in awhile and just talk about the old days. He tried a couple of times, but just couldn't get started. But I have this memory of him, now maybe in his upper 70s, sitting in his favorite recliner in the living room in Abilene, maybe with a glass of wine in an old preserves glass, and chuckling and telling a story of days gone by. There was so much more they both could have told.

5. THE FARM HOUSE

The old farm house from the front porch, 1940s

The farm house with new asbestos siding, Jo Anne's days

We lived in a white, wood frame, two-story farmhouse. It originally had a coal stove, which I can just barely remember, and few amenities, this in 1942. I was born in 1941, but we lived at the edge of the city limits of nearby Abilene, Kansas. I think it was that same year that Dad bought the farm one-half mile east of the city limits on old U.S. Highway 40. I said few amenities, thus introducing the classic outhouse some twenty yards to the north of the farmhouse. Time spent there was preoccupied with the spider webs, wondering just when I would be bitten, and with the door open looking out over the vegetable garden, the alfalfa and corn fields to the east and the distant highway beyond, strangely enough with memories of breezes and birds and their singing. I can vaguely remember the remodeling of the farmhouse that took place when I must have been 4 or 5 years old--a new electric stove and remodeled plumbing in kitchen and bathroom and a gas or electric furnace replacing an old coal stove. There was one bathroom for six of us; I can remember lots of shouting and pounding on the door of that busy place.

The foundation of the house was stone and mortar, the stones from the earth surrounding the place. It was understood that the foundation was laid over one hundred years earlier. The basement of the house was where you could see the stone and mortar walls; it was always cooler in that basement which was used for storage of canned goods, for eggs before taking to market at the general store in Abilene and for the cream separator. The rocks always seemed to me to be solid as the earth, but you could put a finger in between them and the mortar would crumble to powder. (I think this was among the reasons Jo Anne's husband Paul decided it best to tear down the old place and build a new house on the farm.) Many chores took place in the basement: I can remember the candling of eggs into crates that must have held about twenty dozen or so. Eggs were at a premium of about 40 cents a dozen then, and Dad and Mom received somewhat less than that at a general store in town. The cream was primarily for our own use, although I can remember Dad selling it in very small amounts at the same general store in Abilene. This was the time before homogenized or pasteurized milk. The milk was put in bowls in the old electric refrigerator to cool, and the cream of course came to the top. I hated the cream, totally opposite to my parents who loved rich cream on cereal, strawberries and the like, and had to stir the milk in a bowl or put it into a bottle and shake it up before drinking or putting on cereal.

Dad had run a creamery or cream station as they called it on the south side of Abilene during the years prior to buying our half-section of land, this in 1941. (Joe Zey whose father Louie had a grocery store on the same block reminisced with me about this in April, 1991, when I sat next to him and Donna at my niece Lori Whitehair's wedding.) The creamery made him a good living for the time, perhaps better than later years on the farm. It became less profitable when things modernized, when even small town farmers no longer sold milk or cream but bought homogenized and pasteurized products in the grocery stores. I can remember the large steel milk cans, the kind they used to ship on the railway that were collected from all of western and central Kansas, the kind you can find in an auction or antique shop today for a premium. One of the few, old photos is of brother Tom teasing me outside the door of the creamery, for what reason I do not know.

Anyway, it was damp, dank and cool in the basement or cellar as we called it; basements were more for town folks, and there also were spider webs down there. I never went down there to play, but was generally sent there to get some canned food by Mom or to help with the eggs. One time when the pump to our well went out, I recall hours in the basement, helping Dad with the pipes.

The house was divided on the ground floor into a large kitchen with a dining nook where we ate most of our meals, a bathroom with a tub and no shower, my parents' bedroom, the "music" room with the piano (Mom played as a child and lessons were made mandatory for Jo Anne and me), the "front" or living room facing the yard and long lane that stretched some 150 yards down to old U.S. Highway 40, at one time the main east-west road through Kansas, now a county highway with local traffic since the new Interstate 70 was finished at the north fringe of our farm in the late 1950s. There was a large dining room to finish out the first floor. Like many farm families of the times, rooms in the house were also known by direction. My Dad would say, "Go bring me the newspaper; it's in the south room."

The floors of the house themselves were hardwood, what kind I do not know, but we never thought a floor could or should be made out of anything else, certainly not concrete as in Arizona. Carpeted houses in town seemed like a luxury. On the hardwood floor there were homemade, quilted throw rugs woven slowly and ever so carefully by my Mom, made of long strips of material, and called rag rugs I think. I know she spent long hours at them, a fact I did appreciate at the time, but even more in later years when I found they were of high value in country fairs throughout the land. Floor polishing was a regular part of Mom's housecleaning.

The upstairs in the rectangular floor plan was large as well, with five rooms, four of them used at one time or another as bedrooms for us kids, and one for storage. The attic was also large and was used for storage; it was a mysterious, curious place to visit with lots of heavy, old trunks, not the cardboard boxes we use these days. At one time I was afraid to go up there alone, for once again it was full of musty, dusty, spider webs, but it had so many curious things to see that I was able to overcome the fear and climb on up the narrow stairs.

The house had a wood shingle roof with gables on three sides. In Kansas then and now there was an obligatory lightning rod. It was only in 1955 that we added a large television antennae, one of the most exciting days of growing up when the TV set suddenly changed our whole perspective and vision of the world. Until then we used the radio with its altogether different dimensions of a different time, an important part of growing up on the farm in the 1940s and 50s.

I was the baby of the family, my brother Tom four years older, my sister Jo Anne five and older brother Jim, fifteen. I always thought of Jim like the others, but he really was a half-brother by Mom's first marriage to a man named George Phelps, but that is another story. I slept in the same room with Tom when I was a wee fellow. Wee is the key word here. I remember the wallpaper (the entire house was papered as I recall) with different types of airplanes, most of them with propellers. There was an old bureau for clothes. I can't help but have an immediate flashback to it when I read Flannery O' Connor's "Wise Blood" when the antihero comes home from the army to his abandoned farm house, finds an old shiffarobe and leaves a note on it: (paraphrasing) "This here shiffarobe is private property; don't touch it; whoever does will be hunted down and kilt.".

Obviously, Flannery O'Connor has nothing to do with the bureau in my bed room on the farm; it was a light colored wood (my Mom and Dad knew all kinds of wood, the particular grains, and ways to stain, varnish or just leave it alone). There were hooks on the wall to hang clothes on, but I cannot remember using them much; I do recall all dirty clothes being tossed on the floor into the corner. I wonder when I became fastidious as I now am with clothes?

There was a tiny night table by the bed, a bookcase with shelves in the corner where I kept scrapbooks of baseball players, baseball cards and a set of Billy Whiskers storybooks, a late present from Santa Claus one year. The light in the room was a bare bulb hanging from the ceiling that you switched on and off at the bulb, not from the wall. It's funny how just a simple thing like wall switches today makes me so aware of the "niceties" of city living.

Tom was soon to move to his own room, either because he was growing up or more likely because of me. I was a notorious bed wetter and can recall that in spite of a rubber sheet beneath the regular sheets things got uncomfortable. And it smelled. After eating too much watermelon on a summer evening, I sometimes just peed out the window. Years later I did the same thing, maybe from drinking too much beer in town with buddies while carousing in the hot summer evenings of Abilene. I was just too lazy to go all the way downstairs in the dark to the bathroom. Strangely enough, I was never caught in the act and can't recall any scolding. But now as an adult and parent I cannot imagine how my folks did not hear or even smell since their bedroom was immediately below mine. It's amazing that screen never rusted out. I recall today the minor things that upset me about our pre-teen and then teenager daughter's behavior (hairstyle hopelessly out of sync with the type my generation would prefer), and wonder how in the devil my parents managed to put up with my shenanigans.

Mark, looking to the southeast, alfalfa field, later days

These notes are obviously a bit out of order; they are not at all chronological since it's the memory that is in charge. A more pleasant memory of that screen on the east window (we grew up using directions: the south 40, the north 80, and even to sit at the "south end" of the dining table) was that in Kansas in the summer there was a prevailing southeastern breeze, and I used to sleep with my head at the foot of the bed just to feel that soothing breeze. There was no air conditioning in the farm house except a small window unit added later to the dining room west window on the first floor of the house. In the dog days of summer we had our unusually hot days when nothing stirred, but I recall the occasional cool evening breeze, zephyr like, which carried pleasant smells from the alfalfa field immediately to the east and especially the sounds of the summer night.

I can recall the wail of the train whistles, first of the old steam engines in use up until the end of World War II and perhaps a bit beyond, and then the diesels that followed. More than once there was a fire in the fields across the highway to the south of our farm. There the wheat fields were near the tracks, and it seemed to always be near harvest time when a spark from the old engines started the flames. But for a young boy the sounds of the train whistle were soothing, music to my ears, evoking imaginary ideas of where the trains had come from or were going, places I had only read about or perhaps heard of.

I can only vaguely recall my older brother Jim coming home from the War in 1945 on the train. The memory was repeated again in the early 1950s when he came from Korea.

An aside: one of my favorite play toys was the army helmet brother Jim brought home from Korea. I would put on the helmet, a munitions belt with a real bayonet, and grab the single-shot rifle, and off I would go into the fields to fight the North Koreans and Chinese from Korean War days (the comic books "GI Joe" and "Blackhawk" come to mind). We were in the Joe McCarthy era, and the evil yellow peril of communism was an undercurrent of the times.

The other sound from the highway in the night was the hum of the tires of the semis, small versions of today's 18 wheelers, the approach and then a gradual weakening of the sound of engines as the trucks faded into the distance. Maybe the reason I like the road songs and the truckers from country music is somehow linked to those purely audible memories.

The highway itself evokes many memories. The blizzards that we had only infrequently, perhaps every five to ten years, were memorable, and one picture in my mind is that of dozens of stranded cars and semi trucks on a road thick with ice and snow, all traffic coming to a thudding halt. That was when I learned what "jack knifed" meant. And there was the memory of the deep drifts in the culverts alongside the road. We did not use snow fences as in Western Kansas or Eastern Colorado, but a storm like one of these would obliterate any sign of highway. And for me, not involved with the serious adult consequences of the storms, the more snow the better. I can also remember playing in the rushing waters of runoff along old Highway 40 when the big snows would melt.

A different memory, of different times, was that of the occasional poor people who walked the highway picking up beer bottles that had a two-cent deposit in those days prior to the throwaway society. I think there were still people riding the rails in those days, but I had no direct experience of it. The area in Abilene near the railroad tracks was vaguely pointed out as dangerous, and I had little to do with it. In our small town, living close to the tracks was also a definite social statement and disadvantage. We kids picked up some of the bottles along the highway ourselves, for bubblegum and baseball card money. But I never really allowed myself to think seriously about the people who walked the road. I do recall however the occasional hobo or bum who would walk up the long lane to our farmhouse and ask for a handout, of how wary my mother would be, but how a plate of food was always offered. There was also the time the "crazy man" from the county farm would wander the property; our farm was only about a half mile distant from the county "poor farm" perched high on a neighboring knoll. The people up there were a mystery to me (and I had not seen "Psycho" yet).

I went to bed early growing up and also got up reasonably early to help with farm work in the summer, so that east window of the farm house is also always associated with the sound of the birds, especially of robins and of Kansas meadowlarks, music to my ears yet today.

In the hallway on the second floor of the farmhouse there were two tiny windows facing the lane and highway, windows opening onto the shingled roof. Sometimes I would crawl out of one of those windows on to the porch roof and watch the traffic down on the road and listen to the sounds. There were always birds on that roof early in the morning. From there you could see south across the fields all the way to the railroad and beyond to the cottonwoods down by the Smokey Hill river.

We had an old style wooden banister from a landing up to the second floor of the house. I never walked the stairs from the second floor down to the landing when I was little; sliding down the banister was the only alternative for a kid. I don't know when I stopped using the banister, but it was probably a lot later in life than you might think.

And it was amazing, or at least it seemed to me at the time, that if you were downstairs, you could tell who was going up or coming down from the second floor just by the sound of the footsteps. Everybody had his style or way of walking. I never thought of how I must have sounded--a whoosh down the banister and the bam, bam, bam of steps taken two at a time. Boundless energy, it's true.

The "middle room" upstairs was used as a storage room, but when I was about eleven, all that changed. My Dad managed to bring home an old pinball machine from the local Elks Club. We kids soon mastered the tricks enabling us to get the highest scores, including lifting the front of the machine carefully up in the air enough to allow the pinball to roll back to the top and replay the play, thus avoiding the terrible "tilt." Every kid of my generation must remember the malt shops and student hangouts where you went after school to flirt, read the comic books, sneak looks at the girlie magazines and of course play the pinball machines, a nickel in those days as were the single tunes on the jukebox, five for a quarter if you could spare the change. Many Sunday afternoons, especially in the wintertime, we spent tilting with tilts and loving it. My buddy growing up on a nearby farm, Mike Kippenberger, joined me at times.

But the best part of that same storage room was our old Edison Phonograph, an antique passed down on my mother's side through Grandma Cusick to my brother Jim. Jim had a terrific voice, a deep baritone, good enough I understand to consider some type of professional singing after graduation from high school. He had mastered the songs on the records, many of the pop tunes from the 20s and 30s and with an abundance of Irish melodies. We would play the machine and Jim would sing along on the old records. Those melodies are still with me today, not the lyrics, but the tunes are in my head, perhaps because of untold hours of riding a tractor doing field work and whistling the same tunes to keep from falling asleep. A few years ago I taped them on cassetes and gave copies to the brothers and sister. The records on the old Edison were the width of the early '78s, but perhaps one-quarter inch thick. There was a crank on the side of the Edison to wind the machine and move the turntable. In all our years of growing up and listening to those records I never recall anyone changing the needle. I know myself there was little concern for preserving anything but only the fun of mimicking the corny songs. And the arm with the needle had to be moved manually, reaching up into a very narrow spot between the oval horn that served as a speaker and sliding a gismo a certain way; that gave cause to endless scratching of the records. It just was not a priority, and the amazing thing is that so many of the records continued to be playable. Divided into instrumental and voice, the sounds of the twenties are on them, with a preponderance of Irish melodies, voices like you might hear from the hero or heroine in the old W.C. Fields movies depicting the vaudeville troupes (the "Great McGonagle" and baby Leroy and a rich widow who sang "Gathering up the Seashells by the Seashore" to an admiring Fields who needed her dough to keep the show going). Without getting out the tapes today I cannot recall too many titles, but "My Little Bimbo Down on the Bamboo Wire," "Get out of my Cellar," "Parade of the Wooden Soldiers" and many old Irish ditties were among them. Eventually all of us kids, but especially Jim, Tom and I would learn enough of the words to sing along or parody the originals.

There were a total of four bedrooms upstairs in the old farmhouse, five if you counted the "middle" room with the pinball machine and Edison. Each evokes memories: my sister's all frilly and feminine, today I would say in pink, but can't really remember; brother Jim's on the southwest side facing the barnyard and corral where he would hear the farm dog yapping and barking at night at strange noises. I can still hear his yelling trying to quiet the farm dog. That room became Tom's at one point in time, but he left home early, spending summers as a lifeguard at the county 4-H camp (he had terrific allergies which helped to keep him off the farm and out of the corn and alfalfa fields) and off to college at 18. The final room was the "north" room, a bedroom at times, if I recall correctly, at one time for my grandmother on Mom's side, Minnie Cusick. The Cusick name came from her first marriage; her second marriage was to Mr. Kelly after her first husband Cusick died. It was Kelly who owned the farm east of Abilene that my Dad would eventually buy and we were raised on. Minnie was a kindly lady I scarcely recall who died in a serious car accident when I was nine.

Aside: I don't know if I wrote about this. Grandma was dear to me in a couple of ways–I remember her rubbing my hand as we said prayers before bedtime and can also remember her giving me the shiny nickel to buy an ice-cream cone when we all went to town. And I can remember crying my heart out when they told me of her death in the car accident of 1949 when I suffered a fractured skull and almost had the same fate, or so they said.

But there is an important memory from that north room: it was 1951, summertime, and I was lying on the floor listening to the radio with its Mutual Game of the Week and hearing a Yankee game with Joe Dimaggio and Mickey Mantle in the same outfield! My lifelong devotion to baseball dates from that memory. There were other radio programs too: "The Shadow," "Gangbusters" and more I will talk about later.

There was a door out that room onto the roof of the bathroom, and the roof was tin. I hated walking it and was sure it would cave in under the weight. I can recall the roof being used for sun tanning, mainly by sister Jo Anne, and also for looking out over the huge vegetable garden where either Mom or Dad spent hours. But the horrible noise walking made on that roof kept me off of it most of the time.

Back to the downstairs of the farmhouse where another set of memories really tells you about our life in the 40s and 50s. The kitchen had been remodeled in the late 40s and a breakfast nook was added with a dining table where we could really fit six people around if we had to. We ate most of our meals at this table, the general exception being Sunday dinner (at noon as the farm people correctly said; supper was indeed in the evening). I can remember lots of laughter at our table, even with the hard times and family misfortunes that were to come. There were arguments and squabbles too, and tattle tales. It was there Mom corrected my grammar, the "ain'ts," "don't gots," "ain't got nos" and all the rest; I guess that was the main time she could corner me in a captive audience situation, because I never missed a meal. And that was when Dad would thunder "Listen!" as he tried to hear the weather, the farm news, or the evening news in the winter with Gabriel Heater, all on the little table radio on the kitchen counter, all essential to him at the time. Conversation seemed to be mainly about what happened that day at school with three of us at one stage or another at the time. Jim worked in a nearby town with a good job and relatively good pay but lived at home. There was of course a lot of talk about the farm, farm matters, but I was oblivious to most of it except for much later on, late teen years, when I finally began to realize the struggle to keep it all going. But anecdotes from a lot of those conversations will fill this book.

It seemed like all the food was fried in a skillet on the electric stove or baked in a large oven or prepared for canning in a huge pressure cooker that scared me to death. We did not own an outdoor grill or cooker; maybe that's why I grew up not really knowing or appreciating a good charcoaled steak until I had one in a restaurant. The kitchen sink had a large window above it that looked out on a clothesline, the lawn and flower garden and part of the big vegetable garden. Funny, but my memories of the seasons are tied to that window--leaves just coming out in Spring, early tulips, hot sticky summers, falling leaves and brilliant colors in Fall and especially bleak, windy, snowy bareness with bare trees in winter, at times with ice on the clothesline and tree branches. In the wintertime you could see out to the pasture beyond the garden and windbreak, and it was bleak.

The bathroom, once again with the bare light bulb dangling from the electric wire in the middle of the room, the old style bathtub, one wash sink, a vanity jammed with stuff from six family members; it all made for a busy place. I can't recall for certain, but I think the ceiling of the bathroom was tin as well. But it was there I shaved for the first time and all the juices began to flow.

Mom and Dad's bedroom in the northeast corner of the downstairs was off limits, kind of a private place for them. But I do recall when very, very tiny coming to the side of the bed when afraid. A few years later I would sneak into the room, look at the top of the bureau where Dad kept his billfold, loose change and stuff and what's the word, not malicious stealing, I would avail myself of part of my Dad's pocket change for treats at school. I always thought they never knew it. I grew up scrupulously honest, perhaps to a fault (the worst sin was any kind of lying), from their moral upbringing, so the peccadilloes of the change on the bureau must have been just that. In the city, forty years later, our daughter gets an allowance and so far my change lies undisturbed. Now, I was the last child born in 1941 with my Mom that age (born in 1900) and my Dad 47. I cannot imagine how they must have had to schedule or fit in any lovemaking with all that went on in that house. But the idea never occurred to me when I was very young, and later I rarely allowed myself to think about it--imagine your own parents doing that!

To the south of their bedroom was the "music" room with the old upright piano, stacks of music, mom's sewing machine, and other stuff. I originally played the old piano that was barely serviceable for lessons and badly out of tune and later used just the piano bench and propped my guitar music on the piano music stand. But the colonial style glass doors between that room and the living room never really did shut out practice noise of piano, violin, trumpet and guitar from Jo Anne, Tom or me during those years.

The living room in the early days was used for visiting; people came to see each other in those days, primarily on a Sunday afternoon, and the room became a "parlor" of sorts. We also used to socialize a lot on Sunday nights with friends and neighbors, the adults playing cards, the kids various games, Monopoly and the like. Later on, specifically in 1955, the living room became the center for watching our new black and white television. The negative connotations of television I have now are not at all from those days. TV was almost totally a positive experience for the family, at least from my memories and perspective from those times. I remember lots of laughter and fun from shows like Ed Sullivan, Red Skelton, and GE Theater, and on Saturday and Sunday afternoon, baseball or football. I'll say more later on that.

But the divan was used for naps and for reading. Our family read like crazy, everyone included. We used the city library for as long as I can remember, and Jim mainly bought paperbacks, 25 cents, 35 cents, even 50 cents in those days. There was also the arrival of a recliner that became everybody's favorite chair for TV or for naps. To my brother Jim's credit, several of the new furnishings for the house in those days were brought home by him from an appliance store in the little town where he commuted to work for so many years, but not "commuting" in today's sense; imagine driving a country highway 5 miles to a town of 500 population with one factory and sales office.

What I most remember about the dining room were the huge meals on Sunday afternoon, often with company (I'll tell more about our food later). And there seemed to be continual wall-papering of that room over the years. And at some point there was a brand new walnut table and chairs, a lace tablecloth, and the "good" dishes for special occasions. But there was still a bare light bulb hanging from the ceiling in the middle of the room as the only lighting fixture. At one time there was an old, huge "gothic" radio to one side of the dining table and a beautiful antique wooden bureau at the other. But a lasting memory was the west window facing the barnyard and corral, and the dust that gathered on the windowsill after the strong winds and dust storms so frequent in windy central Kansas. And I may be repeating myself, but a rocker stood in one corner at one time, and I remember a cantankerous uncle who came to visit one Sunday, rocking and chewing on a cigar the whole time. He left a ring of wet smelly tobacco in a perfect circle around the rocker. The floor was hardwood with throw rugs, and to his credit he did not spit on the rug.

Finally, the front porch. It's funny but I don't think there was a swing. I mainly remember sitting on the steps looking at the trees and the birds, down the lane to the highway. We would drag mattresses (the family did not own a sleeping bag; all this was prior to camping days, and, besides, the rare, farm family vacation was to the city to see the sights, not to spend more time outdoors) out in the summertime and sleep out, that is, until the mosquitoes or other flying bugs would get us.

6. MODERN APPLICANCES IN THE FARM HOUSE

I can't recall when I saw my first automatic clothes washer and dryer, but I do remember the new washer Dad got for Mom perhaps still in the late 1940s or early 1950s. It looked like some kind of space ship from the early Jules Verne sketches, a round tub on four long legs with a small roller under each wheel, and the wringer, a hand-cranked contraption up above. I do not know what this machine replaced, but we did have the old wash boards (which hillbilly bands use for a funny percussion instrument today). Somewhere way back I think I recall Mom with the galvanized wash tub all full of soap suds with the wash board in it, scrubbing away. A more accurate memory of the tub was that we used it upon occasion to cool watermelons during the hot months of July and August. The scene comes back today: out on the old concrete back "stoop" with cool well water in the tub and a great big green watermelon ever so slowly being cooled.

And that makes me think of the old wooden crank ice cream maker that was used during the same weather. Dad and Mom bought salt and ice in town, thick cream, and would make the ice cream on a hot evening in summertime. It seemed like it was always vanilla, but we absolutely loved it. However our less than efficient electric refrigerator (we all called it the "icebox") and its freezer would not freeze it solid; but it did not seem to matter because it just tasted so good. My favorite part was getting to lick the beaters. Nowadays, with all the flavors possible, and yet with all the fresh strawberries we had during summer, I'm surprised the only option was vanilla.

Let's get back to the old washing machine. Even with the new device, the time spent washing for four, five or six people must have been incredible, particularly when you think of the dirt from farm work and the clothes we would peel off after a hot day in the fields. I think that Mom used that old machine and wringer until they moved into town when Dad sold the farm and retired in 1959. But the drying was the part I remember more because there was no automatic dryer, and everything had to be taken outside to the clotheslines located just north of the kitchen. One of my chores growing up was to help take out the clothes and hang up for drying, but more often to go out and get the clothes, put them in old wooden baskets (the same ones peaches and apples came in from the store) and bring them into the house. The matter was complicated to no end in wintertime; I can recall many times bringing in blue jeans stiff as a board from freezing overnight. Mom would iron them quickly, trying to dry them out some, but I can recall often going to school with very cool, wet shorts particularly from the pocket area and the crotch of the still wet jeans. I can also recall bed sheets frozen over night.

My Mom was a very tiny lady, perhaps five feet tall at most and weighing not much over one hundred pounds. The physical energy it must have taken for the washing, the drying on the line, and then the ironing (because nothing was perma-press then) of clothes for six just overwhelms me today. Mom was typical of her times and peers; the farm ladies worked as hard as their men. With cleaning, washing, cooking and being the "nurse" and "doctor" to all of us, no wonder Mom was worn out a good deal of the time.

The other electrical appliances in the farmhouse were up to date (for the 1940s): a modern electric stove, electric hot water heater, a mixer for blending, electric iron, and a vacuum cleaner (I cannot remember the brands, but a "Hoover" in think). But there was no blender, no automatic dish washer, no garbage disposal (except for the Collie dogs and diverse cats swarming outside the porch door after meals), and certainly no microwave. And little help to boot. Although my sister learned to cook well and sew well from her Mother, it was Mom who prepared most of the meals and did the necessary sewing. No wonder she was tired and worn out so often. The kids were enlisted to help with dishes, and I did a lot of drying and banging them around.

I can't remember if I wrote about the telephone. Ours originally was the wall mounted variety with the receiver hanging on a hook from the main wooden box containing the mouthpiece and innards of the thing. There was a crank on the right side to turn in order to get the operator. Ours was, like most everyone else's then, a party line. So I think our "number" was signaled by a long and two shorts from the bell. We became familiar with the "ring" for the neighbors as well, so you would know who was being called, and when you picked up the receiver to make a call, likely as not, there was someone already on the line. At some point, I think I was well into junior high or high school, the telephone company replaced the old phone with a desk model, no crank involved, but the party line continued for some time. Being not quite a saint, I will admit I did listen in a bit, but just a bit. But when you were talking there were always these mysterious "clicks" letting you know someone had been listening in to your own conversation. I get tickled yet today when I see the "custom" telephones which are meant to look exactly like the one we used for so many years. And now, Keah and I in 2010 are among the select few in the world without cell phones.

I will talk of radio and television in another section, but needless to say, they were the most fun and added totally different dimensions to our lives in rural Kansas.

7. FOOD AND HOW WE GOT IT

The farm was not totally self-sufficient in food, but was not far from it. Meat came from the chickens we raised, tiny from the hatchery, pork and beef butchered on the farm in the open driveway of the granary, later to be packaged and frozen in the old locker plant located on the south side of the Union Pacific tracks in old Abilene. There were lots of vegetables in season from a large, one acre garden immediately to the northeast of the farm house, and many of these were canned for winter usage. Fruit had to be purchased in the local grocery stores and was seasonal, but it also was canned.

We had eggs from the chickens and dairy products from the one or two milk cows (milk, butter, cream) Dad kept around most of the time. We had homemade ice cream once in awhile in the summer time, but most desserts were baked goods: pies, cakes, cookies, and homemade bread, much of it out of Mom's oven. In spite of being a wheat farmer, Dad always purchased flour in town in five or ten-pound bags, just like most farmers in the region. Spices, coffee, and sugar were all bought in town. I recall that shopping or "trading" as Dad liked to call it, was done generally on Saturdays and almost always, in part, paid with store money at the RHV Store ("Real Honest Value," by the Viola Brothers) in exchange for eggs and cream brought in each week by Dad. I am fairly sure my brother Tom worked for some time at the store during high school years; sister Jo Anne worked at J.C. Penney's which still had the overhead cable system for sending receipts, change etc. to cashiers sitting upstairs in the office as well as the old style tin ceiling, and I spent part time and Saturdays in high school at the Gambles Store. I don't know if I told elsewhere, but you can imagine my mechanical ability. One Saturday the boss took me off the sales floor and put me and a buddy down in the basement to put together bicycles and other toys for Christmas. By the time I had looked at the instructions, my buddy Don had a bicycle together and was working on another one. He made Ds in school and owns a successful construction company in Topeka, Kansas. End of story. I probably worked more on the farm than any of my brothers or sister due to one reason or another, but more on that later.

I remember the RHV store, a type of general store in its time. There was the feed part out back with high stacks of 50 and 100 pound bags of grain and feed for all animals, the creamery part with scales, etc. Inside, the appliances, the long hardware part, but my favorite was the sports section where I would ogle the new leather baseball gloves that smelled so good and had names like Stan Musial, Mickey Mantle, Ted Williams or Allie Reynolds on them, and the real Louisville Sluggers autographed by the same heroes. Viola's also had a shoe store across the street, a clothing store and a grocery. We bought shoes there, but groceries were at the old A & P, famous then for its low profit margin; I guess that's why they went out of business, and Zey's food store on the south side, close to the old creamery and the locker plant where we kept frozen meat from butchering on the farm, and besides, they were Catholics.

Back to food and how we got it. Butcher day was a big event, almost always in cold weather as I recall (I guess to help with keeping the meat cool, fewer flies or insects, etc.). The hog or steer was killed by a blow to the head with a hammer or perhaps a bullet to the brain, was strung up on a pulley attached to the scaffolding of the granary, in the driveway, the blood drained, and Dad and his helper(s) would butcher, trim the hide and fat away and make the big cuts. I don't know where Dad learned all that, I guess by helping others and doing. There are so many skills that were lost when he died, skills none of us has today. It seemed like I was always too young, too immature or just plain disinterested to learn much. The whole experience of growing up on the farm was a mainly pleasant one and obviously a good memory, but I am amazed at how little I learned that stuck with me, at least in practical skills. I can recall getting close to being nauseated with I had to stand around and help Dad with a mechanical task, as a "gofer" or whatever. I guess I had the strong genes in other areas like music, languages, history, and book-learning.

I can remember one cold, icy day when you could see your breath in the cold air, butcher day for a steer. I stood by watching when all of a sudden Dad handed me this steamy, warm object, saying, "Here. Hold this". I can't describe the sensation; I didn't feel like fainting, but I guess the word is squeamish (I should have known then that I had no aptitude for medical school). It was the liver, a large hunk of mass, a pleasantly warm, pliable, mysterious piece of flesh. I have never been particularly fond of that organ since, and I always think of the short story by Monteiro Lobato, the Brazilian writer, "The Indiscrete Liver" telling of a young man's aversion to liver and how it threw a monkey wrench into his engagement plans when his fiancé's mother served liver for lunch at the engagement party.

Other things I remember of butchering day were the final product, the nicely packaged meat in the cold storage locker in old Abilene near the railroad tracks. I can recall innumerable times accompanying Mom or Dad into that frozen room to our locker to pick out meat to take home for meals. I always had a real fear the freezer door would close and we would not able to get out, even though there was a large knob contraption to open the door from the inside.

Another memory, this when butchering a pig or hog, was that of the fresh pork tenderloin that I enjoyed more than any other cut of meat. I also liked the thick bacon with real flavor which we always had for breakfast. Related, but unrelated: there is a single memory of high school days when we went over to Solomon, Kansas, to drink beer in the tavern; one night they served "mountain oysters" in the bar; served with ice cold beer. There were days on the farm designated as "castration" days--I can remember watching but not doing, a good thing. In those days the tenderloin tasted to me like the finest cut of beef steak today. Charcoal cookers and outside barbecues were unheard of then; all meat was fried, boiled, broiled or baked on the kitchen stove. For that reason I cannot recall eating much beef steak growing up, in spite of raising and butchering the beef. We ate lots of roasts, hamburger (the kids liked it) and only an occasional fried steak, usually overdone. I am always amazed that the lack of charcoaling persists on the farm today, with my sister's family, this even though they have a substantially sized feedlot with hundreds of head of cattle on hand. (It could be this changed or only was my impression after a certain visit).

But I am sure we ate far more chicken than beef or pork. We killed the chickens by cutting off their heads with an ax, later dunking the rest of the chicken in boiling water to take off the feathers, cleaning out the insides, cutting up and frying. Dad would do the honors with the ax. I can remember like yesterday the big shade tree by the chicken house, the big stump under that tree, the ax planted in the middle awaiting the task. Dad would catch the squawking victim for that Sunday with a long "chicken hook", an affair with a round wooden handle, a long, semi-flexible steel rod with a curved hook on the end, much like the curve of the old shepherd's staff. Often I was sent with the hook to catch the chicken and bring it squawking to Dad. Our Border Collie "Lady," a black and white sheepdog, loved this part and always seemed to know when the fatal moment would be, barking close by in excited anticipation. Between the squawking of the chicken and the barking of the dog, it was a lively scene. Dad with one swift blow would part the head from the body and sling the body away. That's when the show started. The decapitated bird would bounce, stumble, jump and bound (is this St. Vitus' dance?) for what seemed an eternity, the dog jumping and barking nearby, until the body of the chicken finally fell motionless to the ground. I've heard tell and have seen those farmers who put the chicken under their arm, grab the head and neck, and pop it, instantly (I surmise) killing the chicken. For some reason we never used that method.

My time came. "Mark, go get us a chicken for supper". The problem was I could never seem to accomplish the swift killing with one blow of the ax. It was either a series of blows, some of them striking the chicken in the middle of the head, or missing all together. I can recall a time or two of a leaping chicken, head half on, half off, me chasing it trying to give it the "coup de grace". That was just one of my adventures with the chickens while growing up. It's amazing I still love to eat them.

Mom did the plucking of the chicken in big pans outside the house (for obvious reasons), although there were times when all of us plucked as well, I guess when we had sold several fryers to town people, another small source of farm income. If it was cold at all you see the steam coming from the boiling water in the crisp, icy air. It there was any dietary staple in the family, it was chicken, fried in the warm months, and baked with wonderful dressing, like a Thanksgiving turkey, especially on Sunday in the Fall and Winter. Both remain favorites in spite of literally hundreds of such meals growing up. In this paranoid society we all face now I see friends cutting out beef, taking the skin off the chicken. So far I have not succumbed. How is it my parents, and their brothers and sisters, lived to ripe old ages with this diet? At any rate I was a klutz with the ax, but hey, I did it right once in awhile.

I am amazed in the big city today, in the supermarket where you see the neat packages of chicken, some pre-cut into select pieces, all the same size and neatly in a row. It is progress to be sure, but a slice of life is missing. And some flavor too. (See the movie, "Food.Inc. for the way it is really done today.) There were vegetables, fresh in season, canned during the winter.

Garden Day was an annual and important event. Hopefully after the last frost (and you never knew for sure when that would be), it was a family enterprise of sorts, that is, when any of the kids could be rounded up to help. Jim at this point in his life helped little, was more like a boarder with his job in the business world. Tom and Jo Anne helped for sure when they were younger. There's got to be a lot I am not old enough to remember, but by the time I do remember they were often gone on many weekend activities from school or were working in town. It was always on a Saturday. Dad would plow the entire area with our little Ford tractor, approximately an acre immediately east and northeast of the farmhouse. Then rows would be set for beans, onions, radishes and the like. A very large area was set aside for potatoes; I can recall watching Dad or Mom cut up the seed potatoes, always with an "eye" in each bit, and planting. (I also helped dig potatoes, small ones were eaten with sweet peas for a delicious plate in late summer if I'm not mistaken; and the big potatoes were dug during the fall, often with the field muddy with fall rains, to be stored in the cool and damp basement of the house.) I would do a lot of the hoeing, making the rows, planting seeds or onion sets or the like.

We had an annual strawberry patch grown in the shade of big elm trees near the house, and had wonderful strawberries in season. I loved them mashed up on vanilla ice cream or on angel food cake. But I could never eat them like my parents: in a bowl with rich farm cream. Strawberry jam, jelly and preserves however became a lifelong favorite.

Like most kids I did not like many of the vegetables while growing up, but can remember delicious, fresh, tasty, "real" tomatoes, a luxury today. Ah, cucumbers and sliced onions with vinegar. There were lots of green beans, peas, carrots, and radishes. But I did not like beets, spinach, turnips, most of the stuff my parents really enjoyed. But then there was the sweet corn! It was always planted in the far reaches of the garden, to be ready a bit ahead of the field corn grown in large fields on the farm well east of the garden. They always said the sweet corn was better, more tender and with more flavor, but I liked it all, able to devour three or four large ears at a sitting. I can recall being sent to the cornfield with a paper grocery bag, filling up the bag, shucking the husks and getting the ears ready for the boiling pot. My interest in biology and particularly entomology started and ended there with the variety of bugs, worms, and caterpillars working the field corn. But this was deemed normal and doing little harm. You picked out the bugs, lopped off the bad part of the ear and got on with it. That fresh corn was one of the joys of my youth.

Mark J. Curran

    Canning took place throughout the summer when the vegetables were ready, another incredibly busy and hard-working day for my mother. We stored the mason jars in the cool basement. It became a matter of bringing up the empty jars, cobwebby and dusty, washing and sterilizing them, cooking the vegetables and doing the actual canning. Mom used paraffin to seal the lids. I recall lots of fruit canning--peaches, plums, apricots, cherries and the making of jams and preserves. Mom and Dad would bring home bushel baskets of a given fruit in season and do the canning. It was a day-long project, hard work most unappreciated by me at that time. I wonder now why they did all that and am sure it was a combination of factors. They loved the taste of those goodies in off season, in the middle of winter. It was also a custom, the way farm folks had been doing it for generations. However, I am sure the economic factor had to do with it also. It was probably cheaper to buy in quantity during season than buying canned goods that did not taste as good or were not as fresh. I recall they used a very large, heavy duty pressure cooker for a lot of the canning, and I grew up with the fear of that thing exploding, a fear I'm sure I got from talk of the actual thing happening. I have not got within striking distance of one since.

8. WHEAT HARVEST AND FIELDWORK ON THE FARM

Wheat harvest time was important, an event much anticipated, with joy when a bumper crop was expected, with sadness when the wheat was thin. In the 1940s and 50s only the very prosperous farmers had their own big, self-propelled combines; the small family farms still used the old pull-type combines in some cases, but more than likely hired the professional harvest crews on a share basis. These latter were medium to big operations, generally consisting in two or three or more large self-propelled models like Massey Harris, John Deere, or International Harvester. Also, the crews had to have several large grain trucks. The combines sometimes were driven along the country highways at about 25 to 30 miles per hour, but for long distances were transported on the same large grain trucks. Living quarters in the early 50s was generally a modified school bus with bunks. Cooking facilities were at a minimum also since main meals were prepared by the farmer's wife, or were taken in small country cafes in the neighboring towns. Local farm kids often joined a crew and worked from June through early August on the route which started in Texas or Oklahoma, worked its way through central and western Kansas, on up into Nebraska, eastern Colorado and perhaps Wyoming or the Dakotas. (Recall that Dad in 1925 worked a harvest in eastern Washington with its rolling hills, the combines pulled by huge teams of mules or horses, with some rigs up to 36 head.)

I never worked with the custom cutters, primarily because I was needed by Dad to help with the local farm work all summer long. I can recall using an old yellow pull-type combine for awhile, but it was not reliable, constantly under repair, and Dad with the frustration of it all relented to hire a professional crew, but at a high cost. I can remember some of the breakdowns, a frustrating and nervous time, eventually not to be tolerated. The wheat was ripe, and it was also rain, hail, and tornado season. An entire crop in the field could be obliterated or at least partially ruined with much lower yield with additional rain that would cause the wheat to lie down and not be high enough for the combine pickup to get it.

Time was of the essence, thus harvest crews worked long days. Starting time was dictated by humidity and moisture content in the wheat; the grain elevator would take wheat only with low moisture content, and penalize the farmer at a certain point. Thus, if you began to cut too early in the day, you could lose out. Once the drying started, however, cutting went on into the late hours of the night, some times all night long. The crews had a reputation for some raucous living; supposedly a lot of beer drinking and womanizing went on after hours, or on the rainy days when work was impossible, although I think a lot more sitting around waiting or work repairing machinery was more likely. Mike Kippenberger's cousins from Thomas, Oklahoma, ran such a crew, a sad story for me one year. One of the crew, a big tough Oklahoma farmer-football player had a short flirtation with a local girl I had been dating. There wasn't much I could do about it, and it turned out for the best, but I didn't think so at the time. It hurt way down deep.

I believe the harvesters would charge according to the acre, so many dollars per acre. Thus the local farmer's net depended on how many bushels he got to the acre and the price of wheat. There were times when he did not make much, but in the case of the small farmer there was little choice. Dad could not afford to buy a big combine himself, and the old, worn out pull model just did not get the job done. But, in general harvest was a happy time, a lot of hard work to be sure, but the big pay day of the year in Kansas. I can recall the thrill of riding up on the combine while they cut; I never did drive one since I was too young when Dad combined and later on the custom crews handled it.

One of my jobs during Dad's days was to drive the truck or trailer under the combine chute to empty the grain into the trailer for hauling to town. You could drive at age 14 in Kansas if you lived on a farm, so between the tractor and all you learned in a hurry.

There was constant talk of wheat prices, from around a dollar a bushel in bad times when Dad farmed in the 50s to over four dollars a bushel a few years after Dad had quit. The high price must have been the early 70s. But since those days, as expensive as farm machinery was then, prices for equipment have skyrocketed, many farmers including old friends of mine from high school days in Abilene have been forced to sell out, and only the largest can remain. I think it was this situation that brought Willie Nelson's Farm Aid concerts in more recent years. They tell me a good combine today (1988) can run a hundred thousand dollars, about twice what Dad received when he sold the arable part of the farm in the late 50s. The new ones have cabs with air conditioning, radios or tape decks, everything controlled from inside the cab. Keah and Katie got to ride in one at my brother-in-law Paul L. Whitehair's in Abilene; visiting the farm was always a thrill whenever we would go back there.

My memories of harvest are more of the earlier period when Dad cut his own wheat or traded off with a neighbor who had a combine. I generally helped by driving a truck to the grain elevator in town where there were always long lines waiting to dump the wheat. When I was very tiny, I used to ride along with Dad or Mom when they hauled the wheat to town in a trailer pulled by the car or a borrowed truck, a small but workable arrangement. I was always scared when they lifted the truck or trailer up on the hoist to dump the wheat, and was also a bit pensive thinking what would happen if you fell into the pit. Stories abounded about deaths in the grain elevators, generally when moving grain or the like, sometimes an explosion or sometimes by poisonous air.

But the trip into town was fun for a country boy. First of all, you got a change of scene from the farm and got to talk to people, and I generally got a bottle of pop or a pop cycle when I went along for the ride. I can recall the long waits at the railroad tracks while all the switching of cars took place. There were three railroads through Abilene in those days, the Union Pacific, the Rock Island and the Santa Fe. The grain elevators were located by the tracks since all grain was eventually transported by rail. The elevators had to empty storage space for harvest of the new crop, and the wheat was transferred to Kansas City. There was a constant switching process going on; it seemed like that should all have been done ahead of time, long before harvest, but it never seemed to work out that way.

Oftentimes it was dry, hot, perfect weather for harvest. But sometimes there was rain and the combines would get stuck in the fields. The crews began to use huge tires, "airplane tires" (the huge tubes were a mainstay at the local swimming pool where we played "king of the mountain" on them for years), to get through the mud in the fields. This of course left the fields in an incredible mess when they dried and made the plowing a lot tougher later on.

PLOWING. I helped Dad with the fieldwork for many summers. There never was an exact wage scale; I think our system was that he gave me an allowance for incidentals, but that the wages were to go into an account to pay for college. I don't think any figures were actually kept, but he certainly kept his end of the bargain, although I don't know where the money came from at the time. I'm sure he borrowed at the local bank. Summer earnings from the farm and later the ice plant in town helped to pay for tuition and board and room in the dormitory of a Jesuit college in Kansas City, Missouri from 1959 to 1963. In college at one time I had three part-time jobs to help out, and I got a tuition scholarship in one or two of the final years, but the main money came from Mom and Dad.

Mark on the old Ford tractor

Mark inspecting a restored Ford tractor at the county fair

The Farm

When I did farm work it was still accepted practice to totally turn the soil under, the idea being to return the straw, etc. to the soil for mulch. That meant plowing. All those years we used a tiny Ford tractor with a two-bottom plow, turning over maybe a two-foot width of soil each round. I can't remember well, but I think it did an acre an hour. The years varied greatly, not only with the amount of wheat harvested, but the kind of stubble or growth left after cutting: some years, stubble was so thick and damp it was almost impossible to turn under. So we often would disk the field first to break up the stubble, and then plow. I remember that one of the most disagreeable parts of that job was the plow getting all jammed up with the stubble and I would have to stop the tractor, get off and manually pull the stubble out. (In the latter 1960s they began to use a "chisel" plow instead of the old plowing, a sort of long tooth affair that would break up the soil, allow for rain to soak, but leaving much of the stubble still on the surface; I did this type of plowing for Gordon Kippenberger in 1968 after getting a Ph.D. and waiting three months to start school in Arizona.)

So we would disk, plow, disk later to break up the big clods and eventually harrow until the field was a soft, fine consistency. All this was to prepare the soil for planting that fall. I can't believe the number of times we went over the same ground. And like everything else, there was a fine line between preparing the soil properly and not. If it was too fine and you got strong winds, always a possibility in Kansas, it would blow, and the irreplaceable top soil would head off toward Missouri and eventually end up as silt in the Mississippi. I have read statistics of how many tons of top soil is still lost each year in the Plains, another something to worry about if you can't sleep at night. There were times when it would start to blow and we would rush to the field to disk, thus breaking the surface into clods and bringing a bit of moisture to the surface.

Weather was always a primary subject on the farm, and although we had the rain gage, Dad was uncanny after a rain, estimating the amount closely. He also seemed to know how much moisture was in the soil, even when it appeared totally dry on top.

Given my 'iffens, I probably would have preferred a nice job in town to the farm work. Much of it was boring to me, and I regret to this day not "applying myself," working harder and "doing it right." But Dad had little choice; if he wanted the help he had to accept my less than perfect work patterns. It wasn't that I was lazy, but rather I just sometimes didn't get the hang of it. I used to get bored silly out on that tractor, and some of the antics I pulled must have appalled him. For starters, I would sing or whistle every song I had ever heard on the radio, sing until my throat got too sore, and then whistle. I used to pride myself on my whistling, like the theme from the "High and the Mighty" a great adventure airline pilot film with John Wayne. If I'm no expert today, it certainly is not for a lack of practice time then.

I sang pop songs, country songs, church songs and whistled classic melodies, overtures to Operas from brother Jim's record collection, show tunes and the like. "South Pacific" and "Carousel" were from that period.

When plowing, for those of you blessed with no knowledge of it, the right tractor wheels are in the furrow, inclined slightly, so only a little pressure on the steering wheel was necessary. I used to close my eyes and see how far and long I could go without opening my eyes and/or getting out of the furrow. It even got to the point sometimes when I would intentionally try to fall asleep for brief moments until I would wake up and find myself, tractor and plow heading off down the middle of the field, out of the furrow. It only happened a time or two, but it demonstrates my keen concentration and state of mind at the time.

Now, if it rained enough, it got too muddy to plow. I was the quickest "tractor" west of the Mississippi to get back to the house when there was scarcely a sprinkle. I recall once or twice when they sent me back out to the field.

You get mighty thirsty out in that sun, heat and dirt. I carried ice water in a jug that most farmers would carry on the tractor. Not me. I would leave it in a place where there was at least a little shade under a solitary tree or some tall brome grass. That meant stopping the tractor ever so often for a drink. Sometimes it was the only way I could manage to make another long round around the field (like W.C. Fields and his martini at the front of the rowing machine, sort of, you see what I mean).

What I really liked was plowing down by the highway; I knew most of the local cars and would wave at each when I made a round near the highway. There was a cute girl in my class at school who lived just down the highway, and when their old 49' Chevy went by, it would brighten my day. I doubt that she ever realized that, but on the other hand, oftentimes her mother would be along with her.

Another diversion, such as it was, in plowing as you leave a smaller and smaller plot of ground toward the center of the field, all the tiny wild life retreats to the center or the unplowed section. As you finished a given field there was considerable to watch: small field mice, ground squirrels, and hawks circling to dive for the rodents.

Eventually I covered all our arable land. Over the course of several years, working for neighbors and friends, I figure I farmed several thousand acres in Dickinson County which kind of gave me a nice feeling to dream in some way that it was mine and that I had dominion over it. I farmed north, northeast, southeast, south, southwest and northwest of Abilene one time or another. I plowed, disked, cultivated corn, harrowed, and helped bale hay, fill silo, most of the really unskilled work that was needed in those parts. Early on, wages were one dollar an hour and eventually in my time went up to about a dollar and a half. It made spending money during the summer and a little bit toward clothes for school. I never had a car during those years, so there really were no big expenses until I went to college.

The big event of my plowing days was the "Great Enterprise Bank Robbery." Enterprise is a tiny town some five miles east of Abilene along the Smokey Hill River. It must have had maybe 500 people in those days, with a tiny business district. It turns out some local bank robbers made a heist one hot summer day and fled toward Abilene, heading in the general direction of our half-section. All of a sudden there were police cars, highway patrol and even an airplane or two all in the very close vicinity of the east part of our farm and the graveled county roads along side it. I still don't know if they caught them, or where they caught them, but it livened up my day anyway.

HAY BALING. It was another of the big jobs in summer. In that part of Kansas we could cut three or perhaps four hay crops each summer, all depending on the weather. Each cutting was a bit less than the previous as summer went along. A vague, hazy memory is that of an old fashioned threshing machine, not a steam thresher, but a gasoline-driven thresher driven by a belt from an old "Johnny Popper" or old time John Deere tractor with a pulley that drove the belt. This was for alfalfa seed harvesting. The residual, or the hay itself, came out loose and was stacked by hand using pitchforks. I am sure I did witness that as a very young boy.

But the more normal way was of course to mow the hay, rake it into windrows, then bale with a semi-automatic baler. I worked for one neighbor down by the river on one of the old block and tie jobs where the crew in the field was four: one man on the tractor, two on the baler, one to tie the baling wire around the bale, the other to block or section each bale, and a fourth on the hayrack pulled behind the baler. It was all hot, dirty and sweaty, but particularly so on the baler. I was a hired hand in this case, but Dad also used the old block and tie baler in the earlier days. It was borrowed, traded or leased, one farmer who owned the baler doing the work in exchange for help on his own hay or fieldwork.

An aside: the old barn dances of 4-H days. Hay baling makes me think of the dances. They were big affairs: held at night in the haymow or barn of a local farmer, they were a cause for a gathering of many, many local folks. There may have been a square dance caller, perhaps with a little record player and p.a. system, but there were at least a few times when we had a real "live" band: fiddle, guitar or two, maybe a banjo, drums. I was too tiny to dance, but enjoyed the milling around and camaraderie with other buddies, all of us too young for girls at the time.

Back to the hay. Later on came the automatic baler that did the tying and blocking automatically, thus eliminating two men from the crew. But even then it seemed the bailers were constantly jamming, breaking the wires or something. Even with the new balers you still needed quite a crew: one group in the field baling, one or two driving the tractor and hauling the hayracks between the field and the barn, and a crew up in the barn stacking the bales as they came in. That's where our old-fashioned barn and haymow came in.

The barn seemed to be to be a huge old place, two stories high with the hayloft up above with an inclined driveway to a big open door so you could drive a small tractor and hayrack inside, a smaller door on the opposite end for ventilation, and a few windows on the sides.

The memories are many from several summers of working up there: the sweet smell of the hay, but the incredible heat and humidity, the flies and the sweat. We did not have fans, so the only ventilation was an occasional breeze, such as it was. But I remember a lot of small talk, banter, joking, laughing and good times during those days. As usual there was a scary part for a kid: after the hayrack was empty, someone had to grab the tongue of the rack, all would give a push, and it gradually gained speed, seeming to zoom down the incline and in between the silo and the granary before coming to a stop and then being hitched to the little Ford tractor for another run to the field. I think I eventually could handle that part, but only when I was older. It's funny how things like that, so seemingly minute and unimportant, really marked one's growing up.

Dad did all our hay mowing with the little Ford and sometimes I would rake. I had trouble making the windrows straight enough and botched up the corners, still easier said than done to do a good job, but I worked mainly on the hay rack or in the barn. I have always thought there was a big difference between the Irish and German immigrant farmers around Abilene. I still think the Irish all in all did it right (they had more fun but made less money). Our bales were lighter by a few pounds, easier to handle, and we took it a bit easier. Dad would work on Sunday only out of absolute necessity, like during wheat harvest. He always took Sunday off whenever possible, and I am convinced it saved his sanity and also added years to his life. There were German farmers south of town (river bottom land, the best around) I worked for at times; I could barely lift their bales. They were larger, more efficient, more hay in them, and greener sometimes. The green hay reminds me of barn fires. We never had one, but they were not all that uncommon. If the hay was too wet when baled and was stacked tightly in the barn, sometimes the process of spontaneous combustion could start a spark, and the whole crop and barn would burn down. There was one German south of town that we always marveled at, how he never managed to have a fire since he always was in a big hurry to bale. Since then I have realized that most of the German farmers worked the same way. I do recall seeing a humongous barn fire near Enterprise when I was very little, and wet hay was the cause. There were huge flames in the night sky and no rural fire department to take care of it.

But one of the joys of being a small boy or even a teenager on the farm was that during slack times during the summer or later on in the year I would have buddies over to play, and inevitably we would build hay forts in the barn. We had tunnels, forts with windows, etc. and used two tin cans with a taut string between them for a walkie-talkie (remember I read comic books and Blackhawk and GI Joe that were still big, Korean War days). Most of the time it was friends from town that came out, because buddies who lived on farms had enough of it already and preferred to play sports. That barn played a big role in my growing up. But that's another story. Little Jimmie Dickens had a song "Out behind the barn," and with some truth to it.

During all this time Jim was not around much; he was 15 years older than I and was already working as an estimator and then salesman at Ehrsams' Mfg. Company in Enterprise. Tom had a horrible case of hay fever and although he did some work on the farm in earlier years, he flew the coop by getting a job at the State 4-H Camp near Rock Springs, a few miles from Abilene, a place where I think he had a chance to become quite a ladies' man and also where he sunburned his body a few too many times as a lifeguard (Tom died of melanoma in 1985 at the tender age of 49). I always envied that job: great food, meeting all the girls, horseback riding and swimming, and fun nights carousing.

But I had nary a bit of hay fever, don't think I got stuffed up or even sneezed much. Destiny.

But there's a story about Tom when he still worked on the farm. During one of the hay baling times he was introduced to chewing tobacco, once again by my old friend of the 12 gage shotgun days, cousin Kenny Tyrell. (Kenny had taught me how to shoot the gun with the recoil knocking me to the ground and giving me a black and blue face the next day.) I recall Tom coming in from the field at noon for the big farm meal for all the workers, and he could handle a big plate loaded up with fried chicken, mounds of mashed potatoes, tomatoes, heaping the plate high. Suddenly Tom grew quiet and then "blam!" headed for the bathroom. We laughed and laughed. For that reason and who knows what else I never tried chewing tobacco or snuff. Dad once said that when he was twenty--two, fresh out of the Merchant Marine during World War I days, he smoked cigarettes, pipe and chewed, all during the same years. Later he went cold turkey, gave it all up and never smoked again. I never saw him use tobacco.

CORN. Another mainstay on the farm, when there was sufficient rain and a good year, was corn. The "South Pacific" song "I'm as corny as Kansas in August" is a misnomer, at least as dry land farming goes (try Nebraska or Iowa). There was no way we could grow a good corn crop without an unusually wet year, and those were few and far between. I recall many years when the corn would begin to dry up, a decision was made to cut it all up for ensilage, at least that way, salvaging some of the crop. But there were good years too.

I can recall one very disagreeable job in those times: after corn gets to a certain height, it is no longer possible to run a cultivator through it without knocking down the corn. So there was only one way: Dad, Tom and I would walk the field row by row with hoes to cut out sunflowers and cockle burrs. That was when Tom's hay fever acted up most, he was truly miserable.

I also remember that in those days Dad kept a lot of hogs and fed them field corn; my job was to drive the tractor pulling the trailer, the same one we hauled wheat in July, but now with a sideboard attached. Dad and Tom too I think would walk alongside the wagon with shucking gloves on, a leather glove with a metal protrusion, much like the end of a beer opener. They would shuck the corn, that is, pick it and throw the ear against the sideboard and bounce it into the wagon. I eventually did some shucking myself but was not too handy at it. Dad talked of the old days and shucking contests back in Nebraska. He was fast and good. I can remember bringing the corn to the storage bins in the hog house and having a machine that would shell it and put it into the bin. We fed bushels and bushels to the hogs in those days, and to the cattle too. That was what we used to call real "corn fed" livestock.

The actual corn picking or harvesting was done by a neighbor who had a corn picker or harvester. We never had one. It was common in those days to hear about farmers who had horrendous accidents--the corn picker would jam, they would not turn it off, would stick a hand or an arm in to pull out the jammed stocks, the machine would unclog and the farmer's arm or hand would get caught by the sleeve. We had three or four one-armed or one-handed farmers in the town. I had great fear and respect instilled in me about machines, and we never had a serious accident on our farm (from machinery that is; there were plenty of others.) Tom fell out of the granary once and broke an arm, Tom fell on a board with a nail in it and we had to take him, board, nail and all to the hospital, Jo Anne was bitten in the stomach by one of the horses. My accidents all seemed to happen away from the farm itself.

CONSERVATION AND CROP ROTATION

It seemed like we would plant milo or sorgum more than corn, and I am not exactly sure why, because all the row crops needed copious amounts of rain. But Dad was very up to date in his crop rotation techniques and also the care of the land. Mom often spoke of what terrible shape the farm was in 1941 when Dad got it and how he improved it by terracing, contour farming (planting along the sides of the terraces instead of perpendicular to them, up and down the hills, thus saving moisture and preventing soil erosion. I recall we would go through a cycle of wheat or corn, then alfalfa which would put nitrogen back into the soil. My Dad's proudest and finest achievement was with waterways allowing proper run off, good terracing, planting of windbreaks and creating what we called "the pond" at the north end of the farm, an eroded area he turned into a lush haven for birds, squirrels and an abundance of black walnut producing trees. It was all done through good management. I am not sure where he learned all that, but I know he subscribed to farm journals and kept in close contact with county farm extension people. You figure, he lived on a farm his entire life, from the time in SE Nebraska and the move by "immigrant" train car to the homestead north of Abilene in the early 1900s. I was always very proud of our farm and the way Dad ran it, how it looked, even though we did not have the resources others did. He had a balance in farming and in life that many did not have. He worked to the best of his abilities, but managed to enjoy life along the way, something I did not see in many of the families we knew.

9. CHORES

There was no lack of work to do on the farm as a boy; Dad could always find chores for us to do. When less than ten years of age, I can recall one of my jobs was to take the trash out to a barrel north of the house and burn it. When enough non-burnable stuff had accumulated, we hauled the whole kit and kaboodle up to the pasture to a spot we called the "dump," on a hill on the north 80 acres. From there you had a marvelous view of the whole Smokey Hill River Valley below, the town of Abilene to the southwest. The top of the hill would be a great site for a farm home for the right person. Both Jim and Tom talked about building up there one day, but it was pretty much "pie in the sky" dreaming. Tom came back home years later and during one summer dug up the dump hunting for old barbed wire, antique bottles and the like, but I don't think it made him rich. But there was lots of old wire, pop bottles, cans and plain junk at the dump, a perfect spot for cottontail rabbits to hide, so when we went rabbit hunting, that was always a mandatory stop along the route. One of us kids would jump on the top to scare out the rabbits and the farm dog would chase them down.

I also soon was in charge of gathering the eggs. We gathered two or three times a day; if you did not, the breakage would be up, and that meant lost money. I can recall those clucking Leghorns or Plymouth Rock hens pecking at me while I tried to maneuver a hand under their soft undersides and snatch away the eggs. Inevitably I would forget to do this chore, or put it off and play instead, so then there was a mess in the nests. The hens would peck open the eggs. We had to keep fresh straw baled from wheat stubble after harvest in the nests, so that too was a job. It meant cleaning out the old soiled straw and replacing it with new.

Later on, now perhaps 12 or 13 years of age, I was gradually given a whole series of outside chores, at first less in the morning because of school I guess, then both morning and night. I can recall most of that routine like it were today: feeding grain to the chickens, chicken mash or the like and making sure the water pans were full. Then moving on over to the silo where I would climb up in the silo and shovel ensilage down the chute and then on to a long feed bunk for the cattle. I spent many hours inside that silo when filling time came in the Summer, my job being to guide the filler or blower with a long rope attached to it and get the silage spread evenly throughout the silo, then tramping it down. You had to wear goggles and a face mask to protect your eyes since it was very dirty. There was always talk of the danger of poisonous gases building up in the silo, but I never experienced any of that. They mixed a type of molasses with the ensilage and I can recall vividly the sweet smell when months later I would be inside pitching the now well-matured stuff down the chute to the cattle.

A digression on silo filling (with corn, sorgum or maybe milo). It was an exciting time for me and a bit dangerous I thought. Someone (I never did it) had to climb the silo, perhaps with a height equivalent to a six or seven story building, make his way around the top, let down a rope and attach it to a pulley to pull the blower pipe up to the top. I have always been afraid of heights, so that moment terrified me. One time neighbor Gordon Kippenberger scooted up the outside of the silo like a mountain goat, using the steel tie bars as grips and steps. I was sure he was going to fall. The normal way to do the task was to climb up the steps of the silo which were generally enclosed by an oval brick wall, then walk the edge of the top of the silo which had a steel railing and attach the pulley. Gordon did it differently. When very young I used to climb those steps, almost too far apart to get from one to the next, scared to death at first, with a pair of binoculars around my neck, and when I got to the top I would play army "scout" searching the whole area for Apaches, Cherokees, Cheyenne or Sioux. Sometimes I was on the lookout for North Koreans or Chinese Communists. This was when I wore the Army helmet liner brother Jim brought home from the service.

The morning chores also included walking south from the silo, past the big barn and on to the hog house to take care of the pigs. The hog house was located a little away from everything else, maybe due to the prevailing winds. I can recall at different times feeding corn, oats and particularly buttermilk to the pigs. A smelly, disagreeable place it was. The buttermilk was stored in a fifty gallon barrel, and it always seemed like there were millions of flies around, and we would dip in the bucket and pour the stuff into the troughs below the swinging doors of each pen. And just outside was the "waller" that the hogs had to have in warm weather to cool off. This was a place into which we intentionally would run a hose to make mud to cool them off. It was a sight to behold to go out there and see thirty or forty hogs up to their ears or eyes in mud, grunting, snorting and enjoying themselves. The stench of the place was almost unbearable to me.

A Saturday affair: I can't decide which was more disagreeable to me, but as you might imagine, with all the diverse animals around and the diverse pens, a day of reckoning had to come for all. That was the day designated to clean out the chicken house, the barn (cattle or horses) or even worse, the hog house. More than likely it seemed to fall on Saturdays. I can recall over the years how the town kids looked forward to the weekend and Saturdays to hikes, picnics, ball games, but me and my buddy Mike Kippenberger would say on Monday, "Well, what kind of manure was it this weekend?" I shoveled chicken manure, hog manure, cow manure and even horse manure according to the occasion. Only a farm boy can tell you about the experience of working loose a shovelful of dung of some kind and see the steam come off it from the winter air, ah life. Dad had one of the old fashioned manure spreaders, so we would pitch the stuff directly, if the aim was good, out the windows or the doors into the manure spreader. Once again, the odor was evil; often we had to clear out for a while, breathe a bit of fresh air before attacking it again. I tried to invent reasons to be busy on those Saturdays, and I got out of it sometimes, more often than Mike Kippenberger who seemed to do it every weekend. That was either because the Germans kept their barns cleaner than the Irish, or maybe they liked to shovel shit more than we did.

After the hog house it was on to the barn for more chores. When we had sheep, you had to go up above into the haymow and break open several bales of hay to toss down into the manger for the sheep. I can recall as a very small boy, well, maybe not so small, of riding the bigger ones much like a small horse, including getting tossed off. I received more than one lecture about that since it was entirely possible to injure the poor things, but what a fun time that was. We also broke open bales of hay for the cows and the horses. We only kept two or three milk cows at a time, the same with horses. Dad boarded horses for people in town, but that's another story.

I don't know if I was naive or what, but I can recall many, many years later being kidded by city kids at college about what we farm kids were supposed to have been doing with the animals. I didn't even understand at first what they were getting at, but then could not believe anyone would do such a thing. Then I ran across the term "bestiality" in college ethics class or something and then allusions to it in classic literature, so maybe I missed out on part of Western Civilization huh?

The main chore in the barn was the milking. We always kept one or two milk cows for personal use. Eventually it became my chore to milk them. I have vivid recollections of those old cows, especially an old white one which eventually died after ingesting some metal or baling wire. Since we ran no dairy or sold to a dairy, we did not quite have the same standards as a dairy. You learned how to keep the milk clean, and most often it was, unless a stray fly would fall in and get wet and could not get out. But the barn was not exactly a sparkling place. We kept the place shoveled and swept, but it was not exactly "antiseptic". Flies abounded in summer. We had old wooden stanchions where we could lock the cow's head into place; we had metal leg chains, which were not always so easy to attach, to keep the cow from kicking the bucket over or from kicking us. I dodged many a blow. The milking stool was a t-shaped contraption, very simple, of two boards, perpendicular to each other, so you had to balance yourself, the bucket and be in the right vicinity to do the job.

I can recall town kids who would come to visit and would always want to help milk the cows. It never seemed a difficult task for us, but they seemed to have trouble getting the hang of it. For you rookies I can only describe the motion as a slow squeezing and gentle pulling at the same time. Anyway, we had to spray the area in the summertime and spray the animals before milking because the flies were so bad. But that did not keep the old cow from constantly switching her tail. The personal hygiene of cattle being what it is, the tail was, let's say, hardened with fecal material at its tip. That's the part that bats you in the face. So I devised a way to tie the tail in the sections of the metal leg chains, thus keeping her from switching me, but then the flies would drive her to distraction and I might still get a leg in my direction with spilt milk the result.

Mark J. Curran

The other reason I often did not get a full pail of milk up to the house and the cream separator was the cats. Lots of them. We always had a cat or two for catching mice, but they proliferated as nothing else on the farm. I delighted in aiming a spurt of milk at their faces, watching them lick it all off and do it all over again. In spite of all the above we did seem to have enough milk and cream for home consumption, a good thing Dad was not into anything more than that, because we would have gone broke. A lingering memory was the cold, cold days when my hands were darn near frozen, sitting down to milk the old cow. I never considered it might hurt her worse than me.

Those icy mornings when the barnyard was semi frozen remind me of a story.
I never wore work shoes to school and used rubber galoshes in the barn most of the time. But my buddy Mike one time had a pair of cowboy boots he wore doing chores, including the aforementioned cleaning out barns, and for some reason ended up wearing them to school. It was one thing to be out in the frozen barnyard and another to come into a super heated Kansas school building during the winter. The cow manure thawed and he felt a bit like others were staring at him.

Those were the main chores; there were probably others, but that's another story. There were times when I did all the above morning and night, particularly during the time Dad was in Florida in the winter of 1955. And once or twice I neglected them. Imagine a milk cow that must be milked twice a day after a time is missed. I caught holy hell for that. I don't know where it is in this chronicle, but I vividly recall the day when I was old enough and fast enough that Dad could not catch me to give me a whipping for such times when I "blew off" the chores.

10. ACCIDENTS

I think I mentioned there were never any serious accidents on the farm, but I guess I meant machinery-related. If my Dad had any close calls with machinery, he never talked about them. But it was not uncommon in Dickinson County to meet one-armed, one-handed, or three or four fingered farmers who had lost limbs to corn pickers, combines, mowers and the like. I only had one such accident but of a different sort. During my days of fieldwork after wheat harvest, one day I pulled the tractor into its parking spot, next to two fifty-gallon gas barrels. For some reason, and I still do not know why or how today, the tractor caught fire directly above the gas tank. I recall it all now as though it were a dream. I believe it must have been the grease and oil residue on the engine or top of the tank which was directly in front of the steering wheel. It seemed like I was moving in slow motion. I think I grabbed a gunny sack and tried to beat it out, then thinking that was not too safe, jumped off the tractor and ran.

No one was there to help and I think I was pretty young, but the flame eventually died out. I casually mentioned the fire to Mom once inside the house and cannot remember her response other than a "Be careful." Who says only the British are masters of understatement!

But we had lots of other kinds of accidents and my brother Tom, or "Tommy" at the time, had his share. He was climbing in the rafters of the granary one time, fell and somehow ran a rusty nail through the palm of his hand. We had to take him, nail, and the long board it was attached to, all together, to the hospital. Tetanus shots followed. It scared the daylights out of me at the time.

I mentioned somewhere else about Jo Anne and the horse; she was bitten on the stomach while leaning over the barnyard fence to pet the Palomino horse, and that ended any attachment to horses.

There was a serious accident involving me, but my memories of it are so foggy. It is one of those times that you remember something not from experiencing it but from others telling and retelling it. We used to "ice skate" on the water tank down by the barn, that is, slide around in our shoes. I must have been about five years old at the time. I fell through the ice; Jim heard my cries and ran down and pulled me out, cold, wet and crying. That's how he used to tell it anyway.

My accidents were rather at school--a broken arm when pushed against a brick wall in the first grade and another broken arm when pole vaulting in Jr. High and finally a concussion from freshman football at AHS. Here are a couple of details as I digress. I was a better than average distance runner on the high school track team, participating in the half-mile run in those days before the switch to "meters." I think my best quarter mile was a loping 63 seconds and my best half mile run at the state track meet in Wichita, a 2:28 something. But one day when I was bored some with running laps in spring track practice, I decided to mess around at the pole vault pit. In those days the pole vault pole was not fiber glass but actually heavy bamboo. I prepared for the vault, ran down the runway and completely missed setting the pole in the hole. Instead, I fell across the hole with my right arm out to break my fall, and the result was a broken wrist, the arm bent up at a perfect 45 degree angle above the wrist. It was painful to be sure, but funny to see. My buddies saw it and heehawed.

A related incident took place one other p.m. All the stud football players were required to go out for track just to keep in shape for the football season in the fall. One of the slow linemen was placed in the mile run and in one of the meets was so far behind that he "ran" the last lap backwards. It cost him about two hours of extra laps after the meet.

The third broken arm was in the '49 car accident which I think I tell of elsewhere.

I think there was the usual appendicitis, maybe tonsillitis for either Jo Anne or Tom, but I can't recall for sure. There was the mysterious time when Mom went for surgery at St. Joseph's in Salina, a surgery which turned out to be a hysterectomy. But I only understood about that vaguely, such was the explanation given.

Cars and Accidents. There used to be a standing joke about getting your car stuck out in the middle of the country when dating one of those country girls. That never happened to me, although I remember slipping and sliding around a lot. I always fancied myself to be an excellent "mudder," this from driving tractors all those years. (A flash forward--I had a real chance to test my "mudding" in the summer of 2004 when I got our pickup truck and Scamp trailer stuck almost to the axles near Pierre, South Dakota, trying to find Kevin Costner's buffaloes from "Dances with wolves.") I can recall on our own farm that we must have averaged once or twice a year pulling motorists out of the mud trying to come up our lane, this with the tractor.

I did get into it one time. It was early summer and I was driving around in farm country northeast of Abilene in the process of contacting farmers for a prospective job that summer. I was driving my brother Tom's 49 Chevy. It had some noisy pipes on it, pin striping on the side, certainly not his handy work. But I think I was paying a lot more attention to the noise of the pipes backing off than driving so I ended up in mud to the axle. I can't recall if I got out by myself or had to call on the local farmer.

Speaking of that, the jokes about the traveling salesman and the farmers' daughters were a standard while growing up. The old classic of the three salesmen, the three daughters and "It's the cat" punch line was one of them. I can recall literally hours sitting on top of the city swimming pool in the snack bar area and hearing Jerry Collins and Jack Kippenberger swap dirty jokes. They were in no small part my sex education, poor as it was. There was no formal training then, and a poor farm boy just had to keep his eyes and ears open. I thank my lucky stars and who knows who else looking after me today for not having the troubles I could have had with all that, but a staunch Catholic upbringing, which included the fear of a fiery hell, probably saved the day. But that's another story.

11. FLOWERS AND BIRDS

Mom had a great love of flowers, birds and just being out of doors. She always had some flowers out each spring, this aside from the annuals. There were beautiful lilacs north of the house, tulips for a short time each spring, jonquils, lots of multi-colored iris, and lots of roses. There was a slight incline in the yard to the north of the farm house; the mound was above the storm cellar, another creepy place for me, used to store potatoes and theoretically protect us all from Kansas tornadoes. Mom used this area and worked off and on for years there on her rock garden with all kinds of flowers and plants. I have the impression she received little help with all that, not much cooperation on the part of the kids. But I know she loved it. After retirement to Abilene in 1959 Dad had more time to help her, and their vegetable and flower gardens were spectacular. On the original farm, Dad kept a large plot on the north 40 that he did not sell to Paul Whitehair and planted garden and roses there as well. Katie saw these gardens when she was just a toddler when we would come to visit.

Mom loved the birds, the sounds of each, and tried to instill an appreciation of them in us, again not very successfully at the time. But the love I have today of the mockingbird and my favorite song of the meadowlark were garnered from her lessons I think. When we would go back to visit Abilene with visits to the old farm, I still associated the meadows and fields where we worked with the Meadowlark and love the sound. Fortunately there is a Western Meadow Lark on the west slope of Colorado where we spend part of each summer; you can see and hear them in the pastures near Bayfield and a meadow across from the country church we have attended since 1972. It always takes me back home when I hear it. It's been so long now. But the most beautiful birds were the red Cardinal which stayed into the winter and would eat seed or scraps we put out, or the Blue Jay, a feisty bird along the line of the Mockingbird which would play with and fool the cats we always had around the farm. We also had Turtle Doves and Whippoorwills with their plaintive song.

But as a general rule I was not particularly attuned to wildlife. We had pheasants in the fields, but generally saw them when on drives in the country, along the two lane highways or gravel roads. Once in awhile an old hoot owl would appear in the trees out by the barn. There were lots of cottontail rabbits in the fields as well as the prairie jack rabbit. I can recall a time when we would go crazily bouncing over the pastures in a pickup truck with a spot light and net to catch the jacks and get a premium for them from the coursing park where they used them live for greyhound racing. My best hunting shot ever was a long shot of a lone jack on a ridge after a winter snowstorm, went in one eye and out the other, a grizzly affair.

The Farm

We would see an occasional garter snake or bull snake (one big one wrapped itself around the telephone wire entering the house and we had to knock it down with a hoe), but I never did see a prairie rattler and am not sure they were in our part of the country. Dad used to talk about the blue snake or blue racer and tell tales of them chasing you in the field. I don't know yet if that is true.

I can remember the excitement in 1951 when there was flooding around the valley with the high water from the Smokey Hill River south of Abilene. I do not know how or why, but we had several deer in our upland pasture that summer, and it was fun to see them easily leap the fences that had barbed wire on top for keeping cattle in. I would grow to love deer on our place on Deer Trail Lane in Colorado twenty years later.

We heard coyotes, but rarely saw them. I can only remember once or twice seeing them in the daytime, once while riding the school bus north of town. Antelope I never saw on the farm, but only on those times on the western plains of Kansas or eastern Colorado on trips to Colorado Springs or Denver.

There would be an occasional possum, and one time we had a badger making mounds up in the wheat field near the pond; I believe it was either trapped or poisoned. That reminds me of the bounty money the county had put on such animals, including gophers. It must have been a dollar or two per animal. Brother Tom spent a lot of time and energy setting traps out in the alfalfa fields, in the mounds and tunnels they made in the fields. He did not get rich. They could absolutely ruin a good, level field in a short time. So it was a declared war.

12. PETS ON THE FARM AND 4-H ANIMALS

Brother Jim and Ginger the dog who had a "Catholic" funeral

We always had a pet of some kind or other, but in a very different sense than pets in the city. A pet had to also have some primary use or function; there had to be some good out of it. So, our dogs were always work dogs, at least to some degree. We did have a little terrier, Ginger I think was its name; I was so tiny I can hardly remember. But I do know that when Ginger died, we had a doggy funeral and buried the animal on the north side of the barn near the corral with a wooden cross to mark the spot.

I remember better our beautiful Collie "Carlo," a wonderful farm dog that went with Dad to the fields each day, loping alongside the little Ford tractor Dad used to farm an entire half section of land. The dog would follow the tractor or whatever stirring up rabbits. But its life ended tragically, like most of the animals I remember loving on the farm.

I can recall one time when Carlo came home, not really seriously sick, but just below par. We discovered a spent bullet in its hide, shot perhaps accidentally, perhaps not, by a hunter's bullet. The wound was not bleeding and healed shortly, but Carlo's end came soon after that. One day while keeping Dad company in the field (this day Dad was mowing hay and had a mower attached to the rear of the tractor with a blade running to the side), the dog ran too close once too often and the mower of course clipped its legs. Dad quickly grabbed a hammer out of the tractor tool box and put the poor animal out of its misery with a quick blow to the head. But a more faithful companion he never had, and although I was very young I mourned old Carlo.

The next farm dog was the one I recall best, a black and white Border Collie called "Lady." Lady was a good dog. All our pets lived on table scraps and their own initiative as hunters. We never purchased dog food in town. Lady often would come home with a rabbit from the field, and it was just expected that she would fend for herself most of the time. She had good blood from the Border Collie line, but never did have the proper training to go along with it. Yet instinct took her a long way. I recall particularly when Dad ran sheep for a few years and the dog would run along behind, nipping their hind feet, helping to herd them into the corral. The same with cattle, when I used to go up to the pasture with the Ford tractor to bring in the cattle, Lady would accompany me, a joy for a young boy. She did not have any particular shelter during bad weather, but would craw under the front porch of the house in inclement weather. But never was a farm dog allowed inside the house, no matter what.

Lady had one fault -- she loved to bark at cars coming up the driveway or in the parking area in front of the house. And occasionally she would get all the way down the lane and bark at cars as they passed on old Highway 40. That was how she met her end, hit by a car she barked at and chased. I believe I was away at college and was just told about it.

There were also the cats, anywhere from two or three up to over a dozen, they seemed to proliferate on the farm. They lived largely from hunting rodents, small mice in the barns, table scraps and some milk. They got plenty of the latter whenever I milked the cows; only later did I realize the loss to Dad when I brought far less milk than actually given by the cow to the house, having either given it to or squirted the cats in the barn.

The 4-H animals came to be a sort of pet, though not in the same sense as the dogs or cats. There was the most famous, Wilhemina, the Sears Gilt. Sears funded a program locally in which a 4-H er received a gilt, sent it to be bred and when it farrowed, could keep all but one gilt of the new letter which was passed on to the next boy or girl. They were Durocs in my day, a deep red or rust colored, or Hampshires, black with white stripe along the back. I can remember getting mine with the promise of a good project, getting her ready for the county fair and also making some money. This involved feeding the animal and particularly preparing it for the fair. We would arrive at the latter sometime in late summer, but the animal's time was competitive with summer baseball, farm work and other affairs. I can recall making a short board about two by three feet, out of thin plywood, painting our name on it and the name of the local 4-H club "Abilene Aggies". The idea was to practice moving the pig around a small area or enclosure with the help of this board and a long stick (maybe like a broom handle) in the other hand. The idea was to show off the pig's best qualities, whatever they were, to the judge of the competition. I know you did not want the pig to be too fat, too skinny and you had to have it clean, so there were faucets and a wash area or pen at the fairgrounds in the pig barn. We are talking serious business here, but I was serious only up to a point. I had much more fun having balloon fights, playing, flirting with the girls and eating delicious hamburgers at the outdoor food stands at the fairgrounds, great days! I cannot recall but I think my Sears Gilt won a red ribbon standing for second class. And I know I had more than one pig so I may be confusing them.

We never had a pickup truck while Dad had the farm; the main reason I think was money. Instead we had a trailer of sorts we could put sides on and haul one or two animals, towing with the old car, a late 1940s Plymouth. That's how Wilhemina and others made it to the fair. I can't recall if it was she or not, but I did sell one pig in the annual 4-H sale making a few bucks.

The most memorable time with Wilhemina was later on in her illustrious career. Breeding time came, so we loaded her into the same rickety trailer and took her down the road to visit the local stud hog. It came time to pick her up; the owner of the stud hog had called saying she was ready to come home. I remember the trip home yet today. Mom and Dad were in the car, but I was driving. We were heading home, having crossed the Smokey Hill river bridge south and east of town. The pig somehow uprooted the gate of the trailer. I was tooling along and happened to look in the rear view mirror and saw this cloud of dust on the road behind the car and trailer. Wilhemina had literally "hit the road" in a cloud of dust and was rolling over and over. By the time we braked the car and backed up, she was running lickety-split off in the middle of a milo field by the river. I guess she was heading back to her lover boy. We spent the next hour, and it was quite cold as I recall, sometime in the fall, chasing that damned fool hog across the milo field. We finally caught it, had no rope in the car or truck but did have some baling wire in the trunk (no farmer would be without it) and managed to get her back in the trailer and home.

Evidently she was unhurt because several months later she farrowed a huge litter of pigs, but Wilhemina did not end up with a happy family situation. The hog decided to farrow on the coldest night of the winter, well below zero. Dad was not at home for this was the winter he was in Florida doing carpentry work to keep things going. But at about two in the morning Mom woke me up and said we had better be checking on the hog. We went out and tried to save the pig. Wilhemina had sixteen I think. All seemed to go well so we went back to the house, still in the middle of the night. The next morning when we went out to the hog house, the scene was a disaster: there were frozen pigs all up and down the alleyway, strewn all over the hog house, and only three alive. Most had crept out from under the heat lamp that was in the middle of the farrowing pen, down into the feeding trough, and under the swinging door that separated it from the alleyway. That disaster marked my last experience I recall with pigs. Wilhemina herself was either eventually butchered or sold at market. I cannot recall exactly when, but we knew it was bound to happen sooner or later.

The entire experience with the farm animals, especially the 4-H animals is a delicate subject with me yet. Not that I never liked or resented the work associated with them, but I never did seem to have a talent for it, never really got the hang of it. I suppose I learned something from it all, but darned little. For sure, nothing from my Dad's great knowledge rubbed off on me. I could do the chores, knew how to take care of the animals' feed, but never really understood the biological part of it including the breeding. Not that I was ignorant of the main facts of breeding, but I did not understand a lot of the whys and wherefores and whens. And it was not indifference as much as it was an absolutely untalented area for me. My life seems to run to those extremes. I think I have written how I would become almost physically sick when I had to play the role of "gofer" when Dad worked on machinery; such was my lack of interest and absolute lack of inclination toward anything mechanical.

But I do laugh when I think of the cloud of dust in the road or me trying to herd a hog around at the fair or of Gus Goose, a main character in it all.

Gus Goose and the geese. Gus was the "most unforgettable character" of the farm animals. It all goes back to my early teen years when I became excited with the idea of raising geese for the 4-H project. I would start out small, but I figured that about 3000 geese would be the goal. We reached about 24 I think, but that was enough! I'll tell you about the great enterprise. I can recall like yesterday Dad going into town and getting the goose eggs. I think he used chicken hens to sit on them and hatch them. Anyway it started with two or three geese and a gander, of the Grey Toulouse variety. Little by little we ended with about 24. The geese had no specific place to be or be found, but were allowed to roam the place. There is a scotch whiskey, Ballantine's I believe, which advertised for some time using white geese as "watchdogs" for the distillery. Ours could have applied for the job. Any unusual noise, any stranger or car coming up the lane and it sounded like a migration of Canadas, honking by all sizes and shapes of the geese. If especially excited they would all set off running and a few would actually fly a bit across the barnyard.

The geese would nest each spring, and one fine day the goose would appear with several little goslings trailing behind her. We decided to help out and raise the little ones in the warm house (it must have been early spring because it was still quite cold outside). The place was a corner in the warm kitchen. A cardboard box was placed in the corner which contained plenty of fresh newspaper for them, and we gave them plenty of water and feed. So I was in business. They were so darned cute, small, cuddly, warm, and just kind of cooing at that age. We soon discovered that the babies could not walk properly on the slick linoleum of the kitchen floor. But if you took tiny strips of cloth and tied their legs together they could stand up and get along just fine. Fun times.

But live and learn on the farm. Some time later we saw these geese now grown weaving drunkenly all over the barn yard like they'd been eating sour mash instead of chicken mash. It took awhile, but it turns out something in the formula was actually blinding the poor things. Once we figured it out, we saved the rest. But it did rather inhibit the flock size.

The geese loved a rainy day, and that is when we discovered Gus Goose, the big gander, and his wonderful personality. One day during a particularly strong rain, the kind that came with rivulets of water running all across the yard, we found him rolling a five-gallon bucket along the ground, pushing it along with his beak. What prompted the behavior I cannot say, but every time it rained he was out there with the bucket. Gus came to be the true leader of the flock, the head gander. In the haymow of our old fashioned barn there was a wooden floor, and in the center we had some time ago put up a basketball goal so I played continually for years, certainly all through junior high and high school. At one end of this floor there was a door which could be slid open, and the view outside was a nice one, encompassing the farm to the south, all the way to and beyond the highway. At that time I either rode a bicycle or walked to school in good weather. I can recall many an afternoon while still walking along the highway heading for the lane and home to the farm house, I would see all the geese, with Gus at their head, blissfully gazing out the haymow door as if surveying all their domain. They never voluntarily flew out that door, but I chased them out a time or two, just to see what would happen. They could not really fly long distances, but would flap their wings and make it safely to the ground.

On one of those occasions home from school, I went out to the barn to play basketball, and when I came into the haymow from the door on the other end, Gus was perfectly balanced up on the basketball left on the floor. I ask myself today, so many years later, was it my imagination? I swear I saw it. Gus was only beginning to come into his glory. In later times, and no thanks to me, he won the Grand Champion Purple ribbon in the gander category of the Dickinson County Free Fair in Abilene, his crowning glory. His end, not different from lesser geese, was the dinner table. That was after my original dream of a flock of three thousand had ebbed with the passing of time. I do recall in this instance that I would not partake of that meal.

What remains of the goose chronicle are memories of incredible noise, a real racket when they would get started, and goose doodoo all over the place. And that strange behavior.

Over the years there were constantly either cattle, horses or sheep pastured on our farm. The pasture area was actually fairly large, or so it seemed to me, significant in the total 320 acres. It stretched due north of the house and farm buildings all the way to the new interstate highway located on the north 40. I can remember having sheep for several years, cattle even more and horses off and on, these pastured for a fee by my Dad. We never had a lot of any of them, but it came to be one of my jobs to "bring in the cattle" or sheep.

Now it was important to know exactly where they were located in the pasture, because it could be a long, long walk to get them. At different times I rode our Palomino horse to get them, but really this was seldom, since the horse bucked me off a time or two and I never did feel comfortable with it thereafter. I often walked to get the cattle or sheep, sometimes carrying a single shot rifle in case of a rabbit or two, but most often I would drive the little Ford tractor. It was great fun and really for me was a substitute for the hot rods and crazy driving of some of my friends in town. The tractor had four forward speeds, and the fourth gear was highway gear, reaching perhaps fifteen or twenty miles per hour. I would hot rod that tractor all over the pasture, making sharp turns, careening over terraces, never once turning it over, perhaps due to the great advantage of the spread front wheels on the Ford. Looking back, it easily could have happened, and that would "have been that" as Mom used to say. More often than not the cattle would be way up on the northeast corner of the farm, the longest distance from the barn. I was often accompanied by the Border Collie Lady. I used to get some help from her, but just as often it seemed she would send the animals running off in the opposite direction, back up to the other corner of the pasture, but with no lack of enthusiasm on her part. Anyway it was great fun. I never thought about the wear and tear on the tractor or the wasted gasoline, or of flipping it over.

I guess I was a rascal, don't know if there was a genuine cruel streak, or if that was just what farm kids did. I would unnecessarily pull at the dogs' ears or tails, or pick up a kitty cat and toss it into the air to see if it would land on its feet, which it always did. I cannot explain the how or why I did such things other than just plain devilment, and nothing ever carried past that early age. As I review this today on the computer, I am horrified. There were many spankings as a child; well deserved for sure. I knew I had "grown up" when the day came when Dad was going to give me a spanking with his belt, and I outran him, running out into the alfalfa field east of the farm house For some reason, he did not pursue the subject when I sheepishly and cautiously returned to the farm house, probably afraid I was going to miss dinner.

I don't know if I ever told of my temper tantrums and packing things to "run away." I never made it beyond the end of the lane. I'm sure Mom and Dad got a lot of laughs at those escapades. I have this vague memory, maybe from Little Rascals Movies, of the little boy in overalls, a long stick with a bandana wrapped around it with his "stuff" while running away. I understand I was not the only little fellow who made such threats.

13. 4-H DAYS

Mark in 4-H T-shirt leaning on the Chevy

I've talked about some of the projects that involved animals, but there is more to say. Growing up on a small farm in Dickinson County left no choice but for all of the kids in our family to be in 4-H. I think we all participated to some degree in scouting, me only a year or two in the Cubs, but that was basically for the town kids. 4-H was the way you did it on the farm. But we had a curious situation, living so close to town. We were all members of the local club which belonged to the town of Abilene, the Abilene Aggies. I do not recall if I ever had a choice in the matter, if I was asked if I wanted to be in 4-H. I just followed along in Jo Anne's and Tom's footsteps. Keep in mind that Jim was fifteen years older than myself, "grown up" and working in business in a nearby town most of my childhood years on the farm; he may have done a lot of this, but I don't know.

Tom and Jo Anne had both excelled in 4-H on both the local and state levels, participating in livestock projects, animal judging, but also in sewing and cooking in Jo Anne's case and in woodworking with Tom. Perhaps his ongoing love for furniture finishing and antique furniture explain why he got back into that endeavor with an antique store in San Diego, this in the final years of his life after leaving civil service.

The Farm

I believe the 4-H meetings were held once a month, always in the city hall in Eisenhower park in the fairgrounds and adjacent to the local armory and the old CCC baseball stadium. I can never remember a time when one of us was not an important officer in the club. Both Tom and Jo Anne were role models for me in later years, although you never put it in those terms or thought about it that way then. Tom was president for a couple of terms, Jo Anne secretary. I later was president during my time. There were so many instances when I followed in Tom's footsteps, in 4-H, in academics and in sports to some extent, and in Jim's when it came to debate in high school. I believe the club had a sergeant at arms, a song leader, secretary, treasurer, vice president and president. Also there was the customary reporter -- there were always the mandatory reports for the "Abilene Reflector Chronicle," the local small town newspaper dominated by one Henry B. Jameson who definitely represented the "town" opinion and the right side of the tracks folks, the country club set. All this was not consciously opposed by most kids who were largely unaware of class in those days, but this was probably not the case with their more aware parents. Suffice to say, in Kansas farm country and even more, in Eisenhower country, the political slant was always conservative or moderate Republican.

The meetings were a social situation for us kids. Because it was a town club, the members were by and large not "country" and had more of a small town makeup. I believe Abilene had 7000 people at the time. For whatever reason, there was a tone, a lack of "country" and a bit more sophistication to the club. I can remember we started the meeting with the 4-H pledge: "I pledge my heart to greater loyalty, my head to greater thinking, my hands to greater service and my health to better living, for my club, my community and my country." Then came the inevitable songs to be sung with great gusto, or giggling by some of us: "You are my sunshine," "Sunflower State", "Tell me why" and many other rousing ditties. Then came old business, then new business, then the treasurer's report. It was the closest thing to the atmosphere of an old fashioned town meeting I have ever experienced; there truly was a democratic tone. And parliamentary procedure ruled the day. Each year the county had a 4-H Model Meeting Day, and clubs would compete with the goal to hold the niftiest "model" meeting according to correct procedures. It seemed like the Aggies always did well along that line.

Another of our fortés was the little plays clubs would put on in a county competition. All the clubs in the county would compete. The Aggies were outstanding in my time. My brother Jim who had considerable experience in acting, drama and music in high school, and you got to be known for such things in the small towns, was our director for many years. I can recall the fun and the excitement each year when the club would compete for the prize and most often win it. Later on I became a regular cast member, with some success as I recall. Drama was a big extra-curricular activity in jr. high and high school in those days, and I got the lead in two or three of the plays, including one or two in 4-H. I can remember one title--"Auggie Evans Private Eye." I cannot for the life of me remember where they dug up those plays, but somebody must have done some research. Anyway it was great fun.

I am constantly amazed these past few years when it seems so hard to memorize anymore. The Catholic Church screwed up most of us in my generation by slightly changing the wording of most of the memorized prayers after Vatican II, the changes resulting from the changes in liturgy from the Latin to English. In terms of music I can remember only bits and pieces of the lyrics to songs I knew in the 50s and 60s. But in 4-H days it seemed easy to memorize the lines to those plays and also to dramatic readings we did in speech class in public school. I can recall one of the highlights of meetings on summer nights was to hurry out of the meeting and go over to the ballpark where the Jr. Legion or someone would be in the middle of a night baseball game. And often someone would be selling homemade pie, cake and ice cream outside the band shell; it seems like a big piece of chocolate cake and a bowl of home made ice cream were about 25 to 50 cents. My mouth still waters when I think of that; I have not had such good tasting ice cream in stores since. The foamy excuse for flavor in most city places leaves me disappointed. Maybe that's why, later on, we bought an electric ice cream maker and used it regularly at the cabin near Durango; the ritual is still one of Katie's best memories of growing up. Oh, I just remembered the cocoanut ice cream in Manaus on the Amazon River in Brazil … a bit off the beaten track, but worth it.

Sheep in the barnyard on 4-H Project Day

There were other fun moments of 4-H; the "4-H Day or "Project Day," generally in mid-summer when we would all pile in the back of a big open bed truck and drive all around the county to the different farms to see each others' projects, the best part of the day being the great picnic afterwards out at Eisenhower Park. The food was the usual rural fare, fried chicken, potato salad, farm tomatoes, corn I think, cake, pie, and ice cold watermelon. We also drank Iced tea or soft drinks (no appetite whetted for beer yet in those days). I forgot, part of it all too was we went swimming in the big pool in the park before eating; swimming too soon after eating was feared in those days, and then there were the baseball games later on in the evening. And memories are vague, but I think a lot of early teen age flirting took place then too. All I know is my memories are great. But we had fun. I guess some people had more fun than others. The teen age pregnancy was still really frowned upon; the girl generally just "disappeared" for a few months and maybe or maybe not returned to school. Babies were given up for adoption in the great majority of cases. And everyone knew the "good' and "bad" girls, and the "good" girls who were bad some times, and how all you needed to do was get a couple of beers down the girl, and how you better have a condom in your billfold. It was all pretty much folklore. This did not at all coincide with being Catholic, naive, and scared shitless of the consequences if you were in my shoes.

14. CARS AND MEMORIES

Jo Anne, Mark, and the old Buick on a snowy day

We did not get around in the newest of cars; there was just no way Dad could afford them. My earliest recollection is a late 40s vintage Buick which was also the car in which we had the bad wreck in 1949. It was black, had four doors and a running board, a slick car, I guess, for the times. Abilene lacked items for shopping, at least the variety and sales prices that Salina offered, so there were always occasional shopping trips to the "big" town some twenty-five miles away. Memories are vague, but the forays seemed to consist in visiting the Singer Sewing Shop (Mom always preferred the Singer machine and that was what Jo Anne learned on). But I remember the dime store, Woolworth's I believe. They sold these huge tall sacks of popcorn for a dime and had an incredible variety of stuff for a kid. There were always treats of ice cream, or candy on that trip.

I was in third grade I believe. We all went to Salina that day, most likely a Saturday since school was in session. Dad was not with us, probably because of work of some kind on the farm. Mom was driving; I was in the middle in the front seat and Grandma Cusick on the right. Jo Anne and Tom were in back. I never have remembered the accident; all I know is from what they told me later in the hospital. At New Cambria, a tiny burg, a spot in the road east of Salina on old Highway 40, apparently the brakes went out on the Buick. Mom had two choices: the ditch on the right and the chance of rolling the automobile, or trying to pass. There was some kind of a truck ahead of us. So she risked passing, pulled out and another vehicle was coming head on. I went through the windshield (there were no seat belts in those days) and received a broken arm and a fractured skull. Grandma was killed. Mom suffered a severely broken collarbone, multiple rib injuries and some internal injuries, enough to put her in the hospital for some time. Jo and Tom with the protection of those old high seats suffered only bruises in the back seat. I recall waking in the hospital, feeling no pain whatsoever, and Jim and also Dad were there. They waited until I was better before rolling me down to Mom's room and I think staying there until I was discharged. Jim told of the vigil prayers all through the first night at St. Andrew's Church in Abilene. I was close to death for some time. It must not have been my designated time; the prayers and the medicine worked. I felt nary a pain through it all other than the emotions a few days later when they told me Grandma had died. It was one of those times when you just cry your heart out, not that frequent a thing. But I can surely remember my grief, such soul rendering crying when I found out the news. At the age of eight or nine this was my first time realizing the deep pain of death. The feeling was agonizing, my first time around with such emotions, a deep, suffocating painful hurt of losing that dear old lady who used to buy me ice cream cones on each trip to town, rub my hand at night as we said bedtime prayers.

There was shock too when they gave me a mirror in the hospital for the first time: my face was black with the stitches from the cuts on the face and head (and some of the scars are still there). It was Jim who told me later that my favorite winter coat (I still have a picture of that coat in my mind, corduroy with bands of leather) was totally blood soaked after the accident. This was perhaps the second time, or third if you count my birth and stay in an incubator at 3 plus pounds, I had been close to death (breaking through the ice on the stock tank at about age five was yet another close call). It simply was not my time. I have always felt protected by God at those times.

Mark J. Curran

The old 1940s Plymouth, the Chevy, Mark, and the cat

The next car I recall was an old Plymouth, green if I'm not mistaken. This must have been a late 40s model as well. It's the one we were hauling the trailer with when Wilhemina my Sears Gilt 4-H hog hit the road. I was aware we had these old vehicles and to this day regret my immaturity because I recall bugging Dad to do this and that about the cars, and I am sure the maintenance he did or did not do depended much on the little money he had available. But we never had the shiny new cars around.

There may have been another car or two, but never a new one, that is, until Jim bought Mom and Dad a new 1958 Chevrolet. It was a stripped down model, but it was new and ran terrific, the first new car the family had ever experienced. I had the use of it whenever I needed it.

It was only upon retirement that Dad could get a new vehicle. He got a 1962 yellow Chevy Impala after selling the farm, and that was the one we drove on a long, long trip to San Diego in 1963. It was kind of a graduation trip, in part for me, having just finished at Rockhurst College in Kansas City, Missouri. I remember certain parts of the trip, the Grand Canyon, driving through the gorgeous Gunnison River country in Colorado (this was before they dammed it up for Blue Mesa) a wild night in Las Vegas where I couldn't seem to lose on the nickel machines, and finally the time in San Diego where Tom at that time was on top of the world. We went to his girlfriend Valerie Hamilton's parents' house on the hill overlooking La Jolla. It was a beautiful place with a terrific view overlooking the Pacific. The Currans had never seen such a place. And there was much more. My immaturity showed on that trip; I can recall driving entirely too fast perhaps 90 miles per hour on a two-lane road east of San Diego. I shudder to think what could have happened.

Dad and Mom's last car was the 1973 green Dodge. I can recall coming home to Abilene and the back end of the car would be full of garden tools and gunny sacks, always fairly dirty from going out to the farm. For this was the car Dad would use at the pasture during retirement. (How he would have loved to have our shiny Chevy pickup of current days.) It ran great but was hard to keep clean from use on the country roads. The kitchen on the house in town jutted out a bit into the driveway; you had to maneuver slightly around it to get the car into the garage. I guess that explains why the Dodge had several scrapes on the side, and Mom and Dad would discuss who had put them there. I don't know, but I do know that Dad would back out of there without always knowing exactly where he was going. Keep in mind he was in his late 70s or early 80s by then. It was the last car, the last memories.

15. DAD, HORSES AND THE PALOMINOS

My Dad knew horses, had been around them all his life, including using them for recreation, farm work and transportation as well in the earlier part of the twentieth century. They were a mainstay on the original farm at Buckeye that his Mom and the sons farmed for so many years. He in fact was somewhat of a horse trader I think, able to spot some good horse flesh and knew the tricks of the trade. He told of all the workhorses on the farm growing up in southeast Nebraska and then on the homestead north of Abilene. (See "Neal" in this book.) So I guess he wanted us to respect and love them the way he did. It never happened as far as I know.

We had some beautiful Palominos while growing up, the mare a dark palomino with a beautiful white blaze down her forehead, thus the name "Blaze;" the offspring a mare of the classic golden palomino mold. Dad kept good equipment around for use of the horses: reins, bridle, and a good saddle. I rode one of the Palominos a time or two in the pasture to bring in the cattle, one of the chores while growing up, but preferred to careen around on the Ford tractor. I don't remember any of the kids or grandchildren really being crazy about horses like the town kids seemed to be, or wanting to ride or even be around the horses.

Jo Anne was petting one of them down by the barn one time and it bit her on the stomach, the end of any attachment there. I loved looking at them and did some riding, but still remember being bucked off in the alfalfa field east of the farmhouse (History repeats itself; I had exactly the same feeling in March, 1991, when I went sailing over the top of my bicycle in Tempe while trying to avoid a little old lady on the sidewalk. But that's another story from another time). But I can also remember one day riding the young mare as fast as she could go over the plowed fields and cultivated water ways, the only time in my life I think when I got a horse out of a gallop into a full run. But I was scared to death the whole time.

More memorable was the death of one of the horses, another sad time on the farm. I was outside that morning; it must have been spring time or early summer since there was heavy dew on the ground. The horse was outside the corral, as frisky as I had ever seen her, running all over the big space between barn and granary. It was then she slipped, and we ran up to see the horse, silent and hobbling. The broken bone showed several inches outside the skin above the knee. There was only one thing to do under the circumstances. Dad sent me into the house for one of the rifles to put her out of her misery. There was a moment of panic; none of the rifles was there, seems like Tom had taken them all on a hunting trip. So reluctantly Dad used one of the shotguns; I can still see the hole about the size of a quarter in that beautiful horse's forehead. Dad assured me that it was quick, as painless as possible under the circumstances. I guess you never considered a veterinarian under those circumstances, not with a riding horse and on a limited budget.

Dad, Keah, and the horse barn in the 1970s

Years later after Dad retired and sold all of the farm except the north 40 acres, he built a shed and boarded horses for town kids, and he always kept one or two around for what he hoped would be the use of the grandchildren, Jo and Johnny's kids. But it sticks in my mind that they never took much of an interest either, like Jo Anne, Tommy or me in our day. It must have really been disappointing to Dad, but I think he enjoyed just having the horses around. The picture above depicts one cold wintry day when he took Keah and me up to the barn and talked and talked about those horses.

Horses must have been in his Irish blood; years later while on visits to Phoenix to see us he loved to go to the races. He would get the racing guide, try to figure out the winners, and then make his bets. This event only took place once or twice that I remember, but the day at the track was fun for all.

As an adult I love to watch horses today, especially when you see them loose on the range or running friskily in pastures; we see a lot in the mountains and ranch country of Colorado in the summer.

16. FEARS FOR MOM AND DAD

There were times when I was terrified for Dad, not in a way that I would wonder "what's to become of us if something happens to him?" but simply for his physical safety. The little Ford tractor was versatile, and there was a way to switch the very heavy back tires around for working row crops- -cultivating corn, weeding milo, and the like. But the process was arduous, tricky and dangerous. It involved setting up a sort of jack, using the hydraulic system and the power takeoff to lift up the entire rear part of the tractor resulting in the big heavy rear wheels off the ground. Dad would have to loosen and take off all the big bolts on the tires and then manhandle the big tire loose, slowly turn it around and put it back on the tractor in the new position. It was a job involving two people, one person to sit on the tractor seat and run the control for the power takeoff, the other to move the wheel. So I helped Dad many times and was scared to death for him. I can recall what seemed to me as quiet desperation and effort that it took to move the tires, Dad's face and upper body totally bathed in sweat through a blue work shirt, how he had to move so slowly and carefully or the tire could go toppling off in the opposite direction to the ground, or worse yet, falling on him to break a leg or worse. The tire never fell; but there were close calls. There were times like that when I saw Dad try to fix equipment, mend things and I realized the struggle it was to keep things going.

It is very, very difficult to explain, but when I had to help him with something mechanical, I would almost get sick to my stomach, such was the aversion I had to things mechanical. I guess that explains my total lack of mechanical aptitude yet today. (People talk of right-side and left-side of the brain; I still don't get it, but something has to explain the way I am.) I can remember a time or two with the tiny Ford tractor torn completely apart up in the haymow, some kind of an overhaul operation I think. There was no alternative for Dad -- either do the work himself, or at least most of it, or quit farming. The thing was, he never had a particularly mechanical aptitude himself; I think it was pure necessity that made him keep going.

The other time I had serious fears for Dad's safety that sticks in my mind was during the drought years when our well seemed to fail; that, or the pump at the bottom stopped. Whichever, it meant that Dad had to tie one end of a long rope to a tree, wrap the other end around his waist, and lower himself down into the dark, damp hole. I guess it was approximately 40 to 50 feet down, but it seemed like half-way to China to me. I would watch him lower himself ever so carefully over the edge and on down. The feeling of relief was overpowering when he climbed back out the top later. I do not remember yet the problem at that specific time, if we needed a new pump or what, but it got fixed. As I put this on the computer in May, 1991, I think maybe it goes a way to explain many of my own fears yet today--what if the one-ton dually truck has a flat, what if the trailer has a flat, what if my water shutoff valve goes bad at the acre in Colorado, what if the well pump acts up, what will I do? All are traceable I'm sure back to the lack of mechanical aptitude or know-how.

I think Mom and Dad were good managers of the little they had to work with. I know they had to be frugal and wise or they would not have made it. They had limited experience about money matters (in an urban, educated sense of investments today), because they had little money or opportunity to use it. But I know Dad studied a lot about farming methods, farm management and kept an open ear to new techniques. He kept a close eye on farm market conditions and prices. He would attend the county extension meetings for stuff like that and always had a couple of farm magazines on subscription. And he never missed the farm and Farm Bureau news on the radio.

There is only one time I can remember him being bilked. One day this motley crew drove into the barn yard, a spray-painting outfit that specialized in painting farm buildings, a specialization that should have put them in jail. Evidently they caught Dad at a bad moment. Our old barn, originally red, was badly in need of a paint job. They offered some outstandingly cheap price to do the whole thing in grey. Dad took them up on it; they painted it in a flash using a spray gun and it looked pretty good, a pale grey. But that paint quickly faded, in fact, washed off with the rains and weather and Dad was out his money. I know it was a sore point for a long time, and we did not talk much about it.

But simply raising four children and putting them through private college was a phenomenal achievement, and enjoying life as well was proof enough that Dad and Mom must have done something right. We should do so well.

With Mom I can remember a couple of accidents. One time a Coca Cola bottle exploded when she opened the icebox door, cutting her severely on the shins and legs. But a scarier time was when she choked on a fishbone at supper one night. It seemed like it all was in slow motion--she coughed and coughed, gagged, turned red and I was scared to death. It turned out all right of course, but put a healthy respect for fish bones in my mind to the present.

17. THE FLOOD OF '51

One of the most exciting times growing up on the farm once again was related to the elements. In 1951 we had the granddaddy of all floods in our area. Incessant rains caused all the small streams and the Smokey Hill River to rise; there were not that many rivers and streams around, but it doesn't take many. The biggest stream was the Smokey Hill River just south of Abilene, perhaps a couple of miles from the south city limits. But there were small tributaries to it that could do more damage, like Mud Creek that flowed through the middle of town and Turkey Creek running through Brown's Park south of town.

The river and streams went well out of their banks that summer. From the high ground in the pasture in the upper part of our farm you could look south and see a huge band of muddy, brown water. It was of course a disaster for summer crops; the fields were flooded, but that is not the part a small boy remembers.

There were deer in Brown's Park south of town, and for some reason they ended up on the high ground of our farm. For the only time while growing up, we could go to the pasture and see those incredibly beautiful and graceful creatures in the wild. I can remember getting close to them and all of a sudden they would kind of bounce on and easily vault the fence and head into the neighbor's pasture. (I would renew my love of that animal only many, many years later when we began to spend summers in western Colorado. I still tell others about working in my Coleman tent in Colorado, trying to write something sensible about Brazilian folk poetry and its value in the world, and having a deer walk by the window of the tent, what a thrill!)

But it was better than that. The water also flooded the airport south of town, so the private planes had to be moved to higher ground. Our farm was chosen as a temporary landing and storage site, so we had perhaps a half dozen single-engine planes parked on the slopes of the pasture. It was incredibly exciting for me to see them land and take off, and the culmination was a ride in one over all the flooded area, the first time I had flown. It was a scary and exciting experience. I have loved flying ever since; had aptitude and eyesight worked out, I would surely have chosen that for a profession. I wonder if that's why Jerry Rebensdorf, our daughter Katie's deceased godfather and a farm boy from South Dakota, was so enamored of flying, going on to be an advance spotter in a Piper Cub along allied lines in WW II?

Freud, get ready. I can remember a strange, macabre dream I used to have as a boy and am sure it came from those days. It was about a crash landing of a commercial airliner in the pasture with me a hero helping people out of the plane that was a propeller type, maybe a DC-3 or the like.

But there was more fun from the flood. Brother Jim decided he would be a Good Samaritan, or else just tear ass around, so he put the scoop on the back of the little Ford tractor and off we went into the flooded town streets, ostensibly to give people rides across flooded streets and rescue damsels in distress. But from my vantage point, sitting propped up against one of the fenders, it was a neat way to plow through flooded streets, a barrel of fun.

We were also solicited for another reason during the flood. Town water was contaminated and it was known we had very good well-water, so frequent cars from town would drive out to fill their jugs. It was just another bit of added movement and excitement in a small farm boy's existence. Mundane for most I'm sure, such memories are the stuff of Kansas in the 1950s. An aside: one of my favorite of John Denver's songs is "Matthew," his account of growing up on a farm in Colby in western Kansas.

There was little else for me to remember from the flood. Our summer ballgames were of course rained and flooded out, but mainly I remember it as a prelude to those next four or five years of serious drought and the hardships it brought to farmers all over the region, specifically to my Mom and Dad.

18. HARD TIMES

When I was very young and not really until late high school or college days did I realize the fragility of the whole farm operation, the tremendous financial loss when even a few sheep, cows or hogs died for whatever reason. It was clear that a visit from the veterinary was very expensive and kind of a last resort kind of thing, but also a necessity at times. There were times when a milk cow would swallow metal by accident, generally a bit of bailing wire, and die. I can recall the old, beat up truck from the local rendering service that would come out to pick up the carcass, no longer of any use for butchering. The main thing that impressed me was the horrible smell of the truck and the men associated with it. It never struck me as a tiny boy how that must have hurt my Dad in the pocketbook, since he worked on a very close margin at best.

It was clear there was a financial loss when prime cattle would occasionally get out of the pasture or corral and slip into an alfalfa field in summer. They would eat uncontrollably, bloat up and die if immediate veterinary help did not arrive. I can recall this happening several times over the years. Once again, I did not really become aware of the financial loss until I was much older. But a dead heifer or two, or a milk cow or even a hog could make the difference between a profit or loss that year. I guess my slight awareness changed only much later when I talked of such things to Mom and Dad in the house on Rogers Street in Abilene after he had retired. We talked a lot more then, good days and good visits after I married Keah and we came to visit.

There are two or three moments when I recall Mom's anguish and crying as she washed dishes in the kitchen of the farm house, lamenting how difficult it was and wondering when things would get better. I never saw Dad cry, and he complained little as I recall, but it was usually the same complaint: "We can't ever seem to get ahead." Mom repeated that too, so I was at least aware to a degree that they were just making it.

I know that like on many other family farms, a way of life was the annual loans Dad would get to keep going, loans for supplies, seed, or machinery which had to be paid after harvest.

I also know that Dad farmed the entire half-section with a tiny, 2-bottom plow Ford tractor, the kind some people might have used for truck farming. We never had the larger tractors that neighbors did, many who farmed little more ground than Dad. Also I do not recall having new equipment; we did not even have a pickup truck or a grain truck. As I wrote in another section, we had an old trailer that we hitched up to the car to haul wheat to the grain elevator in town, and there once was an old model-t truck of some kind, but I am not sure if it belonged to Dad.

But what we had was enough; Dad made do. He made a living for us all, and I cannot say I lacked for anything growing up. The food was always good, good tasting and plentiful. There was allowance money, maybe just twenty-fie cents, to go into town to the movies or get a coke or ice cream. Our cars were always old, a fact I lamented more than once, but we always got where we needed to go.

I can only remember two real "vacations" with my parents while growing up on the farm, both of them rather vague memories now. We traveled once to Omaha, Nebraska, and to the farm area of southeast Nebraska where Dad was born--the Dawson, Pawnee City area, retraced by Keah and me only in the summer of 2004. I have a vague memory of trolley cars and noise and busy, busy traffic, I think from an open hotel window in a downtown. The other vacation is a bit clearer, a trip to Denver, Colorado, in the late 1940s. How wonderful was the view of the beautifully clear, blue mountains to the west of the city, looking from the street in front of our motel. I think we got to the Buffalo Bill Museum outside the west side of the city. And I visited my first great museum, the Natural History Museum in the Denver city park. The dioramas of bears, seals, walruses, lions, etc. filled me with wonder and happiness. It was a wonderful trip which would always dispose me well to Colorado.

And there were at least one or two other trips to Colorado Springs to visit Mom's brother Leo and family. A lasting impression was swinging a golf club at a driving range with the incredible Rocky Mountains in the distance and a cool shower of rain in the mid-afternoon.

There were no more trips for lots of reasons, the most important that summertime and vacations for farmers, unless they are wealthy with hired hands, do not mix. It was the busiest possible time for Dad. We were in school the rest of the year.

And money was certainly not plentiful. I never heard of skiing trips, travel to big cities in the East and certainly nothing outside the U.S. But I in no way felt deprived and cannot honestly recall ever wanting some big trip or even talking about it.

A real highlight of my early life was when at about the age of 11, brother Jim took Mom and me to Kansas City on a one-day business trip. I remember he said I could choose anything from the menu, and I chose a hamburger. I still remember being enthralled with the small black and white TV set in the restaurant. An even better trip was in 1955, I think, when Jim took me to see my first major league baseball game in Kansas City, more about that later.

I think I did complain about not having enough nice clothes, but the memories are so vague now. Boys wore blue jeans and t-shirts to school, even up through high school in the late 1950s, although I remember dressing more then, partly because I had become very aware of girls. But our jeans were from J.C. Penney and not from Keels which had Levis. I recall Mom buying me a purple corduroy sport coat, grey slacks, pink shirt and dark tie for what I think was my first junior-high dance. My buddy Mike Kippenberger who lived on the farm across the road had the same outfit, so I guess the farm wives got together. I think the colors were "in" then; it might have been influence from Elvis Presley. And I can remember what I thought was an elegant dark striped suit I wore while on the high school debate team that won the state championship in 1959. So I had some good clothes. I can recall that Jo Anne made many of hers; Mom was a good seamstress and with a sewing machine, 4-H and all, girls were expected to learn to sew.

And I never had a car in high school, but a few of my friends did. Thinking back on it, it was the kid from Enterprise whose family owned the elevator company my brother Jim worked for so many years who had the shiny new 56 Chevy, or the farm kid from north of town who had the 57 Ford Fair Lane white convertible. But it was mainly the "less popular" kids who did not do sports or debate or school stuff that had cars, oftentimes "hot rods," and spent their time working to pay off the cars. They tended to be the same ones into drinking and smoking earlier on. But I did have the use of the family car for dating during jr. and sr. years in high school. I cannot recall for sure what kind of car we had then, but cannot remember feeling ashamed of it. I do recall telling Mom or Dad at times that such and such needed to be fixed and getting irritated when it wasn't. Dad did not do car repair as I recall; I think he did not have the tools or know how; he did work on the tractor and combine.

Jim was the one who always had a nice car, but he worked full time as long as I could remember. When he was in one of his prosperous periods (and there were real ups and downs in his life), he bought Dad and Mom a 58 green Chevy, stick shift, pretty plain. That was the first time we had ever had a new shiny car.

But I wasn't always an angel. I can recall a time when Tom was working construction in Lehigh, a little town south of Abilene, near Hillsboro. I drove down to pick him up in that new 58 Chevy. I decided it was a good time to see what the car would do, and I know I had it up to 100 to 105 on a two-lane hilly highway. I was a good driver, careful and not reckless, but when I think of that today I shudder.

Jim once had a tiny, red MG roadster, not the "classic," but the one with rounded fenders, a real beauty. He lent it to me one afternoon and I promptly drove by the local swimming pool where the girls hung out and put a dent in the fender watching them instead of where I was going while backing out. He did not yell, scream or lay hands on me, and I wonder how I would have reacted if in his place. Later on, he also had a 1959 green Mercedes diesel sedan and loaned it to me to take buddies on a graduation trip to Denver and Colorado Springs in late May or June. We stayed at Uncle Walter's old lineman's cabin in Evergreen, visited the Coors brewery, and had a scary moment when the group was divided coming down Pikes Peak. Of significance is the fact Jim put a case of Coors beer in the trunk of the car for the trip; we five boys came home with ¾ of it still unopened. I recall the tiny Mercedes diesel engine would not make it to the top of Pikes Peak with all of us in the car.

My first car was the "Gyro-torque", a pinkish-orange 1953 Dodge I bought with money from working at the local ice plant during summers between college years, in 1960 or 1961. I was allowed to take it to college during junior year. There are lots of stories from all that, partying in it more than once in Kansas City. The next car was a snazzy 1957 two-toned blue and white ford (used of course) which I bought in about 1963 when I was heading off to St. Louis for graduate school. I gave the damned thing away to the Cusack girls (of Chipita Park fame) when I went to Brazil in 1966 for dissertation research (I understand it limped along on a cylinder or two and just died in the street a few months later. I had a one-armed Negro mechanic on Pine Street near St. Louis University that would just listen to the engine and shake his head when I wanted to know why it was just barely clunking along. (Maybe that is somehow related to Flannery O'Connor's short novel "Wise Blood" and Haze and his "rat-colored car" and why I love that story so much.) My next vehicle was a beat up black Chrysler 300, a luxury car at the time, that my brother had left sitting in the barn after he had wrecked it a time or two in the mid-60s. I got it to drive to my first job as assistant professor at Arizona State in 1968 and even courted my future wife Keah in it when she came to Arizona to visit in 1969, including a trip to the Grand Canyon and across gravel roads with bald tires over to Payson along the Mogollon Rim. I believe, in retrospect, it reveals more of Keah's character than mine. She looked at the man and not his car, a sign of things to come.

After Keah and I got married, we drove Keah's new 1966 Chevy Malibu, then a 1964 Pontiac Tempest inherited from her Mom and Dad, and then another pass-me-down from her folks, a Pontiac Catalina vintage 1978, all of which kept local mechanics in the scheckles by virtue of our frequent visits for repairs to keep all of them going. I always said I'll buy a new car before I die. (I did in fact buy one in 1992, our first Subaru). Maybe like Dad I'll get a new one when I retire (he bought a 1962 Chevy with money from the farm sale in 1959 or later). That's the car I drove to San Diego in 1963 after college graduation from Rockhurst, when we saw Tom when he was a naval officer and visited his at that time girl friend Valerie Hamilton at her parents' home on the hillside overlooking La Jolla. The Currans had never seen such a place, but I do not believe we were any the less for it. But I digress. Keah and I did buy a new Chevy Silverado Truck in 1996; this was when Keah had been diagnosed with melanoma and one doctor told us she had a maximum five years to live. So I ordered her a brand new 1996 4X4, her dream. Detroit went on strike so we had to settle for a 2X4, a terrific truck we drive yet today in 2010. We also bought a one-year old Subaru Outback in 1996, pulling out all the stops. And another new Subaru in 2006.

Back to Dad's situation. I think he made a little money in the good years, suffered in the bad years, but managed to keep things afloat. I need to recall that he and Mom grew up during the Depression, so hard times were nothing new.

It always sticks in my mind that good dry land wheat made about 25 to 30 bushels to the acre in those days in the 1940s and 1950s, perhaps at $1.00 per bushel. There was a terrible flood in 1951 that was followed by four or five disastrous years of drought. Those I recall well because I was older and more aware of things.

I can recall the grasshopper years when they came in clouds and destroyed everything, particularly the alfalfa and corn crops. I recall as well the rig Dad used to spray with: a 50 gallon barrel with hoses, etc. on the back hitch of the little Ford tractor, riding along in the field, so tiny he seemed, spraying the fields. It never seemed to do much good. I can still see in mind's eye today the alfalfa sprigs with no leafs on them, with as many as four or five hoppers on each stem. The hoppers came and went, but it was drought that seemed to bring them most.

During the series of bad years, early and mid 1950sm, Tom and Jo Anne were in high school, I was in Junior High, there were wheat crops that came to only 5 to 7 bushels to the acre, and wheat was the primary source of revenue, the cash crop on the farm. And it was not only the drought. One of the most vivid memories of all my childhood also happened just around wheat harvest time in one of those years.

One summer, it must have been late June or even early July, very close to harvest time, the wheat was headed out and Dad expected in fact a bumper crop (this could not have been the dry years, but must have been wet years which immediately followed). We had lots of rain which eventually would knock down the wheat and could cause no end of problems--a rust or growth on the wheat, kernels knocked from the head, etc. The fragility of farming strikes me once again, the fine line between too much rain and not enough, too much sunshine or not enough. The ideal was good rain to start the wheat in the fall, snow cover in the winter for gradual moisture and to protect from blowing winds, steady spring rains in March and April, then lots of sunshine for ripening. This particular day we all saw the cloud coming, Dad, Mom and I. It was grey, almost whitish, and came from the southwest. The cloud advanced slowly, wind and rain preceding it. I was alone with Mom and Dad that day (Tom and Jo Anne by then were working in other towns), and we saw the hail literally mow down the prospective bumper crop. For my Dad, there were no tears, no yelling, no raving or jumping up and down, but just a sad resignation. (I wonder with my own personality how I would have dealt with that.) My worst fears this time were not to come to be. Dad had crop insurance, hail insurance for just such an occasion. Ordinarily this kind of insurance would never insure a profit, but you could at least recoup some of the expenses in planting, tilling the soil, etc. But this time there was a bonus--the hail did not knock the wheat from the head or knock the head off; instead it broke and bent the stalks, bending the head low to the ground. Dad was able to use what we called a "pickup" attached to the front of a combine and recover much of the wheat that went ahead and ripened. But the sight of the force of nature, that white cloud, the heavy hail that clipped the wheat like swinging a baseball bat through a patch of weeds, breaking them off but not cutting them off, remains in my memory.

Worse of course were the droughts when the wheat was thin in the fields, when there was only one crop of alfalfa instead of three or even four cuttings, and when the corn dried up in the fields and the only thing to be done was to cut it for silage, at least partially salvaging the crop.

But Dad survived it, and we grew up well. The kids all excelled in one thing or another. Tom got a full scholarship to Marquette University with a Naval ROTC scholarship, and Jo Anne got a bit of help to attend Marymount College in Salina, Kansas, working a lot along the way to pay bills. I got a tuition scholarship to Rockhurst College in Kansas City my final year or two, but worked each summer and part-time during years to help pay expenses. Jim earlier had the GI Bill after his stint in the Army in the mid-1940s, and went to Creighton University. All the boys attended Jesuit colleges or universities. He did well enough, but decided to quit after two years, not because he could not cut it, but because to him, as he told me in later years, college just did not seem a necessity at the time. He regretted it later when he did the work of an engineer and got paid as a non-college graduate.

But the money we earned or received from partial scholarship was never enough. Dad somehow borrowed or saved enough to see three kids through private, Catholic colleges, a phenomenal feat under the circumstances. Such is the pride I have for my parents and what they did for us.

Yet in the middle of all those years there was one particular period of crisis, a time of severe drought. It was while I was in high school, because I was still living at home on the farm. To keep things going Dad did part-time and even full time carpentry in town, this plus keeping the farm going. He later would lease the farm ground, taking shares, and actually came out better dollar wise than when he had farmed it himself. I think Uncle Bryan farmed it a year or two, the neighbor Carl Buhler the rest, and perhaps Dick and Johnny Whitehair the last years before Dad sold the farm and retired into town. I was happy for Dad in those last years because the backbreaking and frustrating work was over. He told me once that even then he would have continued to farm if he had had the money to get up to date machinery; he simply did not.

But back to 1955; the carpentry jobs became scarce and then suddenly ended. I think Dad was helping Jo Anne in college at the time; things were rough. The only solution was to follow one of the local contractors (Dad had worked for him building houses) to Melbourne, Florida, along the Atlantic coast, where the contractor had work. Dad made the "migration" just to keep working and to keep some money coming in. There is an entire chapter in one of my books on Brazilian folk poetry that tells the sad story of the migrants from rural Brazil to the big cities in the South to hunt for work, this because of the drought in the Northeast and always with the dream of returning home. Dad's story strikes that note.

So that winter while I was in high school Dad left the family on the farm and worked in Florida. I did not, once again, truly realize the gravity of the situation. But I know Mom would get the weekly letters with the check inside and would just say "I wish Dad were here." Indelibly printed on my memory was the morning I came downstairs and saw Dad in the kitchen, looking so much older, tired, oh so tired. He must have been about 63 or 64 at the time. He had been on the bus for two days, arriving from Florida. I cannot even recall why he was home, if the job there had ended, if there still was a need for it, but I was so glad to see him. This, as far as I know, was the only time he and Mom were separated in their marriage. I cannot recall if there was a big hug or even an emotional moment, but only the relief that Dad was home. But that was when I began to realize that he and Mom were not so young anymore.

In later years, after we all were through college (I was supporting myself from 1963 on as a graduate student at St. Louis University.), Dad sold the farm for a good price. He and Mom settled in to almost twenty years of retirement. All did not go well. Jim had a series of problems, Tom as well, and even Jo Anne at times.

What can I say? In spite of all this, I think retirement had its good times. Mom and Dad lived extremely frugally, well within their means. They were able to take a trip by car some of the winters to Arizona to see Keah and me, or to San Diego or Chico to see Tom, Valerie and the boys. They had wonderful, lifelong friends and relatives around Abilene. Dad had his Elks Club gin rummy games, the pasture and horses, the farm garden; Mom had her bridge games with the old gals from years past from church and town, her wonderful vegetable and flower gardens, and church activities. They got to see Jo Anne's kids grow up and were wonderful grandparents to them and always loved the too short visits of Tom's family and later with us.

I recall the joyous moment when after eight years of marriage, Keah and I announced her pregnancy to them in a little modest apartment they had rented for a month that winter in Arizona (oh the times we spent apartment hunting to try to keep within their means!). Happy like never before. Hugging Mom and Dad and even crying I think. Our times together since my marriage were constantly the best. It was in those years when I matured and came to appreciate them and value the heritage I am writing of now.

Later years and aches and pains would take their toll, more with Mom than Dad. He maintained generally excellent health until the last year when he had some high blood pressure and then the abdominal aneurism that killed him, one day's sickness and suffering. Mom suffered more, from serious rheumatism, osteoporosis, and chronic back spasms. Vivid in my memory are the horrible scenes of those times when she could not stand to be touched from the back pain and would end up in the hospital in traction.

But all in all they had I think a good retirement and certainly never complained to us of their hardships, and seemed to enjoy life when we were with them. Their lot was blessed, if not in material riches, in loving each other, in sharing an enthusiasm for life, perseverance and a real joy in the children, and grandchildren. They in my mind deserved that and more.

They were religious in the good sense, of deep faith and loyal to their God. They were strong people of a generation now passed, a rural, farm people, hardy and hard working, lacking in the advantages of wealth or education (Dad more than Mom in schooling) but wise and open to the challenges life presented them. They were friendly consistently to others, rarely if ever speaking ill of others, a model for us. See "growing up Catholic" later on in this book. I still miss them.

19. THE SCHOOL BUS AT THE END OF THE FARM LANE

We kids rode the country school bus for years, this after Jim was gone and working. Tom, Jo Anne and I, the baby of the family, would troop down the lane early in the morning to catch our yellow bus. It really is amazing how little of those times remains with me; we did it every day for so many years. But I recall that often it was very cold and uncomfortable. And you would be bundled up in sweaters, heavy coat, stocking caps, gloves, and galoshes.

We used to play a game while waiting, "Scissor Steps" or "Mama May I," I think it was called, the idea being that each person had to follow the leader in whatever kind of steps the other took. All this took place on the asphalt pavement. I can't even remember the object of the game other than imitating giant steps, scissor steps, etc., but it was great fun. It had the added attraction of building suspense doing it while cars were slowly coming toward you from the distance. We cut it close sometimes.

Because we lived close to town, really only one mile from the east city limit, and because the bus changed its route and direction each six weeks, for six weeks we would be last on in the morning and first off at night; first on and last off the next six weeks. I can't recall exactly how it went, but the idea was that one time we got on the bus and rode for nearly an hour and a half before getting to school, the same getting off the next six weeks. It probably would have been more efficient and better for all of us to walk the mile or mile and a half to school, but I guess we were too small. In later years I did enjoy walking or riding my bike to school in Abilene.

There was always lots of shouting and talking on the bus and a few pranks. Mr. Holt or "Hootie"--our drivers--must have been tolerant people. I can remember one time when some of the older guys, Dale Mills and the Armbrust brothers, started a fire in the back seats. But more often I remember the long rides, reading books or just staring out into space. But on the trip home after school, it was a joyous moment to bound off the bus and start the walk up the lane to see a smiling Mom who always had a treat or snack for me when I got into the house, especially cookies or cake.

It was then that the outside games would come, basketball in the barn, baseball with the lath stick and then the afternoon radio programs. And the chores I've already mentioned were in there some place because there was no way to get out of them. After that, finally, came suppertime with the six o'clock news on the radio.

A last note about the bus days. One morning while waiting for the bus and playing games, my sister Jo Anne left her books and violin (in its case) on the ground near the highway. A neighbor drove in the lane that day and smashed the violin to smithereens! I can only surmise my reaction if such a thing had happened years later to one of our daughter Katie's violins! Or my guitar!

20. BUDDIES, SPORTS AND GAMES ON THE FARM

Mark and Tom on a happy day

As I grew up there was a continual string of buddies I would invite to play on the farm. My nearest brother was Tom, four years older than myself, and by the time I was old enough to play sports, he was already much larger and had other interests. Although I can remember games of basketball and some football with Tom, I had the definite idea most of the time that my older brother and sister really did not want to spend much time with me. So it was simple--either play alone or have friends my age over from town. The games we played were centered on sports and those in season. Baseball was the vacation time sport in the summer and at my place basketball predominated through Fall, Winter and Spring.

Joe Fleagle came to be a good friend. He was not one of the more popular kids in school, was a bit slow in his studies, but his athletic abilities were more on a par with mine, average or a little above, speaking for Abilene. We would spend hours playing ball in the summertime, primarily catch, each pretending to be a major league pitcher.

Joe's Dad was a good man who coached the little kids in summer baseball for years. He had done some semi-pro playing in the area and it was always rumored that he had been big league material until he threw out his arm as a catcher. He coached a couple of the little league teams I played on as a kid. The teams were Ehrsams and Dairy Queen. One memory from the latter is we had a fire balling country pitcher, name of Ronnie Sheets. One time when I was playing third base, he threw to me, a pick off move or something, and the force of the throw literally knocked me to my butt on the bag. He was the pitcher that year with Dairy Queen, I think, because we were undefeated. The fun of it all was that after the game all of us were treated to whatever we wanted at the local DQ--a big strawberry malt or hot chocolate sundae or the likes, a great reward for sitting on third base.

So Joe became a good friend. He spent time in the Army after school and has been with one of the railroads out of Chicago for many years. I have these vague memories of his having learned Morse Code and still using it at work! I understand Art died in a tragic car accident some years ago.

I think I've already mentioned Eddy (Everett) Smith and our music days. I can honestly say that although I was aware of differences between Negro and White then, that there was little or no prejudice in me. Eddy was a good friend with qualities other friends did not have. I recall having him out to the farm to play music, but also for the same sports as with other buddies. Perhaps it was a coincidence, but he was also "just average" in sports. My parents did not object, but it turned out to be an uncommon thing to do in our town in those days, although I certainly did not realize it at the time. I only discovered years later after Eddy's death, a premature death to be sure, while he worked in the foundry of a nearby factory in Enterprise, how much he had enjoyed those times, the only times he had ever in fact been able to visit a farm. Eddie's mother told my mother about this well after his death. And we lived in the middle of the Wheat Belt where most folks were farmers!

Another good buddy, Eddy Jimenez, was a pal from baseball days, sports in school and our common interest in pop music during the time I was beginning the guitar. This coincided with my beginning days in Spanish. Eddy did not admit to knowing the language, but did understand it when relatives spoke. Mexicans-Americans in Central Kansas still were very much a minority group then, and the way out was, contrary to much feeling today, to deny one's roots. I really only began to use my Spanish when I worked at the old Abilene ice plant the first two summers of college when a Mexican co-worker, I think named Hilario Gomez, would chat with me. His family invited me over to the house for dinner one night and served "mole poblano," probably the hottest Mexican food dish that exists! I had to mind my manners on that one. The food was a bit of a contrast to the fried chicken, mashes potatoes and gravy I was used to on the farm.

Catholics were a minority group in the town; I think I once counted some twenty-seven different Protestant denominations in the local phone book. So, many of my friends were Baptist, Methodist, Presbyterian, Episcopalian, and a whole hodgepodge of what we would call fundamentalist groups today, River Brethren, Church of Christ, you name it. This reminds of one of Dad's stories--of the preacher who told his flock to put one hog in a cattle car down at the Union Pacific, pray hard, and by the time the train would get to Kansas City, the hogs would multiply. Dad would laugh until tears ran down his face when he told that story.

One buddy, and a good one too, Gary Alford, used to razz me about the Catholics, constantly asking questions and forcing me to defend my faith , but certainly not in any educated or bookish way, we were only teenagers. Ironically, years later, long after my time in Abilene, he married a Catholic girl from Junction City and converted to the faith. Gary was a good buddy, one of the first who had a car. He had, I believe, an old Pontiac or Oldsmobile or maybe it was a Ford from the 40s, a jewel of a car. Gary was very heavy when he was a kid, in fact fat, and I am sure he suffered a lot from nicknames the kids would call him ("Porky" etc.) . But he had a heart of gold and had good upbringing. He would come out to the farm and we would play baseball or basketball up in the barn. I am trying to remember, but I think it was Gary that I taught to milk the old milk cow. He also was involved with sports through Jr. High and High school, but that is another story.

It just occurred to me I have been talking about an intellectually slow kid, a black kid, a Mexican and a fat kid others called names (and I was not any angel either), but I think there was something in my upbringing or the way I am that considered others, their beliefs and feelings, in a positive way. I could indeed get along with almost everybody if given a chance (in the same way I am able to get along with the Latin Americans over the years at work and sometimes lament never becoming a diplomat. But that's another story for later.)

Jerry Hawks was a good friend; his father was a salesman for Gambles and district manager of the same. He also was a wise guy with a penchant for getting into scrapes. We had our good and bad times and I can remember we must have irritated the hell out of each other off and on. He came out as well and I can recall playing basketball in the barn. We played a lot of military games with forts set up in the hay and tin can and string "walkie-talkies". As I said, he was a bit of a scalawag; tears would come to my eyes when he would fart in Edna Edberg's Latin class. How she put up with us and we did not get kicked out, and how I ever settled down to become one of her prize students in Spanish a year or two later, I'll never know.

I am sure I am leaving some one out. Jimmy Beavers who was from the south side of town, took me out to the Smokey Hill River one time. I had a fear of the river and snakes and all for some reason, perhaps coming from Mom or Dad's warnings. Kenton Sipes, the first in our class to die (in an auto accident on a country road going to see his fiancée south of town; it would have made a good country song) was a friend over the years. His mother was also my 4th grade teacher at Garfield grade school, one of my favorite teachers over the years. Kent also had a car, and did customizing and all. Phil Combs was a good buddy of his and Hawks, and we were all together off and on during high school years. That's also when we first tried beer, drinking and smoking. Neither the beer nor the smokes seemed harmful at the time, and life was a big game and adventure. The scare stories of cancer and smoking had not really become widespread by then; it was grown up to smoke, cool.

I did not have the habit of either smoking or beer drinking in high school although we did a fair amount of each. But I can recall the day I moved into the college dormitory at Rockhurst, going down to the cigarette machine and willfully buying a pack of Viceroys, thinking, "Now I can do what I want and this is what I want to do." And beer drinking during undergraduate years became a Friday night habit with wild rides over to the Kansas line to the local pub, this because you could drink beer at age 18 in Kansas.

Mike Kippenberger was always around, but more with church or family life. Although there was a period in high school when I was much more with the buddies I have mentioned, this because Mike was good in athletics and was in a different crowd for all those activities, we still remained long time friends. All the guys I mentioned were not on the school teams in high school, at least not on the varsity first teams. I never really thought about that then for I wasn't in with a "bad" group, but just a different one.

We used to have great basketball games in the haymow. I can recall getting home from school, practically any time of year, even in freezing weather, and heading for the barn. I had my heroes in those days, some not too recognizable today some 30 or 40 years later, generally high scoring all-Americans: Dick Knostman of K-State the first, Clyde Lovelette of K.U., and Jerry West of West Virginia. I could make baskets from any part of the play area of the barn; you even had to learn to arch the ball over rafters for long shots. Kids were no different then than now; I had it rigged so I could stand on a bale of hay to do dunk shots like Wilt Chamberlain. I probably played more alone than with friends, so that's when the imagination would take over.

21. MIKE KIPPENBERGER AND SUNDAY AFTERNOONS

When I was about five, a new family arrived in town, the Kippenbergers from a little country town in west central Oklahoma, Thomas by name. They bought the farm on the very edge of the east city limits of Abilene, across from the hospital. I can remember yet today going over to their place to visit, waiting outside the yard gate until a little boy my age came out. He was to become, in my judgment, my closest friend growing up in Abilene.

We had much in common, farm background, both Catholic, pretty typical kids, both fond of sports of all kinds and in having a good time. There would be many parallels in our next twenty years and even beyond that in college, yet we were both very different. There were years when we were not close, but I believe in the final analysis there is more to bind us than separate us.

Mom, Dad, Sarah and Joe Kippenberger playing cards in the old farm house

Eventually Mike and his family had to come into this account because profession, faith, schooling and free time brought our families together. Our farm was one mile east of the city limits, its south edge on old Highway 40; the Kippenbergers were, as I said, on the very city limit, a bit south and west of us. The quickest way to get to their house to play when I was little was to walk down the lane, cut across the farm fields of Leckron's and on to the Kippenberger farm, and through the latter's corral. You could walk it all in about ten minutes. While still very little I remember playing over there, different games; I recall popcorn on cold days, all types of sports during season. One funny memory was in their house listening and singing along to the song "Buttons and Bows." Does that date me?

Later on I would work quite a bit for Mike's father, helping out on the farm in summertime. Hay baling mainly. I became a good friend of Gordon, Mike's older brother who stayed in Abilene to farm his Dad's land and another farm up north of town. After finishing my Ph.D. dissertation in fall and winter of 1967-68 and before reporting to my first teaching job at Arizona State University in Tempe in late August of 1968, I worked for Gordon in the summer of 1968. It was a fun summer and I got the lack of physical activity of academia out of my system and just enjoyed being outside. It was a pretty laid back type of farming with Gordon and turned out to be my last serious contact with farming; I have only positive memories.

Back to Mike and the friendship. There were some moments of rivalry, but really very few to my mind; things just seemed to always work out. We were both pretty good in academics, but I always thought he had more native brain matter and that it was more hard work on my part. Since then, I have come to the conclusion it was just different talents in different directions, left brain-right brain, he more toward the sciences and me in humanities and languages.

He was a terrific all around athlete; I was average at best. But we had literally years of contact through sports, little league baseball for many summers, diverse sports in grade school, junior high and high school. I dropped out of sports during freshman year because of a serious concussion from football; Mike continued and dominated the school teams, being offered a sports scholarship to New Mexico State. He was the quarterback, the scoring guard in basketball, the leader. That bothered me very little I guess because I was resigned to the fact that I was just average at best in sports and since I was able to excel in other activities.

I had good roles in plays in 4-H and Jr. High, although I was never too serious about it. But I did have good luck in academics once I got serious about it about sophomore year in high school and in debate in high school. After the brain concussion in freshman football, I concentrated on debate team. I enjoyed public speaking and yet today have no difficulty speaking before others, being totally comfortable in the classroom and always was from the first day.

I was president of the local 4-H club and that involved lots of speaking opportunities, I did some declamation contests in junior high, but the best practice was as student council president in high school when I would introduce all assemblies and was called upon for speaking on all kinds of occasions.

But back to debate. Our debate teams had a good tradition, and we placed in the state tournament my junior year and won first place senior year, my role being fairly significant. I always put that in balance to Mike's athletic achievements since none of our sports teams ever came close to winning state , not his fault for sure. We both were popular with the girls, and that also never created problems. It seemed to turn out in Abilene that before you were done you had dated every cute girl in town some time or other during those years. I think I tell in Part Two of Mike's and my Mom getting together and "suiting us out" for the first jr. high dance, a purple corduroy sport coat, grey flannel slacks, pink shirt and tire! But since high school through the college years and beyond, I think things changed a bit. I am sure Mike caroused a lot more than I during college, and he seemed to attract the ladies, but that's a long story. He was in a fraternity at a party school; I was at a non-coeducational Jesuit College. That says it all since we really had to work to find the girls from other colleges, mainly at mixers and a local girls' international school. I can't really complain, things turning out as they did. And I had my share of adventures in Kansas City, St. Louis and Latin America, but don't believe I could match the tales Mike would tell about dental school days in Kansas City.

The best part of all this is that over the years I think we have developed a mutual respect for each other. Our marriages both turned out well, careers too, but with a certain quantitative difference -- Mike studied dentistry and dabbled a bit in real estate. I took the Ph.D. in languages, make a modest living as a university teacher (pulling "teeth" of my own in most classes), but there are other factors. I've had good professional results with writing and publishing in Brazil, have traveled extensively, have a flexible work schedule and really have most things I want. It has been years now since we spent much time together, and money will dictate differences in our lives, but I think we can both look each other in the eye with respect and a certain degree of admiration. Mike will come into the farm story a good deal. I figure you never have more than three or four "good" friends in life, and I count him as one, this regardless of our destinies in life.

22. GAMES AND HUNTING

SNOW AND THE WINTER TIME

We normally did not get a heavy winter in Abilene; by that, I mean the kind of winter where it snows in November and there is snow on the ground until late April. But you knew when winter had arrived in the area, the first light snow perhaps in December, and always with the hope for a white Christmas. Sometimes a heavy snow would come along. There had been hard freezes since early November. January, February and very early March were plenty cold and potentially nasty with possibilities of heavy snow. We have what they had always called blizzards--that meant a heavy snow storm with strong winds which caused the snow to drift. When that would happen, it could be serious: livestock had to be protected.

And sometimes we could not get the one mile into town for a day or two. Pipes would freeze up, the water tank for the animals too, and a bitter cold would envelop things for a few days. I can remember the ax we would keep down at the stock tank to break up ice so the stock could drink. We kids would play on it too, sliding around the ice. The same stock tank brought one scary occasion; I don't know what age I was, too small to remember, but evidently I fell through the ice one time and screamed and Jim heard me and pulled me out.

The snow cover was always good for the wheat which had been planted in September; it provided slow and easy moisture when it gradually melted in the Spring and protected from blowing dust in dry weather.

There are many memories associated with our winter--freezing hands trying to milk the cow and do other chores in the morning; using the ax to chop the ice on the livestock water tank; frozen clothes on the clothesline, including cold, wet jeans on your body when you were heading off to school; there was no such thing as an electric clothes dryer on the farm. Water pipes even in the house would freeze up; lots of inconvenience to say the least. I wonder how Dad and Mom handled it all. With over twenty years in Arizona it is hard to imagine the winter cold; but I remember particularly getting into freezing cars to go into town. You almost always went out, started the engine and heater just to make it livable. But I can recall often sitting in a freezing car and seeing your breath until the car warmed up.

I can recall two or three bad blizzards, one in 1950 or 1951 when the Wrights were visiting from Goodland, Kansas in their big, shiny Buick. There was one winter when all of us kids got Scarlet Fever; Mom and Dad moved one of the big beds down to the first floor living room. For me it was actually a happy time; no one could go out or leave, so we were forced to play together. I remember long, long Monopoly games, card games. The memories are fuzzy now, but I think Tom, Jo Anne and I were all sick.

I can remember driving on snow and ice to get to school. When the winds and heavy snow combined, inevitably there would be serious traffic problems on old Highway 40, at that time the major east-west road through Kansas. Semi-trucks jack knifed into the ditches, and cars were abandoned and covered with snow. You could not see the ditches or culverts because the wind had drifted snow over them. I can recall one time when the highway was a sheet of ice about 4 to 5 inches thick with snow on the top. We would put on boots, gloves, coats, etc. and go down to the highway to see it all. I guess the people in those vehicles were all right; you heard of people freezing to death in cars and trucks along highways in western Kansas and eastern Colorado, and the panhandle in Oklahoma and western Nebraska.

Midwest ice storms happened less frequently yet, but a freezing rain would leave tree branches, telephone and electric lines coated with ice, and the weight would cause them to break and create problems in the area. A main memory in 1967 was my trek by train from Abilene to St. Louis and the drive by car with Dan Hayes to Chicago so I could attend the MLA convention and do interviews for jobs. I can remember the ice storm and how the entire landscape just shimmered in the reflection on the way back to St. Louis, how I had a terrible case of the flu, and how my dear old Dad picked me up in Abilene down at the U.P. Station very late as I limped home from it all. Never was I so appreciative of a warm home and dear parents as then; one of the last times I really felt dependent on my parents.

But the morning after an ice storm was a beautiful thing to see: the first rays of the morning sun coming through the clouds and the shimmering branches, and even the ice on the grass.

But back to the big snowstorms. After a particularly heavy snow, a day or two later, it was great fun for the kids when we would bundle up in galoshes or boots, and maybe an extra pair of pants (there was no goose down or fiber fill nonsense then, just an extra pair of blue jeans or better yet, corduroy pants), sweaters, coat, gloves and winter hat to play in the big drifts along the road. Later on, when the deep snow would begin to melt, it also was fun to have the rushing water in the culverts and play games jumping across it, or sailing pieces of wood down it. Of course if the storm was bad enough, they would call off school. We always hoped for that and listened to the radio the preceding night or early the following morning for the road and schools closures. That meant a day at home playing in the snow or inside with games. Monopoly was my favorite growing up, and I have good memories of all the kids including Jim in on those games. We never considered the fact that all those days had to be made up later, generally in gorgeous spring weather when we rather would have been outside playing ball.

Tom and Mark's snowman

When we were very young, we would build snowmen in the yard, using a carrot for its nose, and maybe a piece or two of coal for the eyes. But there was one winter we had extra fun; I cannot recall at exactly what age. There was an old sled with runners on it which was stored up above the beams in the granary. Jim pulled it down and hitched it to the little Ford tractor. We drove crazily through the pasture, upsetting and landing in fairly deep snow, but never noticing the wet or the cold, just having a good time. I can only remember one time we did that, but what fun! Jim had a mischievous streak in him, and I think the sharp turns and upsetting us was all part of the plot.

HUNTING AND GAMES

I can remember hunting some in the winter, primarily rabbits. It seemed a lot more fun when you could see the fresh tracks in the snow and follow them to their lairs. I cannot remember hitting many of them, but we did have fried rabbit once in a while, most of them shot by either Tom or Dad. My job was to hold the legs of the rabbit while Tom would skin it, a bit more than I wanted to handle at the time.

But Tom's comeuppance took place shortly after he married Valerie and brought her home for the first time in the wintertime. The idea I think was to show her some winter hunting and what a good shot he was. She, Tom, Dad and I went out with rifles and shotguns to hunt rabbits. It was a good day of sorts; it turned out that Val got about eight, Tom just one and I zero. Turns out she grew up skeet shooting and was an excellent shot. I never knew what Tom had told her of his hunting escapades while growing up, but I surmise he did not have much to say after that day.

Hunting and Games. What I recall more easily and with great relish were my play days on the farm. I was allowed at a certain age, perhaps ten or eleven, to take the Springfield rifle single shot or even the 22 special (shorts, long rifle) pump action out for "hunting." I was careful and had learned good habits with the rifles, but it still was a game to me. Since I never seemed to hit much during hunting, I would rather just shoot ricochet shots to hear the same sound I used to hear in the Roy Rogers movies. You know, the "pteeeerr" sound of the glancing bullet. My favorite game for quite a while was cowboys and Indians, me being the only player and with the only rifle. The villains were Indians – maybe Iriquois or Hurons, the ones I had seen in movies like "The Iriquois Trail" who shaved their heads except for a single swath down the middle. I used to draw marvelous pictures of them in school when I should have been paying attention to the teacher, entire battle scenes with Iriquois and buckskin fringed heroes a la Daniel Boone or Davy Crockett. As I write this, I just remembered the hair cuts in style when I was a kid, the "Mohawks" which meant a shaved head with a swath down the middle; I never had one, can't say if for lack of courage or fear of a spanking at home.

Anyway, I had a set route I would take: through the hole in the fence between the chicken house and the tree stump where we cut off the chicken heads, through the windbreak of cedar trees Dad had painstakingly planted over the years, past the "coffee bean" trees, through the buffalo grass meadows in the long pasture which gradually ascended to a hill from which you could see the entire valley. I always stopped to rest at that point, gazing out over the cropland down toward the highway and the Smokey Hill River beyond. There were little gullies or ravines that inevitably had Indians in them or varmints of one sort or another. I could use half a dozen shells by that time. But the highlight of the game took place near the pond on the north 40 acres. A great place to play, it was surrounded by large elm trees and many other kinds Dad would gradually plant over the years. Generally there was just a little water in the pond since it had always seeped some. Dad spent lots of hard earned money trying to fix that, even going so far as to buy some sealer to put on the bottom of the pond. But there were lots of birds, an occasional duck or crane-like bird, squirrels and the like. My game of Daniel Boone and the Iriquois might be interrupted off and on, perhaps finding an old tin can to use for target practice. But many, many times I would take off alone from the house with the explanation that "I was going hunting," but would play that game instead. (I wonder now as an adult how my folks must have worried with an eleven year old out with the rifle alone; they showed more patience and trust than I do today.) But there were no people around, big distances, and the city is a lot more dangerous today especially when I/we don't have the guns.

The other game, at an earlier age, involved wild animals in an African jungle (a carry over from the black and white Tarzan movies with Johnny Weismuller or the Jungle Jim comics). There was a small field of about 5 acres south of the farmhouse that Dad usually planted in brome grass and let livestock use for pasture. The brome grass grew tall, and even taller was the sunflowers and miscellaneous weeds. I would roam that field playing games of Tarzan and the jungle and did some climbing on a large outdoor sign near the highway, a sign rented by the local Chevy-Cadillac dealership. I must have been ten years old or less for those games. There were all sorts of wild animals and critters lurking behind trees, fence posts, and in the tall grass. At some point I would carry a machete, a real one, another item Jim brought home from the service, and cut my way through the jungle debris.

However the field became less pleasant for me in later days when Mom or Dad would send me along the fence with a hoe or machete to cut down those same weeds, particularly sunflowers or cockleburs which seemed to proliferate along the roads in Kansas.

23. PRETEND GAMES

There was one game in particular that I played alone that sticks in my memory as great fun, a sort of stick baseball. I was totally immersed in baseball in those years, maybe 1951- 1957, probably from about 11 to 16 years of age. I listened to the radio, bought baseball bubble gum cards (giving them all away about Jr.-Sr. Prom time in high school when interests had definitely turned to the girls), collected cards and of course played in the summers in little league.

At home I invented a fantasy game that was the greatest. At least I think I did, I know Mike Kippenberger played it too, so maybe it was his idea. I would stuff my jeans pants legs down into my socks, this to be like the major leaguers looked, and wear my baseball hat. There was a place north of the barn, right beside the silo where I would stand at "home plate." The bat was a lath stick, the handle filed so it would be smooth to hold. The baseballs were small stones about the size of a marble that I would toss up into the air and hit with the stick. I learned to really cream the ball. I don't understand the principle of physics, but if you pulled it just right, you could almost double the distance traveled. A single was anywhere against the wall of the barn, a double on the tin roof either side of the driveway into the haymow, a triple on the top part of the roof, and naturally a home run was over the barn roof.

I would play all summer long, hours at a time, wearing out lath sticks and having to hunt for pebbles to hit. I was Stan Musial, but mainly I was Mickey Mantle. There were no strikeouts, only game winning hits. I would set the scene just like the radio sports announcers, and inevitably, it would be the last of the 9th, two out, a three and two count, and "bam," over the barn roof.

I was a bit sheepish about the game, not the kind of thing you announced to adults or even to people not close friends, but I do remember talking to Mike about it. But mainly, it was for me, for all the years I was just a mediocre player, striking out too much and not ever making the "All-star" team during summer play.

The Farm

Mark in Elks' All-Star baseball uniform

Correction, I did make it once, kind of a last resort player. I will never forget because that was the only time growing up when I was issued a real baseball uniform. The old black and white picture shows me in baggy pants and shirt; the uniform was flannel, just like the major leaguers', not the polyester or whatever they used later on. I wore white sweat socks instead of regular baseball socks, holding a glove and ready to play ball. I recall playing in one game as an all-star, going to bat with a bat with a hunk missing on one side. I hit a solid base hit to right field and got thrown out at first base! I can remember running down the first base line as though it were a dream, one of those nightmares where a monster is chasing you and you can't seem to run. So it was strictly a "good news," "bad news" situation. It really was like a nightmare because just a year to two later I became a respectable if not outstanding middle distance runner and ran a 2:28 half mile in the state track meet.

Baseball by the way was not all bad. I was a pretty good fielder and did get some base hits once in awhile. The highlight of the career was an indeed spectacular catch I made of a potential home run John Anguiano hit over the fence. I backed up gradually on the ball, stuck my glove over the fence and got it. Fame is fleeting.

But my heart was not just in hitting. Another game that lasted all too short a time, this because I broke the "baseball," must have taken place in these same years. I don't remember where I ran across this, maybe in Duckwalls' Five and Dime Store, and have hunted ever since in toy shops for the article. But here was the deal: there was a package you could buy with two baseballs made of Styrofoam, but the balls each had a tiny hole, maybe the size of a rivet, in one side. This allowed a seemingly unlimited variety of ways to throw the ball making it do exactly what the big league pitchers did, or better I suspect. I pitched game after game, throwing the balls against the wooden door of the haymow, being Robin Roberts, Bobby Shantz, Allie Reynolds or Whitey Ford.

It was absolutely incredible, even by the standards of an imagination garnered from years of devotion to the big leaguers! You could make the ball curve a good two feet! I figured out how to vary the spin and make it curve another two feet in the opposite direction. I could throw a fast ball that would rise about a foot and a half, a drop that would fall the same, and an honest to god knuckler that would flutter all over the place. The fun I had!

If I could find some baseballs like that again, I would be out throwing them against a wooden fence right now. Once again, the game scenario was always the most dramatic – World Series, final game, but I always pitched no-hitters, now striking out the same guys I used to be when I smacked rocks over the barn roof. A coincidence--as I write today, Nolan Ryan pitched his seventh no-hitter last night at age 44, striking out sixteen but walking two (the bum!). He was after my time as a kid, but he would have been on the list. The end of the story is that I finally battered the two Styrofoam balls to death against the wood door. I ask myself: where are they today? Why doesn't somebody make them again? Do the little kids know what they are missing? It's worthy of note that when playing "real" baseball, I tried and tried to throw a curve, and it never happened. So make-believe was much nicer than real life, don't ever let them tell you any different.

A variation of the pitching game took place outside the barn in the wide space between it and the farm house. There were three old rickety wooden windows on the east side of the barn; I used to spend hours pitching all sorts of small rocks against them, once again in game situations, striking out the best. But this time I had to develop some control, at least I had to hit the window for it to be a strike. I had the good sense to stick to smaller rocks. But this pitcher did not turn into a country "phe-nom." Maybe that was why I loved the movie "the Natural" years later.

I used to love to climb, yet paradoxically was scared to death of heights. I climbed every possible tree around the place, climbed the steel steps all the way to the top of the silo for my "army scout" game, walked to the top of the hill to spy over the entire area. But once I got myself into a scrape--I climbed up onto the tin roof of the barn on an old, rickety ladder and was afraid to come down (this must be what cats feel like in trees). I must have sat up there for two hours before I got the courage to test the old ladder once more. But once down, I never tried it again.

Talking about fear of heights--the best-paying job I ever had as a boy in Abilene was as part of a construction cleanup crew at a gas booster plant near Enterprise. My job, among other things, was to perch high up on a ladder to wash the dozens of windows in the place. I did not last long;

there always seemed to be a stiff wind making the ladder sway, and all there was below were a steel catwalk and lots of machinery. I was terrified.

I'm sure there were many, many other games, a few of which I have described. I know playing "cowboy" was the favorite of earlier years, and I think my all-time favorite Christmas gift as a child was a gun and holster set, this in the days of seeing the Western B movies and Roy Rogers at the local cinema.

24. MUSIC AND THE FAMILY

We were a musical family, largely through the inspiration of Mom who played the piano growing up. The upright piano we had in the "music room" was not serviceable most of the time as far as I can remember, being at least partially out of tune, with some keys unplayable. But Mom still wanted us to do music, and there was a long sequence of events and instruments.

Jim, as far as I know, never did an instrument, but had the best voice of all of us, but Jo, Tom and I were not bad at all. He sang in the school choir, operetta and in the Catholic Church choir, this back in the pre-Vatican II era when the singing at mass was still based on Gregorian chant. I can still remember the different parts of the high mass, particularly where the bass-baritone voice of my brother came in. He stopped singing a few years ago, several years before his death, and I never did get a good explanation why. Jim sang at weddings, and I of course remember Jo Anne and Paul's in 1959. Jim would sing at the wedding mass, generally doing the Ave Maria. But his real specialty was the "I'll take you home again Kathleen" at the reception, generally after getting well juiced up and lubricating the vocal cords. Although he did not sing at Keah's and my wedding per se, he certainly did sing at the reception.

Tom did the trumpet (he had a good voice as well, more tenor than Jim's, in school chorus and some school plays as well) and was in different local school bands, and I think still played as a NROTC cadet at Marquette in the drum and bugle corps in the late 1950s.

Jo Anne did piano and violin. I've already told the story about the smashed violin at the end of the lane. I think that ended her music days.

My music started with "obligatory" piano lessons from my godmother, Adele Lexow, in the second grade I think. I was not particularly keen about the idea, but Mike Kippenberger was starting at the same time; I think both our mothers were in cahoots about it all. I went mainly for the milk and cookies we got after each lesson. I could handle the right hand just fine, but the left was much harder, kind of uncoordinated at best. Of course my daily practice time was maybe a total of fifteen minutes, so maybe that had something to do with it. I never did succeed in bettering that, but never worked very hard at it either. I think I lasted either two months or two years.

The next disaster was the clarinet. I do not ever remember being asked if I wanted to take and play the clarinet, but the idea was to play in the grade school band. Clarinet was easy enough; reading some basic music from piano days helped. I had one of those silver plated instruments and was always suspicious that it was inferior to the black wooden jobs. The instrument was rented from the band director, a certain Mr. Worman. My memory of him was that he was business like, had a thin mustache (cause for suspicion; the villains in the cowboy movies all had thin mustaches) and was not particularly friendly. But I had little difficulty making first chair in the little grade school band, especially considering that the only time I practiced was at band rehearsal.

But there was a falling out with Mr. Worman; he claimed my instrument needed cleaning, but that was a lot of money and hassle, especially since I didn't give a hoot if it was clean or not. Shortly thereafter my band days were over. There was some time in that period when we seemed to march a lot, an activity I considered a huge waste of time at the time (an idea I howled at in "Catch 22" with Lieutenant Scheisskoph, the marching and the parades.) With a little perspective today, however, I remember with fondness the university bands that actually played marches. The most entertaining university marching band to me is Stanford University's, and if you have seen them, you'll know what I mean.

Something rubbed off, either due to genes or Mom's quiet persistence, but it turned out differently than Mom had planned. I always say Mom because Dad did not speak up on the matter, never expressed himself until many, many years later about it all. When I was a sophomore in high school I became interested in the guitar; it must have been about 1957. At that time the rock-pop thing was just beginning. In our area few people played guitar; Central Kansas in those days was not a country music stronghold although many appreciated it. In our town classic guitar was unheard of, at least by anybody we seemed to know.

I believe it was the music of Chet Atkins that first attracted me to the instrument. We had a record and I heard his "finger pickin'" style, using thumb and all four fingers on the right hand instead of using a single plectrum or pick. The sound was unusual and when he played it sounded like more than one guitar. But it was only later on I heard classical guitar music.

I can't remember if I paid for it myself, but my first instrument was a steel stringed "Stella" bought at the only music store in Abilene, funny now how I remember being so many times in that store looking at music, with Jo Anne, Tom and myself. The guitar's main virtue was that it would stay in tune. A second was the price, $15 I think. I worked alone since no lessons were available locally, and with the method book I had I was able to play with a pick and play some very simple melody lines. Strangely enough, chords and guitar accompaniment escaped me for a long time. It was maybe a year or two after I started, now playing fairly complicated melodies, when I attended a 4-H get together in a little country school house and a local country gal was singing "You are my sunshine" and accompanying herself on the guitar with chords. Once I saw it, I was amazed how simple it was, not at all as difficult as the solo, melody lines I had been working on. In no time I picked it up and was singing ditties.

In the late 1950s there were magazines for about 25 cents which had the lyrics to the top 40. We did not call it "Adult" bookstore at that time, but the vile looking old man who ran it kept special magazines under the counter. How do I know? Through Jerry Collins, my contact with the local underworld. We used to laugh about the place because the old man kept Chihuahua dogs and you would find dog poop on the magazines sometimes. Abilene was a high class place in those days. Said bookstore, unfortunately, was in one of the original historic buildings on 3rd and Buckeye across from the Post Office and just north of the Union Pacific tracks.

Anyway, those were the days when I got the words to songs by Ricky Nelson, the Everly brothers, or maybe Marty Robbins. Many of the songs I thought were "country-pop" like "A White Sport Coat".

About the same time my brother Jim was traveling quite a bit for Ehrsam Mfg. in Enterprise, Kansas. One day he came home from Kansas City and brought me a classical guitar method book, not really knowing too much about it himself. The author was South African or Dutch, Van der … something. I took to it like a duck to water and was delighted to use the finger technique for plucking instead of the pick. It seemed to coincide with Chet Atkins' style, at least a little bit, the little bit I could learn. At that point I began to spend hours listening to a couple of his records trying to imitate the sound, but without a whole lot of success. But I did pick up at least elementary classic technique and could soon play a version of "Malagueña" and a few others.

This coincided during the last two years of high school with yet another effort. A local Negro boy, Everett ("Eddy") Smith, had bought a small amplifier and electric guitar, the first one I had ever seen. He had music in his blood, was talented and also trained classically in music, his instrument the trumpet. But with the guitar he "did his thing" and "wailed". I can't recall how we swung it, but we managed a full hour each school day during study hall time to go down to an empty band room and play guitar. I soon bought an inexpensive amplifier and electric guitar--a "Kay" model I think, bright metallic orange, the sparkly kind you used to see on the hot rods in town. It had a vibrato gismo on the amplifier, and you could make it reverberate like Duane Eddy and his "twangy guitar".

Eddy and I became proficient enough, singing a duet of sorts, to begin to play for groups, the epitome being a performance at Marymount College in Salina, Kansas, for Jo Anne's class. But Eddy also played in a local "jive" group of black kids, and their music was a bit different from ours. They did the Coasters, the Platters, and early black rock with names like Little Richard, Fats Domino, and Chuck Berry. Lord, he turned sixty the other day!

I learned a lot of those old songs and still recall enough bits and pieces to do a "rock" bit at parties. So from a hodgepodge of country music on the radio, lyrics from the pop magazines, and playing with Eddy, I managed to build up a repertoire. I began to play a bit at parties, one a beer blast up at the pond on our farm. I played a bit of basic classic for the annual Spanish Banquet in 1958 or 1959 dressed in a vest Jim brought back from Mexico.

The Farm

Where my music really bloomed was at Rockhurst College in Kansas City, Missouri, from 1959 to 1963. I developed my classic quite a lot, although without instruction, thus learning a lot of "incorrect" positions and bad habits I have to this day, but you don't know it if you don't know guitar. I did have one lesson: Jim I think and Mom took me to Kansas City while I still was in high school, to the nearest classic guitar instructor around. I will never forget: he was an old man, kept this absolutely gorgeous classic guitar in a fine case under a bed, wanted me to spend my first month practicing the right hand, not touching the guitar with the left. That was the end of that. I have regretted since not learning classic technique "properly" but to master the instrument and the style was more of a discipline and time consuming affair than I could manage at the time. And honestly, I believe I was concerned about how we would arrange the trips to Kansas City and the expense.

But at Rockhurst I began to play at a lot or parties, played classic for the variety shows and worked out a great parody of a country radio show with Bill Rost, the "Slim and Curly's Noontime Jamboree" modeled on a real radio show by a local country huckster in Hutchinson and Salina, Kansas. It was good parody with all the facets of the real thing, but I think I already told that story.

I remember many a night at Rockhurst, coming into the dorm late on a Friday or Saturday night, picking up the guitar and going down to an empty room in the basement where the music had a nice echo to it and playing quiet classical music until two or three in the morning. By the way, my first classic guitar was from Sears, via the mail order catalogue, cost about $50, and was a really adequate learners' instrument. During my freshmen year at Rockhurst a buddy from St. Louis told me about a free concert at the University of Kansas City Arts building. I attended and was spell bound by the music and the event; the guitarist was a certain Siegfried Behrend from Germany. Aside from his ability, a smaller matter impressed me: the decals from all over the world he used to decorate his hard case. I may not have mastered the instrument like a professional, but my decals and travels will match them all! That afternoon concert was a really significant moment in my music life.

I forgot to mention that I had graduated from the $15. Stella to a Sears Roebuck Classic I ordered out of the catalogue in Abilene with savings from working at the local ice plant in the summertime. Looking back on it all, some fifty years ago now, the guitar was really quite adequate, very nice tone, too high of fret action, but a wonderful beginner's instrument. A vague memory just came to me of the times in Kansas City when I would go downtown by bus to one of the major music stores and just sit and play the extremely expensive classic guitars. I don't know how I convinced the salesmen I could actually buy one, but that was when I first heard of Goya, Martin and others. What an incredibly beautiful sound and thrill that was.

It's hard to remember what happened to my old guitars. I generally gave them away; I believe that one went to Eduardo Matheu a great friend in Guatemala. The next instrument is a beauty, a Di Giorgio classic I purchased at the "Guitarra de Prata" shop in the Largo do Carioca in Rio de Janeiro in 1966! A long ways from old downtown Kansas City! I bought the guitar for cash on the barrelhead, including a fine solid case, an incredible steal from today's perspective. But however reasonable the price, it was hard earned money--it was bought with the money I scraped together while on a Fulbright Hays research grant in 1966-1967 in Brazil. While living in a broken down boarding house in Recife, the "Chácara das Rosas" near the old Law School, on board and room at US $35 per month, I was constantly thinking of the guitar I would buy when I moved down to Rio six months later.

It is funny how some memories are so indelible. I can recall like today going to the guitar shop, playing all the fine Di Giorgios and Gianninis (rosewood guitars, fine instruments, no longer available because of the wood shortage, rare buys today), buying mine, taking it home like a baby fresh from the hospital in a Rio taxi which made me just as nervous as a mother with a one-week old infant. And finally leaving it under the bed at the Kerti's in Flamengo while I returned to the North for a few months' more research. The rosewood eventually cracked badly in Arizona, was redone and refinished, and is cracking again. I remember the repair in Arizona cost as much as the original cost in Brazil. An appraisal from about 1980 was $1,800. It should be more now.

Anyway, back at Rockhurst I can recall taking the guitar to picnics with the Latinos, including the girls from Notre Dame de Sion, kids from both Spain and Latin America. I always wondered how such people ended up in private schools for high school in Kansas City? Another memory was of a New Years' Eve party on the Paseo in Kansas City when there was a blizzard and we put the guitar on a sled and took off for the party. My cohort in crime was Eduardo Matheu of Guatemala and some TWA stewardesses.

Then there was the "serenata" or serenade when we all jumped the wall at the Notre Dame de Sion prep school for "refined, young ladies," began our serenade, and woke up the Dobermans, the girls and the nuns. We were told to vamoose or else, and that was the last Latino serenade like that I have participated in. Maybe that is why Chico Buarque's song "Juca" is so special to me, and why I like the sernade scenes in Jorge Amado's novel "Dona Flor and Her Two Husbands." I also have played borrowed guitars all over Latin America, in Mexico, Guatemala, Colombia and especially Brazil.

The guitar during St. Louis University days was similar to Rockhurst except I played mainly at parties with the large group of friends I had from graduate school--Dan Hayes, the Cusack girls, and Jorge Negrete from Mexico, the friend who helped me compose a Mexican "corrido" or ballad. The latter took place one night after several beers, and I still remember the filthy lyrics to our "Felipe Bermejo". But I also practiced my classic guitar in the quiet of the lobby of the Coronado Hotel where we had a dorm for a year or so; the beautiful lobby and ornate ball room was the inaugural site of Harry S. Truman when governor of Missouri.

Back at Rockhurst I had played in two different bands, the first a "pop" group playing a lot of Big Band standards. The leader was a Jewish guy from Chicago. I became good friends then with Bill Bockleman of St. Louis and Phil Kezele of Gallup, New Mexico, Bill the pianist, Phil the drummer. We played high school dances, proms, that stuff. We were pretty lousy. I think my big moment was a solo on "Honky Tonk" and I remember I worked hard on "Guitar Boogie Shuffle," but never quite mastered it. But that was an introduction to pure guitar accompaniment to big band standards and the "fake" book.

The second band was more fun, called the "Blue Velvets" where I played rhythm guitar and a few solos. The highlight of that career was a fraternity party at Kansas State in Manhattan where we actually made $25.00 apiece, big dough for a hobby in those days. We played in white dinner jackets with velvet lapels. I wish I had some pictures; I know I had a flattop or crew cut, wore white socks and weighed about 125 lbs in those days. But through the band leader who lived in a wealthy area of Shawnee Mission and through the Latinos and dating girls from Notre Dame de Sion, I was introduced to an altogether different social group from Kansas City and then Latin America. For a totally unsophisticated farm boy from Abilene, the guitar had taken me a long way.

There is a later story: I am sure that my music, languages, and Spanish led me to be offered what would have been my first permanent job, for the "Industria Farmaceutica" in Guatemala. I have offered wondered how different life would have been had I taken that path.

A couple of final notes on music. After graduating from Rockhurst College in 1963, I did not have a summer job. There were no worries about the immediate future since I had a three-year NDEA Fellowship for language and culture study at St. Louis University, to begin in the Fall of 1963. So I taught English in a summer institute at Rockhurst, mainly to the Latino friends I had had at Rockhurst. But after the first year at St. Louis I needed a summer job and ended up playing guitar and singing in a club in Kansas City for the summer. I landed a job at a pizza joint, sort of restaurant-bar called the "5050 Club" on Main south of the Plaza in Kansas City. The owner was Italian of course, and I still believe today he had his mafia connections in town. I know he told me to "relax" and he would "take care" of the ASCII union guys who would show up. The place did burn down two or three times over the years. But I played six nights a week, nine to one a.m. For awhile it was a fun experience; I doubled my singing repertoire to over two hundred tunes; also increased the classical guitar selections. I sang from nine to midnight and did classic from midnight to one a.m. The crowd was a mixed bag; some cronies from college days at Rockhurst, locals, but later on a delightful bunch of Peace Corps trainees for Latin America. I can recall a "hootenanny" type atmosphere, early 60s vintage, good acceptance of my music, mainly folk songs of that period (late Kingston Trio, Limelighters, etc.) some pop and country.

This was during the Kennedy years' enthusiasm, Peace Corps etc. And there was some growing up that took place. It was then I knew I could not do that kind of thing for a living. I can recall the customers buying me beers; the ultimate was one night seeing the drinks lining a little shelf next to the microphone. That kind of partying could not have gone on long. The career came to an abrupt halt one night, this after the Peace Corps contingent had finished their training and the clientele of the bar had slipped back to the normal "regulars" including some obnoxious drunks. My brother Jim came in (I lived with him that summer at his tiny house over on the Kansas side) and told me of a trip planned to the Lake of the Ozarks the next day. I put the guitar in the case, said "let's go fishing" and walked out.

But, back to the original point of music on the farm, Mom's desire for us to play probably turned out beyond her expectations, at least in my case, particularly when you take into account my original lack of interest and enthusiasm and discipline. The instrument has brought me untold days of happiness and am sure it will have some more. In recent years playing with Katie in the Summer has been the highlight, classic and popular music in church in Colorado. I wrote in 1985 that I hoped she had the talent and the discipline for music. Now in 1990 I am sure she does and has long surpassed me in the classic music. I did all my music on plain, ole' desire. I could never have maintained professional discipline, but I had some fun.

As I rewrite this now in 2006 from Colorado and Arizona, there is a whole new chapter since I returned to music upon retirement. I played and sang folk, classic country, John Denver, "Oh Brother where art thou," added Irish later, and did some classic guitar, this until Cristina's Restaurant stopped having music in about 2007. But that's another story for another time.

I realize all this latter chatter really did not involve the farm, but the seed was planted by my Mother on the farm.

25. THE MOVIES AND OLD ABILENE

One of the entertainments that were popular in Abilene in the 1940s and early 1950s prior to television was the movie theater. The old Plaza Theater played an important role, and to a lesser extent the Lyric Theater, a poor cousin, an inferior house with little or no decoration, small screen, and black and white films. I can remember literally falling out of my seat laughing with my buddy Mike Kippenberger at films such as "Francis in the Army", Jerry Lewis and Dean Martin's films, Ma and Pa Kettle movies and the Harlem Globetrotter story, all these at the Lyric. The seats were wooden with an assortment of chewing gum on the bottom, but the price of admission was right, 14 cents admission for children.

We truly passed through the period of the Saturday afternoon matinee and the golden age of the cowboy movies. First of all, even for poor or middle class families it was little or no hardship to attend. Admittance was for the grand total of fourteen cents. My Dad would give me a quarter dollar, and with the other eleven cents I could get a nickel bag of popcorn, or a nickel package of Milk Duds, have a nickel coke or root beer after the movie and still have a penny left over for bubble gum or a root beer barrel. I think there was a time when the quarter represented my week's allowance, but that's foggy now. It amazed me years later to see how long the theater maintained the price at that level or just a bit higher, and, evidently still made money for the two Strowig brothers who owned both movie houses. I think adults paid 35 or 50 cents admission. After I left Abilene for college there was a quantum leap in prices that brought them up to big city standards.

The movies were I suppose like anywhere else in the U.S. small towns at that time. Each session screened a few advertisements, the newsreel of national or international news, a great and it seems to me today truly funny and creative cartoon (Walter Lantz, "Loony Tunes", Disney), previews of coming attractions and finally the feature presentation. My years were a bit late for the Saturday serials although I have vague recollections of them. What I do recall is becoming an expert in my time on the movie cowboys. We had them all and continuous films of each. All of this now seems to be a sort of fantasy age, golden age to me now for it coincided perfectly with vintage Mickey Mantle baseball cards and Blackhawk and Superman comic books.

There was Hopalong Cassady, a grey immanence dressed in black and riding a white horse; Lash Larue, a B-film type but one who could handle himself and had a nasty bullwhip to settle with varmints, sidewinders and others of their ilk. The Lone Ranger and Tonto were around, but not much; they were much more popular as a serial on television in the mid-1950s. Tim Holt was still in some films; Tom Mix had pretty much gone by the way. A favorite of mine was the Durango Kid played by a Charles Stuart, a fellow who had to make a quick change from local citizen to super good guy and bandit chaser. I believe the ever-present Smiley Burnett was a regular as the sidekick and funny man. I have wondered if the hero-sidekick thing evolved from any particular form; the obvious model in my experience would be the hero-comedians from the Spanish "comedia" tradition, maybe just a coincidence. Gabby Hayes was around too, talking through his whiskers to his friend Roy Rogers, but this was a higher budget western.

Two movie-cowboys who remained a notch above the B films of the times were Gene Autry and Roy Rogers, the latter gradually winning out with color films, music, etc. "Back in the saddle again" and Champion were good, but Trigger, Dale Evans and razzmatazz won out for Roy. And there even was a dog, a German Shepherd I think, or was it a Lassie type? Gene's films were more often in black and white while Roy spent more money. His was a semi-modern scene on the ranch, with one of those genuine wood paneled station wagons that used to be the standard thing.

I remember scenes as though it were yesterday, particularly from the B movies: terrific shootouts where the guns rarely or never needed to be reloaded, bullets ricocheting off huge boulders (the likes of which I discovered years later to be common on the Payson-Phoenix or Kingman-Phoenix highways in Arizona), and lots and lots of fistfights. Stagecoach robberies were big, long chases were involved; and there was always the run-away carriage or wagon with the heroine saved by the cowboy who jumped from his horse to the wild stagecoach horse or into the wagon seat and grabbing the reins to gradually slow it all down. A digression: I am one of the great admirers of more recent cinema, particularly the comedy and satire of a Mel Brooks or Steve Martin. Their knowledge of the old Westerns and "plagiarism" of the same are rather apparent if you see "Blazing Saddles," "Three Amigos," my favorite, or "History of the World Part I." They use many of the old B western scenes, and improve on the same.

I think these movies ended with a song. The villains dressed like businessmen, a strange coincidence in these capitalistic times, with suits and string ties; they sported thin mustaches and spoke good, standard, American English, not that of the "cowboy." For a ten year old, what really stood out were the six- guns, the fancier the better; Roy's and Gene's had pearl handles; the villains in these movies all had dark wooden handles. I developed a fairly good trivia mindset seeing so many of the character or minor actors in other films later on, actors like Chill Wills or Andy Devine. Later on, now in my teenage years, the westerns were dominated by John Wayne or even Paul Newman ("Hud") and sophisticated stuff like "Butch Cassidy and the Sundance Kid." Jimmy Stewart in "Winchester 73" was a favorite too. There were many, many more, but their titles escape me now.

I have tried to recall exactly when puberty came and beautiful girls in the films began to draw more interest than the old "shoot 'em ups." I am sure it must have been early junior high or high school years. I can't place a specific film, but I noticed I did not mind the love scenes so much, in those days hugging and a passionate kiss, and in fact looked forward to them. I was before the time of Annette Funicello and the California beach party movies, but I can remember Ester Williams in her swim suits, Doris Day and a particularly young and sultry Liz Taylor in a white swimsuit in "Suddenly Last Summer." "South Pacific" and the Polynesian beauties and Mitzi Gaynor I think were part of it all too.

I can only recall one movie giving me nightmares, one of the early versions of "King Kong" on one of those Saturday afternoons. The nightmares were horrible and lasted several nights. Also wild animals, jaguars, black panthers and the like were a particularly scary thing. I can remember one Tarzan movie when he tackled what must have been a two-foot wide tarantula. And crocodiles and boa constrictors were the norm. I had the creeps for weeks. Then there were the original monsters like Frankenstein, the werewolf and vampires with Lon Chaney staring at the moon.

The movies were just an occasional thing for Mom and Dad. (Mom's favorite was "The Egg and I.") I have vivid memories of Saturday nights in the summertime, people in town at early evening to finish shopping or "trading" as my Dad called it. The local merchants would stay open later on Saturday night. Some folks would take in an early movie or would stay outside talking while the kids were at the theater. There were still iron rails in front of most of the downtown buildings, a throwback to hitching rails I am told. You could sit on the top one and just watch life go on by; I can recall being perched on one while listening to Dad pass the time with another farmer in town for the evening, or sometimes sitting in the back seat of the car, windows down, while Mom talked to an acquaintance from the front seat. As I think about it, Mom and Dad did not really go that much to the movies, but would do the visiting while waiting for the early show to get out. I can recall climbing into the back seat after a movie and be asleep before we had gone three blocks; I guess Dad must have carried me into the farmhouse all those times. Don't know if I ever thanked him.

I don't really have the details on the buildings in town in the mid or late 1940s, but Abilene was founded about 1869, a terminal for the Union Pacific Railroad and an important shipping point for the cattle industry of the times. The Chisholm Trail from Texas to the rail point was the main reason the town became so famous in its day. The Belle Springs Creamery, incidentally of Ike Eisenhower days and where I worked in my teens, had been a drovers' cottage for the cowboys and the streets south of the U.P. tracks, A Street among them, were renowned for taverns where cowboys and prostitutes and gamblers and other varmints could be found.

From that beginning farming began and dominates yet today. The population of Abilene changed little in those years and is not that much different today, some now fifty years later, fluctuating I believe from five to seven thousand people. The main factor in the recent past is that children do not have any decent job opportunities, but must move on to urban areas, that is, unless they inherit a good situation on a local farm or in local commerce. The local class system seemed to revolve basically around that reality: poor, middle and wealthy farmers and local merchants.

But I do remember the old "Toothpick" building on south 2nd Street that dated from the earliest days of Abilene. Like many other buildings it had the tin ceilings inside, ventilator fans and very high ceilings. I recall old barber shops, dry goods stores (Pinkhams, Hamburgs, maybe J. C. Penneys), real drugstores with a soda fountain and accompanying furniture. Architecture in Abilene was Victorian with many beautiful homes, most of them wood frame, but a few of native rock or stone, Elm lined streets were many, altogether a pleasant place. Brick was used to a great extent on the commercial buildings downtown, but wood frame was the rule in residential housing.

There was a blacksmith shop or two, the Viola's feed store, hardware store, appliance store, shoe store, clothing store and grocery store. They in fact had "company" money that you were paid in from bringing in produce and could spend at any of their stores. Several brothers ran the outfit. It was the nearest thing we ever had to the old general store concept.

Got a little sidetracked here, but my idea was the movies.

26. RADIO AND EARLY TELEVISION IN THE 1940S AND 1950S

We did not get television until 1955, a momentous day when my brother Jim brought home a black and white set from an appliance store in Enterprise, Kansas, where he worked at a local small manufacturing plant. And there was also a very tall antenna that had to be attached to the roof in order to pick up signals from far away Hutchinson, Wichita or perhaps Topeka ; Kansas City was too far to pick up anything. Stations were also far enough away so that "rabbit ears" were of no use. Even with the antenna we could receive only three stations, and one of those was marginal.

But radio was an integral part of growing up on the farm. I believe we listened most to the one in the kitchen, on the counter near the breakfast nook where we ate most of our meals except Sunday dinner. It made sense to have it there since Dad could catch his weather, agricultural and other news easily. At one time we had a model that would be antique today: the kind set in a wooden cabinet shaped like the spade of a shovel, "Gothic" perhaps?

I can recall in the winter sitting next to the furnace vent while listening to programs on that radio. I can also remember listening to baseball games in the summertime and especially to the Sunday afternoon programs while spread out on the floor in the upstairs bedrooms and listening to a different radio. During the meals, especially the evening meal, we had the radio on for the news. It was evidently the only time Dad could get the news since he was out of the house so much during the daytime hours. We were silenced, and at times none too gently with "LISTEN!" Then Gabriel Heater or another news commentator would fill us in on the world; my earliest recollection was the news telling of the aerial dogfights during the Korean War, losses of jets in battles over the Yalu, and the Panmunjong peace talks.

I believe it was high noon when all the farm news came: livestock reports, prices from the markets, and weather news. Associated with this was a program I used later on to create a wonderful parody of country-farm radio programs, this for a variety show at college. It was KSAL radio in Salina, Kansas, with a program I think was called the "Noontime Jamboree". It was evidently a poor takeoff on the Grand Ole' Opry type stuff. This show had some local talent, a couple of people "pickin' and singin'" and doing advertisements for feed for cattle, etc. The sponsor was the Gooch Feed Co. of Salina, Kansas, sponsor of the CK Ranch Annual Livestock Sale, a big event for me in my teen years. Each bag of Gooch feed had a red circle on it; you cut it out, saved it for the points on it, and when you had a few million or so could take those points and go to a beautiful ranch west of Salina and bid for real, honest to goodness livestock. I drove out one year with my friend Joe Fleagle in our old green Dodge or Plymouth. I believe my parents sent me on my own; I can't recall how it came out, but I certainly did not come home with any livestock. I think I mainly wanted a chance at the free hot dogs and pop.

Anyway, our parody radio program, the one I referred to earlier on at Rockhurst College, had it all. I still have the original script, a single sheet typed page from about 1960. On the program we advertised hog feed, chicken feed, cattle feed and a special brand of "baby feed". There was a letter segment when listeners would write in with birthday requests. We would sing the "Mom and Dad Waltz" for anniversaries and a corny, made up song for birthdays. We had a heavy dose of local 4-H and farm news with an incredibly distorted use of farm jargon whenever possible, using words like "boar, sow, philly, barrow, steer, heifer" and such as maladroitly as possible. We always closed the program with the religious section and a hymn butchered by us, with some good words to the wise, all of this of course with a smattering of country song hits of the time. It was the Slim and Curly Show on KSAL. I do not believe we ever performed it locally in Abilene, but on stage at the variety show for the sophisticated St. Louis and Kansas City prep schoolers and Jesuits it went over great. Today I realize how much of it was not really parody, but just happy reminiscing.

There was another type of program, associated I think with the top 40 pop songs. I know I heard stuff like "Mockingbird Hill", "How much is that doggy in the window", "On a pawn shop, on a corner, in Pittsburgh, Pennsylvania" and then in teen years what must have amounted to a combination of country, pop and very early rock and roll. I regularly bought a magazine for 25 cents that had all the lyrics of the songs and I would try to learn them on guitar.

Back to the farm and the radio. The favorite programs for me fit into two categories: the daily kids' programs from about 4:30 to 6:00 p. m. before the news and the Sunday programs, afternoon and evening segments. Today in 2010 Public radio, TV and catalogues offer today a smattering of what we took for granted.

Food for thought--why was it I got on our daughter Katie a few years ago for wanting to watch her programs on TV after school or early evening? Was I getting old and cranky? I guess it boils down to the fact that I do believe there was an essential difference in tone for those programs we listened to and the quality of teen sitcoms, quiz shows and all a generation later in Katie's growing up days. The old programs boiled down to "good" and "evil", (just like the Brazilian folk poetry I spent thirty-five years studying), heroes and villains and some fairly innocent humor. Sex was generally taboo and violence was at least not the visual business of today. But the daily radio programs of the 1950s were fantastic and I was a regular. I had lots of farm chores then, so these programs must have been worked in around them, can't say how.

I can recall, among others, "Straight Arrow," "Sergeant Preston of the Yukon," "Bobby Benson and the B Bar B Riders". I swear there are even some episodes I recall, one of them a Chinese water torture with the drip, drip, drip and cries of pain, I think on Bobby Benson. The programs were a wonderful part of my life. I liked the music behind the action, the sound effects, but best of all was the gadgets you could send in for, this with 25 cents and a box top from Cheerios or Wheaties or Shredded Wheat. I was constantly sending in for the prizes, saving allowance money and begging my parents to do it. I received for instance the "Gold Nugget Straight Arrow Ring." It had a hole in it, and when you looked at it in the light you could see ... you guessed it, Straight Arrow's cave! Another one caused me no end of problems at school--trouble for me and several buddies who all ordered it. It was a "cannon" ring: you could make spit balls, pull back the trigger and "bam"-- shoot the girlies. I cannot express the excitement the days I would take the school bus home, get off down the lane, walk up the lane and have the small package waiting for me on the kitchen table. It was heaven!

I don't think it was related to the kids' programs, but evidently a little later on when I began to be interested in music, we could get a country music or gospel station from Del Rio, Texas. It seems like the transmitter was in Mexico, thus they had super wattage and could be heard to the Canadian line. They advertised a harmonica for just one box top and maybe 75 cents or a dollar. Life's tricks and deceptions hit home hard: the harmonica, when it finally arrived, was plastic and worthless. That may have been the end of radio merchandise and promises for me. The story ended years later when I bought a real Chromatic Harmonica, a brand name, and actually learned to play about any song I could whistle on it, that is, once I figured out by chance the technique with the tongue. I could not for the longest time figure out the "knack" of it, but still take it today on camping trips and love to play the old spirituals and down home stuff near the campfire. But if the song is too fast or has a bunch of sharps or flats, forget it.

Sundays were the best for the radio programs, especially Sunday afternoon which was a delight: the crime programs, the mystery programs and some very, very scary shows. I recall the "Shadow" with "Who knows what evil lurks in the hearts of men" and the laugh. There was "Gangbusters" and a couple of private eye shows, "Nick Reynolds"? maybe or Nick Carter, who knows. Man, but were they fun. I can remember Jo Anne and Tom listening sometimes, but my listening companions were more likely buddies I would invite over on Sunday p.m. The radio was interspersed with all kinds of sports activities or playing outside. I get so frustrated today trying to think of stuff for Katie to do; life seemed to be easier and less complicated then.

But the best is for last: the Sunday evening and night programs with comedy shows that I have yet to see matched in any medium: the "Jack Benny Radio Show" and "Amos and Andy." For some reason, perhaps I came along a bit late, I never did catch W.C. Fields and his Lucky Strike Hour. I think "Gracie Allen" and George Burns were on then. And we often heard the Edgar Bergen show with Charlie McCarthy and Mortimer Snerd. The sound effects of radio were absolutely magnificent, particularly on the Jack Benny show (the long trips to his vault with all the closing doors, footsteps, etc.) I recall many of the crazy secondary characters voiced by Mel Blanc: Si, the Mexican Benny would run into in the train station going to Cucamonga, Benny's old Model-T,

Rochester, Mary Livingston, Dennis Day and the "yeeeeeeeeesss" salesman. What writers Benny had! We would see him later on television, and the show was good, but the joy of radio with its singular dimension of sound and the fact that we did the imagining and describing of the characters and scenes, these made it my favorite.

I can recall so well my disillusionment seeing "Superman" on TV in the 50s, and also "Amos and Andy" after the radio shows. I first saw TV at Clarence Gillinger's house up on north Buckeye, almost outside the city limits. The Gillingers had a small six our seven inch screen; the program was "Amos and Andy". Clarence's Dad also kept a pop cooler with big bottles of RC Cola; he charged a nickel to customers at his car repair shop, but they were free to us of course, I was in paradise. I can also remember seeing wrestling, a staple of early TV at Pat McMahon's house and my first trip into Kansas City where I stared at some big band program while we were in a restaurant. It was a whole new world, marvelous and mysterious.

One final memory from the radio days: listening to the Mutual Game of the Week baseball game. I have this vague memory of listening to the Yankees, my favorite team growing up, Mickey Mantle the greatest of heroes, when Mantle and Dimaggio were both in the same outfield, 1951 I think. Mantle was first injured about that time, stepping in a drain in the outfield, and that seemed to be just the start of a long series of ups and downs for him and me. It really was the first in a series of tragic injuries that many say curtailed his career and greatness. But the ballgames came alive for me, a custom which I have kept alive all my life, that is, along with certain periods of detachment when I can't put up with astronomical salaries and spoiled "businessmen" players. I think all the baseball heroes of my youth: Mantle, Mays, Ted Williams, Stan Musial, all topped out at around one hundred thousand dollars per year. Even with approximately 500 hundred per cent inflation since then in the national economy, that would put Canseco, Clemens and friends at about 500,000 per year, probably not an unreasonable figure. What do you think?

Television and Baseball: the mid 1950s. There was a game of the week and for years I saw it off and on while growing up. Early announcers were Dizzy Dean and Pee Wee Reese. Then the trout fisherman from Montana, Curt Gowdy, Joe Garagiola, Tony Kubek (whom I saw walk into the Katz Drugstore on 12th and Main in Kansas City, Missouri, across from the Muelbach Hotel with Moose Skowron and about dropped over with delight. This was approximately 1955.) I still remember Dizzy singing the "Wabash Cannonball" each ball game and all his braggadocio; I never minded because he was such a legend, and was really sorry when he lost the job.

I can also remember other great ballgames, the time Mantle hit the ball over the roof at Briggs Stadium in Detroit, the All-Star game that went into extra innings and Stan Musial won it with a homer, but mainly I remember the Yankee Games. The New York market ran TV and success made the Yankees by far the most televised team. In the later 50s we watched pro football, but it was baseball that enthralled when we first got television.

Other shows. I can recall only vaguely but the fifteen minute Perry Como show was a favorite; he walked out and sang; that was it, no falderal. We also watched another 15 minute show with a magician and comedian named Johnny Carson. I think I saw Jack Parr once in awhile, but it was Steve Allen in the late night slots, along with his sidekicks Don Knotts and the "man on the street" routines that I recall best.

But the most watched show was Sunday night, the "Ed Sullivan" variety show: the Englishman who did the "passing out" ceremony; Señor Wences and his puppet in the box; the man who brought a chair out on stage and began laughing and by the time it was over we were in tears and our stomachs hurt. And of course there were the first appearances of Elvis Presley and the first U.S. appearances of the Beatles.

The Honeymooners. This was the favorite on Saturday nights for years with Jackie Gleason, the fat bus driver; Art Carney his sidekick the sewer worker; Audrey Meadows, the wise, suffering wife. With all these shows I remember the advertising for cars, the only time in my life when I could recognize the models, etc. Ed Sullivan advertised Mercury for years. The commercials actually talked about traits of the cars, their selling points.

The old G.E. Theater was another program we regularly saw on Sunday nights. I can recall a show when Burl Ives played a hangman who would sing a ditty or two. There was the highbrow "Odyssey" on Sunday afternoons with Alistair Cook with dramatized moments of history, like the death of Socrates. There was a lot more live drama on TV than now. "I Love Lucy" as well.

So entertainment in Abilene for us was the weekly movie on Saturday, almost daily radio in its times, TV, and going to a local 4-H play or school function. The basic pattern began to change when I began to date seriously, this in the very late 50s. Drive-in movies, inside movies, high school sports, and lots of dances took up our time. In the summertime when I didn't have a date, we used to go out to Eisenhower park and play basketball or even tennis at times. A funny memory: I remember we played golf during one phase of high school, not at the country club, but rather at a country course out south of town, renting clubs, and playing on sand greens and dodging cow pies in the fields. But a favorite summertime thing, from junior year on was when my old music buddy, Eddy Smith (guitar) and Bob Hensley (bongo drums) and I would go out to the park, maybe in front of the old bandstand, drink beer and play music. One night Mike and Jack Kippenberger joined us; and we had great fun with the music. An aside: Jack was eventually a civil service employee, guarded presidents Agnew, Nixon, Ford, and Kennedy, and later I understand was the head Treasury Man in Miami Florida with the drug busts. More than once the police would drive by and tell us to pipe down. But never was there the slightest troublemaking or vandalism, nor were we bothered by others. I don't know if all that would be possible in a big city today. I can remember the cool night breezes and laid back times.

27. GROWING UP CATHOLIC

St. Andrews's Catholic Church, Abilene

The Curran family is of one hundred per cent Irish background, and the Catholic religion that goes with it was maintained by Mom and Dad. Dad's family was of course Catholic, but he never talked about specific Catholic memories. I know many of his brothers and sisters left the faith. I am not entirely sure why with the exception of Uncle Bryan who left because of some mistreatment by the obstinate, old-time Irish priest in Abilene, Father Roach. Result: not only Bryan's own numerous children were lost to the faith, but all the grandchildren and generations to come. But there were probably two sides to the story.

The Farm

Mom had more education than Dad and spent a few years at the Catholic High School in Salina, Kansas, Sacred Heart Academy. She was the one who verbalized Catholicism more and was responsible for getting us kids to church. But Catholic tradition was equally shared by Dad. He had become a Knight of Columbus at an early age and had taken one of the advanced degrees. I remember the "Napoleon" style hat with the feathers, the cape and especially the sword, that all smelled of mothballs stored upstairs; I loved to play with the sword. He led a life of constant service in the parish, taking up the collection, doing carpentry work, volunteer work with the Knights and later on at the grade school, and in his last years constantly helped as pall bearer at funerals. He was never without his rosary at mass, a fact recalled by Monsignor Wassman in the eulogy at his mass in 1979.

Mom had all her support activities as well, the Altar Society which helped to clean and prepare the church for mass, the D of I's, Daughters of Isabella, whose exact function I am not sure of. There were few of the activities of parishes today other than those mentioned because there were St. Joseph nuns who would come from Salina to teach catechism and summer school. Religious education etc. of today did not exist. But we did have the Missions during Lent by the guest priest, usually a Jesuit from the city, and a bit of fire and brimstone along with it.

But what I'm getting at is that Mom, being more educated, probably verbalized more aspects of "Church", but Dad was no less a practitioner of the faith. Both had what I judge what a very deep faith; I never heard it doubted by either of them in our presence, and I truly believe they doubted little, or if they did, they kept it to themselves. The faith was largely uneducated on their part, a result of tradition and practice and not of any formal study on any advanced level.

But their faith was so important as a part of their lives; you cannot really separate who they were from what they believed and how they lived it out. We were taught to never lie under any circumstances, to "be good," and it had such an effect on me that I honestly believe that I could not possibly choose to do otherwise in my adult years without the incredible guilt trip it would put upon me. This reminds me of the Jesuit Father Mazza's analysis of his students in the diatribes which entertained us and distracted us from weightier matters in the graduate courses at St. Louis Univerity. He spoke of Curran saying: "Yeah, Curran. He's so good he'll probably help a little old lady across the street and she'll stab him with her umbrella." I've thought about that a lot over the years; my life would have been much less troubled if I had been a little thicker skinned. This may just be part of the strict Catholicism my parents lived and passed on to us. I have had to deal with the great negative effect of guilt as taught at weekly confession and all since childhood.

Sunday Mass. We never but never missed Mass on Sunday or a Holy Day. I do remember discussion about missing on those few occasions we were traveling. I can remember stopping at churches in tiny towns in Western Kansas on the way to Colorado, even for what Mom called a "visit." There were times I would wish for a blizzard or some other act of God so I could stay home.

Snow was a good excuse since we had to get down the graveled lane and about two miles on asphalt to church. Due primarily to farm routine, I cannot recall anyone going to daily mass as a regular routine over the years, but there was an effort at daily mass during Lent. But rarely did we miss an evening service such as Benediction, Rosary or Way of the Cross.

The church was built I think in 1916 of a dark brick with a single bell tower and one long nave. The original altar was marble I think, of the style with niches for all the saints, and a crucifix in the center above the tabernacle, a truly mysterious place lined with velvet cloth and perhaps gold walls, where the Holy Eucharist was kept. There was a choir loft, a tiny "crying room" added later but seldom used and a baptismal font in the back. I spent a lot of time in the sacristy as an altar boy, but that's another story for later.

It was a country parish, or better, a small town parish, and each family chose its place to sit and never varied from it. I believe that custom never changed in my twenty years in town, and I imagine a place in the pew is often passed on to the children. I can recall that very few people would sit in the first two or three rows; I always thought they were either those who had contributed more or "extra pious" types who just wanted to be closer to the altar. How different from our big city days where you have to get to church early to sit close enough to the front to see well and feel a part of it! The pews were of a dark hardwood, and there were padded kneelers; Catholics still knelt then! I still cannot properly celebrate mass in a church with wooden kneelers, congenitally weak knees. And I can remember how my mind would wander during church, I had a way of losing myself at night staring at the candles flickering and thinking of who knows what. Funny, but certain images stick with you: one is of my Dad's hands, workers' hands with freckles or moles on them, but with a rosary.

Dad, once again, was firm in his beliefs and did not ever say too much, but he was exemplary in his actions. Rarely would I hear him swear and cannot really ever recall attacks on others, verbal or otherwise. There was absolute honesty in all dealings.

There is a scene etched in my memory. Of cold, cold nights in winter and Mom at home before bedtime huddled into the corner of the dining room with her feet in front of one of the furnace registers, saying the rosary. She often recalled the promises to Bernadette, Fatima and all, and she believed very much in the saying of the Rosary to avoid the victory of communism in the world. This, I think, was again as a result of one of the apparitions of the Virgin at Fatima. I can say that when Keah, Katie, and I visited Fatima in 1987 it was a very moving, a very faith filled experience for me, in large part because of my memories of Mom and all that Fatima meant to her while I grew up.

Mom also believed deeply in the protection of Mary at the hour of death. Our family said the Rosary regularly together. As a little boy I mumbled and rattled off all the prayers, it was so hard to concentrate. In spite of modern times today and the fact we have not maintained the custom of the daily or even monthly rosary in our family, I believe memories of my Mother plus contact with Latins plus so much of the literature I teach in Spanish or Portuguese with such a close link to Mary have left me with a deep feeling that She is our Mother and protects us. I have feelings of consolation and protection and do pray regularly the "Hail Mary".

Along with this custom was that of the scapular medals and others. It is all vague to me now, but we were urged to wear a medal of some kind since childhood. I can recall so vividly our old tarnished St. Christopher medial in the car. It was in the old Buick in the wreck of 1949, and I do believe that my surviving was in part in answer to prayer; who knows, maybe the medal had to do with it also. I can recall some embarrassment at wearing the cloth scapular to school and always preferred the regular metal medals.

Weekly confession. Another custom was almost weekly confession, generally on a Saturday afternoon. The family was in town anyway for shopping or "trading" as Dad liked to call it and then there was the afternoon matinee movie. Diverse memories come from that. I can recall a detailed picture of the confessional itself: the carved wooden outside, the darkness inside, the screen between me and the priest, the kneeler. We experienced three or four priests growing up in my time, but most dominant was of course Monsignor Roach, the old Irishman. I can recall how quiet it would be in the church, how even a whisper seemed to carry far beyond the confessional, and the how the priest seemed to talk in a very loud voice when admonishing me to sin no more and do the penance. Confession was simply not a positive thing. The worst was that I seemed to commit the same sins day after day, week after week, yet felt obliged to confess again and again. It is truly amazing to see the turnaround that the Vatican II Church has made with the sacrament, in particular how it is handled by the Irish priest in our recent parish who was 180 degrees from the old school I experienced. Most of the new vision is simply a matter of semantics, the language used; things are put in the positive, confession being a celebration of reunion with God in grace and not a grievous punishment for past sins. God is forgiving and loving, not cruel and punishing. Is there still a hell of fire and brimstone? Or is it the loneliness of life without God? Very recently our local parish priest in Mesa, Arizona, of Polish extraction but all American and modern, says nothing has really changed but the way we present it and talk about it.

But there was no discussion about going or not going to confession; it was a stated fact and that was all there was to it. Of course we were all taught in those days you would burn in the fires of hell for eternity if you sinned seriously and did not confess it. But there was more to it than that. I recall yet today the solitude, the peace and the quiet joy of sitting in the church on those quiet Saturday afternoons. The church had huge stained glass windows and truly the brilliant late afternoon sun would create an atmosphere of beauty in the church. More than that was the absolutely unique feeling of having gone through the torture of admitting once again one's faults, getting up the courage to confess them and the absolute feeling of relief of being "clean" once again, the feeling you had a direct ticket to heaven should something happen to you. I am convinced yet today that the psychology of confession, the ridding oneself of guilt of faults was and is healthy for us all. What I do not know is if that in any way was outweighed by the incredible guilt we carried with us much of the time. I do know the heavy weight that would fall on me later in the week when I would sin again and feel unsafe until the next confession. There was always the Catholic "out" of the "perfect" Act of Contrition, but you could not bet on it. We had little experience of the God of love in those days; our God was forgiving but severe and never forgetful.

The penance in those days in Abilene was generally a few to a full rosary of "Our Fathers" and "Hail Marys". There could be no fudging on this in my mind because HE knew. This however did not keep me from rattling the prayers of penance off as fast as I could and get the heck out of there. But it was a sort of Catholic magic; just saying the prayers seemed to make it all well. That is, until the next heavy date as a teenager when one was once again faced with the "near occasion" of sin. I can rarely recall any penance of dealing with people; we just prayed.

Tom's First Communion

Holy Communion and First Communion. The Saturday confession was always followed by Sunday communion. But in those days as important as the communion was the fasting that went along with it. There were always rules to be followed, many of them vague to me now. But you absolutely could not eat anything from Midnight Saturday on. And you could not drink anything, even water, one hour before receiving. I can recall how precise we were on this, and that you had to get up early even to have a drink of water. There were prayers you said after communion, a set ritual I followed from the "Sunday Missal", some of them beautiful prayers, most I have forgotten. But there was no real "improvised" or personal prayer other than a "I'm sorry. Please make me do better."

We received First Communion at age seven I think. Once again, we were prepared for it by the nuns in the two-week summer school held after classes in public school got out in late May, this since there was no Catholic school in town. Summer school was dreaded at first, but always turned out to be a lot of fun. And later on it kept me out of the fields and the farm work for an extra two weeks. It was actually held at the old Lincoln Grade School across from the church; in later days that site is the parking lot for the Eisenhower complex. This was the same school that was attended by Ike Eisenhower and his family who lived immediately across the street east from the school playground. The building was old, the steps were creaky and old, but highly polished oak I think. Desks were the old style with ink wells, a fixed top with a place underneath to put books. The seats were straight backed and were attached to the rest of the desk with a somewhat ornate iron grill framework, and several desks were attached to each other on runners. Memories are truly fuzzy of exactly what we learned to prepare for communion, but I know we practiced the actual routine with either unconsecrated hosts or candy or something to be sure we did it right. It was considered a grievous error by the nuns to allow the host to fall out of your mouth, and heaven forbid,! land on the floor. I can remember several times as an altar boy when the host would fall off the paten and the priest would pick it up, crisis time. There was only one way to receive: with your eyes closed and your tongue stuck out, but not too far out.

I know we also had to memorize the "Act of Contrition" and practice going to confession. The "Act" is still with me today. You had to be able to recite the sins, how many, how many times, how long ago you went to confession, a regular shopping list. I had a vague idea of Mortal and Venial sin, the latter should be confessed but it wouldn't "kill you" or make you burn in hell. But look out for the big ones, pain of eternal damnation if you did not "fess up." If you by any chance forgot a biggie, then you were obliged to tell it first thing next time, and not go to communion. Well, that was definitely a bad deal: all the family is sitting in the same pew, and only Mark does not get up to go to communion. Everybody knew he must have been up to something this last week. But in the case of venial sin you could go ahead and receive communion and confess it all later. It was all a bit legalistic.

Then there was that mysterious idea that we actually were receiving the body and blood of Jesus. I had quite a problem with that. That great big word "trans-substantiation" eliminated that problem since you did not have to think about "body" or "blood" or cannibalism any more but you knew it was magically Jesus. I still have difficulty today with the hymns that talk of eating his body and drinking his blood. "Faith" was just a word then and is still difficult now, but we got the idea that the water and wine were turned into the real Jesus, not just bread and wine with "Jesus" attributes. I always expected to feel different after receiving communion and guess I did upon occasion feel a bit "holier," but mainly I recall that a lot of times the host would not leave such a good taste in your mouth. Some of the "real" bread they use nowadays seems to improve on that.

But "first communion" was a big event for us. The boys wore white shirts and ties, the girls pretty white dresses with veils. There are some old pictures with Tom's communion, but none of mine survived.

Confirmation. It also was a big thing. You were confirmed at about age twelve. I cannot remember exactly why it took place, but it was explained that you were in effect becoming a "soldier of Christ." We were taught it was a renewal of baptismal vows, but since we did not remember those, I am afraid that part fell upon shallow soil. But I did have a vague idea it was a kind of growing up in the Church, of taking on more responsibility for one's actions and faith. The preparation was arduous. It consisted primarily in Catechism classes on Saturday mornings for several weeks and the drilling and grilling of questions by either the nuns from Salina or the priests, Monsignor Roach or later on Father Kramer. But great fear was once again instilled in us: on that special Sunday the Bishop would come from Salina to confirm us, there would be a public examination by him of all of us with the catechism questions. The fear of course was that we would be called upon in public (we knew almost everyone in the church) and not know the answer. And there was some vague idea that he would slap our face or something for some reason, to test us, during the process. The Bishop for me was a sort of mysterious dignitary from a far away town who dressed like the Pope with the funny pointed hat and in scarlet. As it turned out, we knew or mumbled our way through most of the questions, no one got slapped hard, and we all got confirmed. I recall I did not feel much different after it was all over. I can't recall any special celebration at home either, but am sure there must have been a treat or the like.

Religious Instruction. The main religious instruction outside the home was in the form of Saturday morning catechism. Since our town was small and there was not sufficient population or money to support a Catholic school, this was our only formal instruction expect for a mandatory two-week summer "Bible" school. I have lots of memories of summer school: the tremendous heat and sweat of playing baseball outside and then having to go in to attend classes in the un-air conditioned building, the great baseball games we would have, the picnic the last day, the nuns who were great hitters, nothing like that to gain our admiration, the beginning of puberty and girls. There were not that many kids, but the few classes were taught by St. Joseph nuns with the old style habits, black and white, floor length, tiny crescent of face showing, not even their hair. We all wondered to ourselves, was it shaved when they became nuns? I thought so at one time. These were the real "nunerroonies" or "penguins." One class would be taught by Monsignor Roach or the assistant pastor.

We hated Catechism for lots of reasons. Only Catholic kids had their Saturdays spoiled by having to go to church. Buddies played ball or whatever. But we had a compromise: arriving a half hour early and having softball games in the church parking lot. I recall the lessons were rote memorization from the famous "Baltimore Catechism." "Who is God?" "God loves me." "God is everywhere." "A sacrament is an outward sign instituted by God to give grace." You were expected to memorize the lesson for the week and then recite it when called upon in class.

I remember Msgr. Roach as both a smiling, lovable old man who talked funny and as a severe person who might slap a lazy or smart-alecky student. I can also recall Father Kramer, the young priest we all liked so much who was later chaplain for the Newman Club at Kansas State University. He was the only priest who ever really seriously mentioned seminary to us when I was in high school. Funny. The priests were always forgiven for having big, nice and new cars. In those days gas was cheap, maybe twenty cents a gallon, so even at a priest's salary, $500 per year sticks in my mind, they could afford gas. Generally the cars were donated by some heavyweights in the parish. And the priest did have to get around quite a lot, saying mass occasionally in little country towns with frequent trips to see the Bishop, etc. It was also frankly a reward for choosing that type of life, celibacy and all. Father Kramer on his day off would play golf, a hobby joked about by many in town, but not maliciously, but also a real extravagance for some of the old workaholic farm types in town. I recall him in his sporty golf hat, a big cigar and smile on his face. I have to admit that he was kind and a sort of hero to us, just what a young priest should be like. He more than once suggested seminary for me and Mike Kippenberger as well. But it was never pushed and I never was inclined.

Monsignor Roach on the other hand was quite elderly with a still huge white shock of hair, a friendly smile and the remains of an Irish brogue, this even after many, many years as a priest in Kansas. He was known for preaching not always so kindly from the pulpit. He once printed a list with all the families in the parish with respective dollar donations, something that would not be done today. But he was in charge and there was damned little anyone could do to protest. The standard joke was that once a year he would announce that he wanted to go back to Ireland "just one more time before I die" to see family, or maybe before "Mother" would die. I do not know the facts, but rumor had it that the parish would get together for a special collection for the one, last trip. He went to Ireland often. It was also known he appreciated a bottle of Scotch, the good kind.

Altar Boy. Like most of the young boys I also was trained to be an altar boy and to help serve mass. Father Kramer trained our group, and we did learn the Latin fairly well; it was memorized for response to the Priest in the mass. We actually understood very little of what was said, but had the English translation like everyone else. I can recall Father Kramer's clear Latin during mass and Father Roach's hurried and slurred version, not from speech defect or liquor, but years and years of hurrying through it. He would come into the sacristy and be dressing for mass and let out outrageous belches that of course caused us to fall into hysterical giggling. We giggled more in mass than you can imagine to the point of being scolded while still shaking with laughter. It was that time in life when anything could set us off -- a belch, a fart, a funny look, whatever. And this included not only the daily mass with small attendance early in the morning, but the Sunday High masses as well. We wore long cassocks buttoned down the front from throat to knee, different colors according to the liturgical season, and white surplices on top. I guess we looked angelic enough. I can remember we were supposed to have our hair combed, and Joe Fleagle came one day with hair oil dripping from his forehead. We heehawed over that. Shoes normally needed to be shined or we wore tennis shoes. Of course someone would always trip over his cassock and something would go flying or be dropped.

It's all fuzzy now, but we took turns with the tasks of mass: one altar boy "got the book," that is, the mass book for scripture readings, one the paten for communion, both the wine and water cruets, towels and water for washing of hands after the offertory. This was prior to Vatican II and the church used the old, beautiful, ornate, tall white marble altar. The steps were marble as well, and we had foam kneeling pads, but it still seemed nigh impossible to kneel through an entire mass. During the Consecration we were to climb up a step or two and hold the chasuble of the priest as he bent over to say the consecration prayers or genuflect. There was no pad on those steps and it was killing. Oh, I forgot. Someone "got the bells" as well for ringing at crucial times throughout the canon of the mass. Each one of us would develop his own style of bell ringing, a big game. Other items were to prepare the incense for the incense boat that was used particularly on High Masses and on Holy Days. Inevitably we would choke and cough with the incense. Then there were the processions with the ciborium when we would hold a cross, candles or whatever. I think if I reread one of the old mass missals, much more would come back to me.

We alternated serving, each one of us would serve daily mass for one week, and three or four of us on Sundays which usually was a high mass sung by the choir, with Gregorian response, and the priest singing the mass, This was one of my most beautiful memories of those times. Our favorite time however was when mass was over, everything put away and our last duty was to take the empty water and wine cruets over to the priests' house and give them to the housekeeper, Ann Hogan, coincidentally also from Ireland. She always had wonderful bakery cookies for us, cookies of the most delicious and fancy kind. Anna, God bless her.

Before I go on to something else, I have some thoughts. For all the fooling around, the laughing and giggling, the making fun of Monsignor Roach and his belching, farting and murdering the Latin, the experience was invaluable in my life. Sleepy, a bit groggy, I can recall the quietness of the daily mass, of that special moment of the Consecration, how special and close it felt to witness that special, magical moment, seeing the reflection of candlelight off the gold chalice (Father Kramer's had emeralds or rubies imbedded). I think then I believed in God, and the Consecration has been special for me since then, though never quite the same when from a distance as in our huge church today.

There was a gift I did not realize for those few boys were serving. There was a wooden altar rail that separated everyone else from the altar, from being so close to the actual celebration of the mass. Today, pondering the matter, I think that was one injustice that I think women truly may have a case on. There was the quiet closeness of the mystery of the presence of God during those moments.

Oh, I forgot the weddings. The altar boys always made a "tip" for serving at weddings, and I can remember Bruce Sexton's when the time came for the wedding ring and they had forgotten it. We all just waited until they went and got it. Katie's Uncle Johnny tells a good story about that day.

When I was smaller someone of course had to bring me to mass to serve, generally Mom. But later on I would actually ride the bicycle the entire way in from the farm to the south side of town where the church is. It was a fine thing in summertime.

Once we reached high school age there was an organization called CYO, Catholic Youth Organization. Something akin to CCD today I guess. I am sure the idea was for additional catholic teaching, but perhaps more so for socializing and keeping the Catholic kids together. I know the adrenalin and hormones were flowing in those days. We had all sorts of parties, dances mainly, and kids from neighboring towns would come. Now, we believed that there was a lack of good looking Catholic girls in Abilene, so we ended up dating the Protestant girls. But in a neighboring town of Chapman ten miles east of Abilene there was an unusually large Catholic population for its size, and the town was known for its rowdy and hard drinkers too. But there were some really cute girls. I can recall meeting one or two of them, liking them well enough, but nothing ever really coming from it, one reason being I had no dependable car of my own, another being I didn't want to have to get in fights with the local ruffians.

The CYO occasionally had conventions, and they were great fun. We went by car, bus and one or twice by train. I can recall a crazy several-hour train trip from Abilene to Hays, Kansas. We all bought water guns before boarding, and the whole trip was a huge water fight. Can't remember a blessed thing about the actual convention, but the train trip was the best. An aside: that convention did involve one of my few early language experiences. I had an acquaintance named Switzer and we went to visit his grandmother in Hays who spoke only German, a great revelation to me.

I have always believed the part of the Bible that talks of the gifts of the Holy Spirit, that each has special talents. I often wonder why I never considered seriously the seminary, particularly when I went on to seven years of study in Jesuit schools. The time ripe for an early vocation would have been during or immediately after high school. Life since has had its religious struggles, struggles of faith, but I always felt that I had some, only a few maybe, but some of the attributes of the making of a good priest. I always felt I could have done well in the speaking, the sermons. But I can see today that the lonely life and more would have probably done me in. Even yet, I believe few people have an inkling of what it takes to lead a priest's life, I mean the total life. They were a special breed. I used to think that if something were to happen to Keah, that I would try it. This was before Katie came. Romantic visions I think. And a lot of water has passed under that bridge.

28. STAYING IN TOUCH WITH THE RELATIVES

One of the things that definitely was lost when my Dad died in 1979 and Mom in 1982 was a sense of extended family with relatives -- I mean aunts and uncles a generation or two removed, cousins of the same. Today I treasure the memory of the drives on Sunday afternoon growing up, something I did not care so much for then when Mom and Dad would set off to visit some of these relatives, most of them usually living in the country or in nearby counties. On one such drive we passed through Kipp, Kansas, south of Solomon and southeast of Salina, where Mom was born. It's all hazy now, but the town itself seemed to be a gas station, a general store and not much else. We also drove by the farmhouse where she was born and even visited with the present owners. It seemed to me to be a typical house of the area: wooden frame, Victorian in style but plain. I have a few more details of her youth in the "Neal" and "Nellie" section of this narrative.

But back to the relatives. I recall frequent visits to Solomon, Kansas, to visit the Enrights, Mom's aunts and uncles on her mother's side. The family, by the way, is buried in the country cemetery near Solomon. It's the Catholic cemetery; religious separatism is still a custom yet today in this regard. After Dad died in 1979, when Keah, Katie and I were visiting Abilene around Memorial Day, we drove Mom to the Solomon cemetery. I find it amazing that at age 79 she could still walk up and down the rows of tombstones and knew almost everyone or something about their family. The same of course was true at the Catholic Cemetery in Abilene with both Dad and Mom. Even in my own case, having lived about 20 years of my life growing up there, I can walk the rows and recall names, faces and events of growing up. A small digression is to be permitted: a thought that may express another facet of growing up in central Kansas is the cemetery itself. Having lived the past forty years in big cities, when I return to Abilene and visit the family graves at the cemetery, it is an emotional experience not just for the memories of the dead, but the atmosphere of actually being present in country cemetery. Coincidentally, Memorial Day may just be the most beautiful time of year on the Kansas plains. Late May presents everything green, colangelas and roses in full bloom wheat coming up, but perhaps not headed out yet. The cemetery is well taken care of, grass clipped for that special occasion. But when you get out of the car, the first thing that strikes you is the smell and the sounds. There is the fresh smell of freshly cut buffalo grass, the original grass on the plains, flowers, alfalfa in nearby fields, and then the birds, particularly the meadowlarks warbling in the warm sun.

There is a peace, a true place of rest there that I have never sensed elsewhere. Emotionalism perhaps, but the idea of being put under in the heat, dust, noise and pollution of the Phoenix metropolitan area seems like a desecration to me. The family plot in Abilene has four places: Dad, Mom, a place now occupied by half-brother Jim who died in 1989 after lung cancer, surgery, and the last for my twin brother Michael who died shortly after birth. We were incubator babies, he being born first. My birth certificate shows a little over three pounds at birth. My knowledge of all that is vague, neither Mom nor Dad ever would talk about it much, but Mom did say shortly before her own death in 1982 that the doctors were perhaps not on top of the situation, and that he could have been saved. I sometimes wonder how he would have been, if we would have been at all alike, and if we would have been competitors and all. I do know we were not identical twins. This was well before the day of automatic lawsuits; you just lived with whatever happened.

Like I said, I never cared much for the visits to the relatives on those drives mainly because there were never young kids around, no one to play with. The relatives all seemed ancient to me, and they never did anything but sit around and talk. I'm still not very good at that, not like Keah and her family, masters of sitting back, relaxing and whiling away an afternoon visiting. On the other hand, I can write about it. And, maybe someone will understand me, the elderly relatives seemed to smell...well...old, if you know what I mean. I was less than ten at the time and probably had some fairly distinct odors about me myself, but they smelled...old! I'm talking about the relatives in Solomon. There was an uncle in particular who wore suspenders and chewed tobacco. I recall one Thanksgiving when he came to our house on the farm, sat in the wooden rocker in the dining room, chewed on a cigar the whole time but never lit it. When he left there was a perfect ring of tobacco bits around the rocker. We are talking country!

So it wasn't that I disliked all those old folks; my own parents did not seem old at all, smelled nice to me, and although farm people, seemed more educated and aware of the world. There was an older cousin in Solomon who ranted and raved on any political subject, local or national, always with a solution to it all. I did not realize then that the world is populated with such people, and it in fact, may run in the family. He became the local trash collector for the town, making I understand a rather good living. Today I realize fortunes can be made along that line, but growing up in a small country town, it was low on the social scale.

Back to the Sunday afternoon visits. Sometimes we traveled farther, to Delia near Topeka to visit one of Dad's sisters. I recall only two or three things there -- eating too many green apples from the orchard and getting puny and playing in an old abandoned Model-T with a wasp's nest in the rumble seat.

Digression: a buddy from high school days in the late 1950s rounded up several of those old cars, buying them from farmers in the region for a pittance, fixing them up and selling them. He has worked for years at the state prison, and I never can figure out if he belongs on the inside or outside. But when I see a restored Model-A or T today, I just shake my head.

There were visits to Council Grove, Kansas, a historic place of the meeting of white and red nations, also perhaps visited by Francisco de Coronado, Spanish explorer, to visit relatives on Dad's side, the Dykes, his mother's maiden name. I cannot recall a date, but I must have been less than ten. But that was a good visit since they lived near a pretty country lake. But those little towns which really are fairly close to Abilene seemed far away in those days. My Dad used to say fifty miles per hour was fast enough for anybody. I tend to agree with him.

As I put all this on the computer in 1990, and edit it once again in 2010, I can't help but remember stories from Flannery O'Connor and the deep South; we in Kansas were very different, but the rural tone is much the same, a bit of Americana perhaps.

There were relatives I did enjoy, more because they were cousins closer to my own age, and it was fun. Mom's brother, Leo Cusick, wife Edith, famous for nonstop talking, and four children, Mary Lee, Mickey, Jane and Ann, lived in Salina, Kansas, while I was growing up. Salina was thirty minutes by car and seemed like a very big place to me in those days; it was about five or six times the size of Abilene. It was Salina where we would go to shop once in awhile and returning from there we had the tragic motor accident of 1949. Sometimes the Cusicks would come to the farm. But we kept in touch, and it was fun. They moved to Colorado Springs when I was a teenager, and gradually we grew apart. All the kids are married, remarried and scattered. One of my favorite memories of Colorado Springs, the mountains and Pikes Peak was when I was 15 or 16 years old and we went to visit. I spent an afternoon at a driving range near their house and recall the beautifully cool, fresh smelling air after an afternoon mountain shower and hitting golf balls in the direction of a splendid mountain range topped by Pikes Peak. You could see the tramway rising from Manitou Springs in the distance. I have always loved the Rockies, and that was one of my earlier memories.

Closer to home, the main relatives we visited were Uncle Bryan and Aunt Marie Curran and their kids who lived on the original homestead when Dad, his mother and brothers moved to Kansas from Nebraska after his father died. Their family was huge, Catholic originally, but all left the church, a story mentioned in "Growing Up Catholic in Abilene." The children were Harold, Dick, Bob, Marvin, Delmar, Duane, Dorothy and Mary Lou (I may be forgetting someone). The farm house was simple, somewhat smaller than ours, about three or four miles farther from Abilene. Curious how the family grew up, but Bryan although looking much like Dad, was a different sort of person, for lack of a better way to say it, more "country", as was his wife Marie. This is not meant to be a criticism, but rather just describing them the way I knew them. I really liked Byran, my favorite Uncle on Dad's side. I worked for him upon occasion while a teenager, doing various farm chores: hay baling, working the rack stacking and also at the barn. I just remembered, I don't think Mom or Dad ever called ahead of time for these visits, but just drove over. I could be wrong about that.

Bryan and Marie's house on the original Curran homestead in Kansas used a cistern for water, but had inside plumbing. I have vague memories of the wonderful aroma of freshly baked bread when we visited them or when I worked there. Farm food was fresh, mostly produced on the farm, long before chemical additives. I still wonder if that food regime will get me through, save me from the various diseases associated with the chemicals we all take in today. It was an incredibly high fat diet, milk and cream, eggs almost every morning cooked with farm bacon, lots of fried foods, fried chicken the most common. A usual summer meal, one that still wakes up my taste buds, was fried chicken and lots of it, sliced tomatoes which tasted like tomatoes, roasting ears in season, green beans, and mounds of mashed potatoes covered with chicken gravy. There was lots of iced tea to drink and homemade fruit pies for dessert -- apple, peach upon occasion and cherry. Most of the food was from the garden, the fields or the livestock. Marie Curran's home cooked meals and home made bread are still in my memories.

I can still picture Bryan, a classic farm image for me, and my Dad too for that matter. in from the fields at noon for one of those huge meals, almost always dressed in blue or grey overalls, faded blue work shirt, arms and face black with dirt to a definite line on his forehead where the straw hat, not cowboy style, but "farm" style, reached, washing up in the little room outside the kitchen in a large wash basin with water pumped from the cistern and lava soap to wash off the grime. He always seemed to have a smile and to laugh a lot.

That's another difference in our families: for some reason Dad and none of us kids ever wore overalls, the outfit that was considered "hick" or "farmer" in town. I am not sure if it was on purpose or not; we all wore work pants, jeans or the like. The other major difference was speech; Dad and his brothers were all of limited education, formal that is. They all had to stop school, generally after 8th grade, to work on the farm, an accepted practice in those days. But Dad was well read, and his speech was correct. You could tell he was from Kansas, from a small town, but he did not sound "country." I probably have more of a Kansas "brogue" than he ever did. Mom was educated for those times, the teens of the early twentieth century, having experienced high school and two years of college in order to be a country school teacher. She was the one who helped us with homework, corrected our speech, and encouraged us in music. I do not recall Dad ever saying much along that line. He was more the visible role model. I heard little profanity, ever, from him, and that on understandable occasions.

But a couple of the cousins up north of town were vulgar in their talk, swore like demons, and spoke fractured English. Once again, I'm not criticizing, for today I know that the way you talk does not necessarily take away from the good inside you. I never in my life consciously looked down on the cousins or Bryan or Marie, but I did see them as different. But in the late 1970s, Dad's last years, when we would come home to Kansas to visit and took short drives to see the relatives, I thoroughly enjoyed them and saw them as good, basic people. I wonder who it was that changed and matured.

But my original point was that this was how Mom and Dad kept in touch, how they kept the circle unbroken, so to speak. It saddens me to realize that it's all over now; the last of the Currans of that generation, my Dad's younger sister Maggie died at the interesting age of 99 this past summer, still bright to the end they say. But a generation and a way of life are gone.

29 THE LAST VISITS WITH MOM AND DAD

Dad and Mom in the house on Rogers Street in Abilene

    I was not around much during those last years, but without fail, our visits were joyful and we really had quality time with Mom and Dad. We never did much in the way of socializing outside the family, but would get up at a reasonable hour, talk over breakfast and lots or coffee. There would be the visiting of the relatives I talked about before, but the best part was early evening when we all would go out on the front porch of the house on Rogers Street and enjoy the beautiful evenings and just talk.

    I can remember practicing the classic guitar out on the porch in the days when I was a home in summer time. Mom particularly would listen and still would have a tip or two from her own music teaching days if I did not have it right. Dad was not much involved with music, but always did enjoy hearing "the Blue Tail Fly". Funny, a memory is him whistling around the farm, but never any melody I had ever heard; I think it might have been his own private tune.

I think those times on the front porch in Abilene are dear to Keah as well, and it was then she came to appreciate my parents so much. The July or August air was generally pleasant, always with a few bugs or mosquitoes in the evening; maybe you could hear the music from the band shell a few blocks away with the Thursday night summer concerts. We talked about everything then, and all was not joyful. There were problems with Jim, Tom and Jo Anne at one time or another, but Keah and I were okay and were a source of minimal worry, and I think we brought many, many good moments to those last years. I would pray for the same in my old age.

Mom and large flower, the garden in Abilene

Mom, the Irises, the garden in Abilene

Oh, another thought about those summer nights visiting Mom and Dad in Abilene: Dad would sit outside awhile, but would often go inside to see a Perry Mason, Bonanza or Gun Smoke on TV; with his deafness the TV would be blaring. And Mom would tire so easily in those last years. But there still were good moments; particularly I think when we brought Katie, this in May of 1979, Dad's last spring. That year Mom's flowers were particularly beautiful, outrageously beautiful, and there were a few strawberry plants ready. Katie gave Mom and Dad the biggest kick by picking and gobbling up the berries; she must have been about one year, ten months of age. And Mom would read to her on the front porch in the evening, the two stretched out on the lounge chair.

Dad, onions in the vegetable garden on the farm

Nell and Neal at the vegetable garden at the farm

We also made a visit to the farm where Dad had a large vegetable garden. Inevitably he would come back in loaded with tomatoes, cucumbers or squash.

Dad inspecting trees at the pond.

Mark and a full pond, the 1970s

And you could not drive to the pasture where the vegetable garden was located without walking down toward the pond to check out the growth of fruit trees or walnut trees. Dad would speculate about how big and how many little bass or channel cats might be left in the seeping water. Only one year did we catch fish while I was living on the farm. We have a wonderful picture of Mom fishing with about a foot of her pole in the water, a bit distracted at the moment. She wanted so badly to catch a fish; I lament they never got up to Vallecito Lake in Colorado with us for the real thing. This makes me recall the time Keah and I came into town for a few days, this back in 1971, fresh from a few weeks at Uncle Walter Wright's cabin west of Denver in Evergreen where I wrote what would become my first publication, in spite of insect infestations in the cabin. We had several tiny but beautiful brook trout which Mom and Dad fried up and seemed to enjoy tremendously.

There was sadness then too, this due to the people who had bought a lot from Dad east of the pond and were quickly turning it into a junk heap. There was nothing he could do, but I know the sight of it deeply hurt their pride. Fortunately for Mom, the particular lot did improve some before she died. It is a pity that part of the farm was ever sold, but I think there were some hard times and Dad had a place for the cash. Jim and Tom were both in difficulty off and on; that may have had something to do with it.

But Mom also had rose bushes and lots of flowers at the vegetable garden on the farm; we would always go for a look, pick some to bring into the house in town. It was a great source of joy for her.

I'm adding this in 1991. After Dad's death in 1979, Mom was of course left alone in the house on Rogers. Jim quit whatever job he had at the time; you could not keep up with either his job or his whereabouts. He worked construction projects in the plains and the West but seemed to spend more time unemployed than at work (a hazard of the trade?). And there were always a lot of unexplained circumstances. He would show up back in Abilene and would live on the second floor of the Abilene house, at times for months until he would get another job. But at this point in time he decided he would take care of Mom. She herself preferred that he have a regular job, a paycheck coming in and said she could get by okay, but he moved in and stayed until she died and beyond. In retrospect I think he really believed he was being good to her and was needed. And, I think it was the right decision, and I respect him for doing it. Whatever the other circumstances, he was there for her in a time of need, and that, I believe, is a basic value in our creed. I don't know if he ever worked steady after that time, but he did provide company for her. It's always good to remember his circumstances anyway -- she was his only blood parent. A long story all in all, but those were the last days.

A bit morbid but it finishes the story. Keah and I were living in Mesa, Arizona, in the house on Palmcroft Street when Dad died in 1979; I can remember being awakened by the phone call, Mom telling me of his death, and me crying in bed that night with Keah doing her best to comfort me. Three years later Mom got strangely ill, her perfectly pronounced speech becoming garbled and incoherent. I went back to Topeka for the brain surgery; all the kids were together for maybe the last time. I can remember being asked to lead us all in prayer before the surgery. (I wonder yet, why me?) Mom survived the surgery but was in a coma several days until her death. I had to return to work after a couple of days so was not there when she died. But I can remember walking into the intensive care unit, her head totally bandaged and she looked, oddly enough, like a little nun in a white habit with the bandages and tape around her head. That is my last memory of her, kind of fitting since she was so religious with such a deep faith.

There is yet another lesson of life here. We had discussed the ramifications if she had lived, probably reduced to near vegetable status and financially unable to handle the full-time nursing care. I remember stewing a lot about all that. It turned out to be unnecessary. You never know. Keah has always said to not worry about what you cannot control and what has not happened yet. My defense is that it is not worry, but being realistic and practical for the future. She seems to be right.

The Farm

The final picture of the family at the farm

The final family picture, 1979.

PART TWO. SCHOOL DAYS AND GROWING UP IN ABILENE, KANSAS, IN THE 1940S AND 1950S

PREFACE

These notes are really a continuation of "The Farm," written some twenty-two years ago as a hobby, a diversion from academic writing, and a gift to my parents, Neal and Nellie Curran, and then to my wife, daughter and relatives. They are meant to tell more of the story of life in a small town in the Kansas wheat belt during the 1940s and 1950s. Like "The Farm," they are based on memories, many now foggy, and are rough in the sense that people and places come from recollection many, many years later. And the language of this Part II as Part I is conversational, meant to simply retell the story. Once again, this is a hobby, now in early retirement from Arizona State University, and only time will tell where these recounted memories will lead. The account may seem unexciting to some perhaps, but perhaps worthwhile, also.

Oh, I must begin with an apology to all the girls, my classmates, and maybe add a disclaimer and some moaning as well. Once girls became important to me, and they surely did, it was too late for much dating until final years of high school. By freshman year in high school, the girls in my class dated upper classmen--they had cars! So it was only by junior or senior year when I could borrow our old family car to go on a date that things evolved a bit. What I mean, girls, is that most high school memories will involve the guys, my buddies, so if you happen to read this, please, please understand! I think, however, that you will share some of the moments I report.

I. GROWING UP: GRADE SCHOOL AT GARFIELD SCHOOL

KINDERGARTEN. 1946. Age 5.

Mark dressed for first day at school, age 5

    We were living on the farm about one mile from the east city limits of Abilene, so I probably was either taken to school by Mom or perhaps began to ride the school bus with older brother Tom and sister Jo Anne. I remember that each of us in kindergarten that year was required to have a rug which we kept in our cubbyhole, and at a given time, all the kids placed the rugs in a big circle and we had naps! (Just like today, 2010, but without the rug.) There seemed to be a lot of horsing around, peeking at others and lots of giggling; laughter was so easy then. I think there was milk and graham crackers around the same time. School, I think, was one-half day. One other odd recollection was the windows in the room; they were squares of glass, allowing light but not being able to see outside, the kind you seen in bathrooms meant I guess to keep the youngsters from being distracted by the playground outside. Recess was probably the highlight of the day with the school "jungle gym" for climbing and swings, and lots of running and kickball.

FIRST GRADE. 1947. Age 6.

An entire year evaporated! Nothing comes to mind. I might as well have skipped it. By the way, skipping grades was a bit of a status symbol in those days, but people were also held back. To recall an adage of the times: if you are held back, do not cross GO and do not collect $200. There must have been some amount of humiliation for those involved and a lot of disappointment and tears.

SECOND GRADE. 1948. Age 7.

Now there's a bit more and always from the mind's eye of a seven-year old. The teacher was "fat, old" Mrs. Hess and in my memory wearing those dresses that one associates with grandmothers in the 1940s. Yours truly received a hard slap on the hands at one time for tracing my pencil or pen on the already carved wooden desk. The infamous ruler used by nuns in Catholic grade schools was not in my memories, but the St. Joseph nuns of Salina, Kansas, did play a role on Saturday mornings and the first two weeks of June when the Catholic kids in town were required to attend Catechism, but more about that later. Suffice to say the downside was that these classes began immediately after public school was out. But returning to the carving on the school desk, at least I didn't do original work, and I surmise this kept me from an even greater penalty if caught, probably a visit to the principal's office.

Another incident, a harbinger of things to come, was the day during recess when I was shoved against the brick wall of the school yard by a young fellow who played rough and fractured my arm. Memories of the cast, the passing of time, and the grime and smell after a few days or weeks, are still with me. It would be just the first of three broken arms while growing up. Funny how the senses come into play--my sticky hand and my cruddy, smelly left arm.

THIRD GRADE. 1949. AGE 8.

The teacher was Mrs. Horn whom I remember as stern and she wore sun glasses in class. She did not have me as a class favorite. What brings you to say this, you may ask. At about this time, each class gave a short "play" for the rest of the grade school in the auditorium-gymnasium. Ours apparently was based on flowers and birds, leading to one of my first disappointments. Good friend Clarence Gillinger was inadvertently involved. Clarence was a school buddy and it was at his house in about 1953 that for the first time ever I experienced the miracle of television. The Gillingers had perhaps an 8 by 10 inch black and white television, and the first programs I remember were "Amos and Andy" and wrestling. I often went to play at his place and we would get big bottles of RC Cola from the cooler in his Dad's auto garage. Unrelated was Clarence's later passion for the Civil Air Cadets in high school during the Cold War years of the 1950s, an organization somehow connected to the "readiness" campaign in the Cold War; Clarence began "marching" everywhere, lots of "straight corners" as he walked, hmmm. I think he later enlisted in the U.S. Air Force and made a career of it, so evidently this early penchant for marching and the military was not unfounded.

To return to the class play, Clarence was named a "star" in the production and got to be a blue bird or blue jay. This was no small matter; the birds in the group were outfitted from head to toe with a large, feathered costume! I think there was a cardinal and maybe a robin; I did not even merit a sparrow. But to keep us all active, if not satisfied, there were flowers in the play. Vaguely enough, I don't remember what kind of flower I played, probably a sun flower, the state flower, or perhaps a daisy. But it was a non-speaking role which I think consisted in standing up and then slowly sinking to the stage, somehow depicting morning sunshine and then sunset. It was one of my first experiences of envy at this early stage in life.

It was in 1949, third grade, that something major happened. The event is in "The Farm," and I repeat it here. I've got to set the scene: Abilene was a town of about 7000 people and most needs were satisfied by the local stores--Viola's RHV, J.C. Penneys, Pinkhams, Royers' Men's Store, Duckwalls, three or four pharmacies and others--but there was a Singer Sewing Machine Store in nearby Salina, some 23 miles west on old Highway 40, a two-lane asphalt national highway west to Denver, long before the U.S. Interstate System. Because Mom was an avid and excellent seamstress, I suspect by necessity as well as design, an occasional trip to Salina was in order. As well, there were larger stores and I even recall she bought groceries as well. Sister Jo Anne, brother Tommy and I would all go along for the ride and treats. A big tall sack of popcorn at the 5 and dime was the main treat. On this occasion my Grandma Minnie, brother Tom and sister Jo Anne were along. On the way home there was a head-on collision. Mom was driving, I was in the middle of the front seat, my Grandma on the right; Jo and Tom in the back seat. We were driving in an old, heavy, black Buick, vintage of 1946 or 1947 with running boards. Mom was behind a highway truck which was going pretty slow; she started to go around, and there was another vehicle coming right at her. At this point the brakes on the car failed, and Mom said later there were only two choices: swerve violently to the right and probably roll the car in the ditch (there were no seat belts in those days) or try to simply swerve and miss the on-coming car. We hit head-on, Grandma was killed, Mom suffered severe shoulder, arm, and back injuries, but I was thrown through the windshield. Tom and Jo Anne suffered only scratches in the back seat; they were protected by the huge padded front seat of those days.

I woke up in Sacred Heart Hospital in Salina, Kansas, some days later with a broken arm and a fractured skull. Mom was in another room in the same hospital. I can remember visits from Tom, Jo Anne, and Dad, but especially Jim. One day they allowed me to see myself in a mirror; my face and head were black with surgical stitches, really black. It was then I realized the severity of it all; Jim told me that I was at the point of dying for several days, that there was a prayer vigil at St. Andrew's Catholic church in Abilene, that the coat I wore the day of the accident (my favorite, felt with some parts leather) was literally soaked and coated with blood, and was of course thrown out. I never felt one twinge of pain, either in the arm or the head, and to this day, I truly believe that I was saved by prayer, that it was God looking after me. I used to remark to my wife Keah that my and our lives have always seemed to be blessed. I did some really stupid things growing up and escaped tragedy more than once; perhaps God's blessing's once again. Our family always believed in and said the Guardian Angel's Prayer; I still pray it. And there was a St. Christopher Medal above the dashboard in the car (but no plastic Jesus). I was nine years old at the time. The most difficult thing was the day, later on in the hospital, when they told me Grandma had died. I remember crying, sobbing; this was the first time I had ever experienced anything so serious in life.

This leads to another important part of our lives; I digress to tell it. What continued to be the greatest miracle in our lives was the birth of daughter Katie (Kathleen) on September 29, 1977. It is a long story, and perhaps Keah could tell it better, but the long and short of it is that we were married for eight years and no child was conceived. In the final part of those years I was tested for sperm count, Keah was examined, and we were talking of adopting. But then we attended a prayer meeting at Brophy's Xavier church in Phoenix by a priest, Father Francis McNutt, a priest known for his "intercession" in healing through prayer and prayer meetings. Keah without previous planning, was moved to pray that if there were any problems, that they be taken away (we went to the meeting for altogether different reasons). The next month Keah became pregnant (we had continued to try harder!) After experiencing a nearly perfect pregnancy and childbirth, Katie was born that September. Months after the birth, Keah still experienced severe monthly problems and finally the doctor recommended surgery and a hysterectomy. They discovered severe and advanced endometriosis. The Dr. simply said, after coming out of surgery, that there was no way that he could imagine that it was possible for Keah to conceive with that much blockage. Enough said.

Back to other times during that year of 1949. There were evening activities throughout the year, all held once again in the school auditorium-gym. At what I recall as the school carnival, I ate too many hot dogs and threw up on that nice hardwood floor of the gymnasium; it was months or years before I could eat the dogs again. Vomiting thereafter would come only upon severe illness or a couple of beer busts in high school. I think they boiled the frankfurters in a big pot; that must have been it. As I write, juncos, jays and other birds cavort outside my office window here in Colorado; a Stellar Jay just took an enormously satisfying bath. Last night on the way into town to play guitar music and sing for the bar flies and others at Christina's, bar/grill in Durango I had to brake hard to avoid a rotund, black bear.

FOURTH GRADE. 1950. Age 9.

The teacher was Mrs. Sipes, one of the nicest teachers who incidentally did not ever smack me but instead encouraged the young scholar. It did not hurt that she was the mother of one of my good buddies, Kenton, later to become one of the first hot-rodders in Abilene with a lowered car, dual pipes and curly cue lines on the side. Customized cars were associated with "hoods," with ducktail haircuts. And I think Elvis Presley's ducktail was in vogue as well. Kent later spent most of his time working on the car and dating a cute farm girl out in the country south of Abilene, Carolyn. It would all end tragically – about one year after high school graduation, on his way for a date, he smashed head-on into another vehicle on one of those blind country intersections. He died, the first death which I experienced of a friend, and with it a realization that life is a bit more fragile than we thought. Maybe we were not going to live forever. Think of the Liam Clancy song "Those were the days." And it led to my caution to this day on the country roads in Kansas. Today someone would probably write a country song about it all.

FIFTH GRADE. 1951. Age 10.

Mark in new clothes, later years

I experienced my first male teacher, Mr. Roberts. What's in a child's memories? He seemed handsome, with a good head of blond hair, wore a suit and tie to school, but most of all, was my first "teacher-jock." He would become the grade school basketball coach, and I guess, a role model for all us guys. Life now would begin to revolve around sports and my first team experiences, namely basketball and then baseball in the spring on the school playground.

We practiced in the aforementioned gymnasium. It must have been a half-size court, but it seemed like Madison Square Garden to me. Memories are sparse, but I do know that I played regularly in practice, was a guard responsible for bringing the ball up court. My budding mediocrity in sports was in evidence, but I was no klutz or slouch either. There was no lack of motivation. Our basketball heroes were from Kansas State and K.U. There is more to tell, much more, but I don't know where in this narrative. But K-State had Dick Knostman, K.U. had Clyde Lavellete and then B. H. Born and then no less than Wilt Chamberlain. Many a night in junior high and high school were marked by my listening to K-State games at the side of the old radio in the family room and scoring with Xs and Os. Good friend Mike Kippenberger was the true athlete, even back then in grade school, the "natural" who was a high scorer and could make those pretty outside shots. I would throw one in just once in awhile. I can remember Bob Hensley, also a natural, playing the forward or center slot.

I can recall only one game, against that powerhouse of Talmage Grade School. For perspective, Talmage is a spot in the road along a paved county road some eight miles north of town, but they had a tall center who would later become a friend in high school, Bud Habacker. All things converge; Bud after high school would take over the family farm, and then years later, sell the farm, with the traditional farm sale of those years with folks from bigger farms coming in to bid (cheaply) on the farm implements. I think the motive was his father's death, but cannot say for sure. Bud would salvage the day by taking a day job at the county grain elevator and then drive a truck for them. His future wife and high school sweetheart, Louis McDowell would become Dickinson County clerk. But only later did we all realize that this was indeed a sign of the times, shades of Willie Nelson's Save the Family Farm Campaign of later years. It was sad, so sad, and representative of things to come. I don't mean Bud's case, because I was not there at the time. But I mean the malaise you read about in the newspapers, a national crisis. I digress; as you drive east from Durango to the East Slope and then across the plains of Eastern Colorado in 1998 you come to small bergs, farm towns highlighted by the tall grain elevators (they used to call them the "skyscrapers of the plains") with one or two short streets with commerce. The streets are commonly dotted with buildings now boarded up, the commerce and life long disappeared, evidence of migration to the city. To my utter shock, even Abilene had some of this during my last visit. As you crossed the state line into western Kansas, there was a pocket of prosperity in Johnson County, the country where niece Lorie, husband J.D. and Kasey, Lindsey and Reilly reside. The prosperity is due to big-time farming, corporate farms and a rich aquifer that supplies large irrigation projects. And it is the land of huge corporate feedlots where thousands of head of cattle eat, drink, and gain weight in large, smelly pens that they leave only for the slaughter house. The debate of large scale beef operations, but more important, pig farms, continues to alarm local farm people --you don't want to live down wind. And see the documentary "Food.Inc." Contrast this to "The Farm" where I describe in detail the old family-farm in Abilene and the self-sufficiency and I believe healthiness of such an operation, one not dissimilar to Bud Habacker's.

Back to the ball games in the fifth and sixth grades. This was my first experience at actually having a uniform for sports! I can't recall the colors, but the jersey and baggy shorts on my, guessing, skinny 70 lb. frame, must have been a sight to see. But we all felt like K-State or K.U. stars in those uniforms.

On the playground, recess was still the most important activity other than sports after school; there were lots of races run, and once again, I turned out to be one slow white boy. There were girls who could beat me and other slowpokes; this brings first mention of Susan Neil, a regular gazelle, one of the class cuties who later would shine as cheer leader, star of the stage in jr. high and high school plays, and strangely enough, one of the few girls I never dated (but brother Tom did have a thing for her older sister in those years). I digress. Her father was an executive, I think, for the only real corporation in Abilene in those days, the Five and Dime Duckwall Stores, later to be named Alco; it is a strange sensation today when Keah and I travel throughout Colorado or Kansas and see that Alco is still in business, a difficult thing with the rise of Walmart Inc.

A big activity in those days on the playground in the 1940s was tether ball, a vigorous competition of two, each trying to bat a soccer ball on a rope around a pole before the other person could wrap it around before you. Kids with creative Dads (and not busy farmers) cajoled ole' Dad to put one up for them at home. My Dad did not do this, but on the other hand, I would have in jr. high and high school the best basketball court ever in the hayloft of our big old hay barn.

A great institution at Garfield Grade School was the end of year picnic. We had an outing to the nearby high school athletic field for baseball or such, and then a sack, picnic lunch. My all-time favorite in those days, was cold fried chicken, bread and butter sandwiches, maybe an apple, and probably cookies or candy bar for dessert. The picnic also seemed to usher in the warm and even hot weather. There was no air conditioning in the school, so those hot spring and fall days meant for lethargy in the class room.

An interesting phenomenon of growing up: the anticipation and envy of growing up, but short-term, of wanting to grow and get to that next level--Junior High and then High School! Immediately next door to Garfield was Abilene Jr. High, formerly Abilene High School. We witnessed the "big" kids each day next door playing baseball, or hanging out in front of the school before classes. It seemed much "cooler" than our lives. There is a famous picture in the annals of Abilene, one Dwight D. Eisenhower in baseball uniform for the Abilene High School Cowboys, taken in front of the same building I describe. I will tell more on that later when I grow to age 12 and move on over to the Junior High, puberty and new times.

The grade school years--lunch at Duckwall's. This is one of the stories that old geezers tell; I can't recall if it is in "The Farm." Our family was truly of modest if not humble means; money was scarce, but between good planning and frugality Mom and Dad were extremely successful in seeing we got the basics and more. In "The Farm" I talk of my parents' accomplishment of sending all four children to private Catholic Schools, all on small to big scholarships to be sure, but amazing just the same. One small example of the "basics:" for a treat about once a week and a diversion from the sack lunch routine at school, I was allowed to walk the five or six blocks to downtown to Duckwall's and eat lunch. I recall Jo Anne being there as well and Tom too. What I remember is the price and the menu: a toasted cheese sandwich with mashed potatoes and gravy on the side, eaten at the lunch counter in the back of the store. Seems like a dill pickle came with it; I don't recall if we drank coca cola or water, but the price was 35 cents. I also seemed to have some pennies or a nickel or dime to buy Double Bubble Gum or maybe later on, baseball cards. There was time to look at the toy section as well. I think cowboy stuff, six-guns and holsters, hat maybe, and Red Ryder B-B guns were hot items at the time.

There was another little café on the corner of Buckeye and 3rd street, the main intersection in town. At some point we would eat there as well, or I would, maybe years later, and always ordered the hamburger, maybe with fries. The customers were strictly working people from the downtown area.

Another place, and definitely associated with religion and the Catholic church was a place over near the Union Pacific tracks, called, I think, Cathy's Kitchen, run by the Callahan girls. It was very popular in its day, very bright and antiseptic as I recall, and a once in awhile spot to eat. But maybe after Catechism; it was always associated with church by me. Helen Callahan had two daughters, Jolene, jet black hair and Tom's age, and Kitty, Irish-red hair and in my class. Tom dated Jolene for some time; I went out with Kitty just a time or two during school, once again, always associated with church, perhaps at the time of the CYO Dances in the church basement while a teenager.

The only other cafe I recall was the working man's café south of the tracks on A Street where Gordon Kippenberger and I would eat lunch almost every day in the summer of 1968 when I helped him farm and got to drive that big dually John Deere Tractor, and when I broke the middle toe of my right foot lowering a big disk from highway travel. It seems like a basic meal was about two or three dollars.

The "in" spot for Abilene folks in those days was to drive old Highway 40 west to Brookville for the family style fried chicken dinners. The place would move to Abilene years after I had left, and the tour buses stop regularly.

The other "old geezer" money story I used to always tell our daughter Katie when she was a tot, supposedly to show what's happened with the value of money, and the idea of being frugal (Katie should get a laugh out of this) was the Saturday movie with a total budget of 25 cents. This was the situation during the same years I describe, probably grade school years in the 1940s. The money for the movie was either earned for chores at home like getting the paper down the lane, or money generously given by Mom and Dad on market day, Saturday in town, described in detail in "The Farm." The movie cost 14 cents, and you often got a double feature for the price, generally an old black and while "oater" or B cowboy movie : Lash Larue, Monty Hale, Lone Ranger, Hopalong Cassady, or on a good day, and perhaps in color, Gene Autry or Roy Rogers. The film was always

The Farm

accompanied by a Woody Woodpecker or Tom and Jerry or Roadrunner cartoon, and the national newsreel; I'd give a bundle to recall what we saw, but I'm sure it included the times of President Harry Truman, the Berlin Airlift, Korean Conflict, Eisenhower days. But the decisions involved the other 11 cents; there were lots of options. You could get a coke in the fancy new machine dispenser, this for a nickel; you could get a nickel bag of popcorn which always seemed delicious (I could stand spellbound and salivating by the popcorn machine with its big metal pot that dumped the fresh corn into a huge pile). But sometimes I would forego one or the other and save the nickel for a small ice cream cone at the nearby drugstore after the movie, and a penny was left – a root beer barrel or a Double Bubble bubble gum.

When I was really young, I can remember more than once going to the 7 p.m. movie at the Plaza Theater on Saturday night, my parents still socializing outside on market day, and piling into the back seat of the car after the movie and immediately being lost to the world. It must have been Dad that carried me in out of the car, into the farm house and up to bed. Sleeping was never ever a problem. Never thanked him for that.

At about this time in life, probably after school, I recall I was allowed to walk downtown or perhaps Mom and Grandma picked me up at Garfield, and we would go downtown where I got that proverbial shiny nickel from Grandma and got an ice cream cone at the Bankes' Drug Store. Chocolate chip, chocolate swirl or the like. (In later days, perhaps now junior high or even high school, there were the cokes, etc. and the flirting at the Malt Shop, a semi-sleazy place on 3rd, or at Callahan's drug store with the big kids, with the pin ball machines and sneaking looks at the girly magazines back in the corner, but also checking the latest football and baseball stories. I still have a few of those sports magazines, particularly anything about the New York Yankees and Mickey Mantle.

But on one of those occasions after school, I must have been in the 2nd or 3rd grade, I got separated from Mom and Grandma, probably in the hustle and bustle of Duckwalls, absolutely panicked when I could not locate them, and walked what seemed like the huge distance, and it was for a small child, all the way from downtown up the main north-south street of Buckeye Avenue, then east on 14th street (or Highway 40 through town), all the way out to the each side of town to the ramshackle house of Mr. and Mrs. (I can't recall their name,) an old couple that actually had bought the house and corner lot where Dad and Mom lived when I was born. I think I was a few months old when they moved to the farm; this only because there was an old photo with brother Jim holding me in his lap, me in huge blond curls, with Jo Anne, Tom in the photo; it seemed pretty "rural" to me when I saw the photo. Anyway, the lady got on the phone, called Mom or Dad, and they came and got me, now calmed down but still frightened by the experience. Is this why I don't want to go to New York or Paris?

SIXTH GRADE. 1952. Age 11.

Mark, 6th grade class, Garfield School, Mr. Horst.

Much previously said may have happened that year too. But the teacher was Mr. Horst (I guess that's German; it fits). Not my favorite, but what can I say, he was probably doing his job.

Did I talk of the grade school days when I sat in the back of the classroom doing these fantastic drawings, probably during penmanship class? I would do panoramic Korean War Scenes with aerial dogfights between US Thunder Jets or Saber Jets and Russian Migs, the skies full of action. Another topic was Indian wars, but based on a movie I saw in those days--either Hurons or Iriquois with the strip of hair in the middle of a shaved head, but with bows and arrows, tomahawks, knives, and pants and shirts with the buckskin fringe on the leggings. But the masterpieces would come with immensely complex drawings of Road Runner cartoons featuring all the gadgets that Wiley Coyote would get from ACME company to try to thwart the roadrunner. With some training I might have made something of that, but alas and alas. Oh, we had races to finish the assignment each day in penmanship class, the "we" being Jerry Hawks, Mike Kippenberger, myself and others. The main result today is my lousy, lousy handwriting.

A moment of hilarity from the same days was the grade school lunchroom scene. Many of us brought sack lunches which in my case would mean a sandwich; perhaps some sliced carrots, some chips, an apple and some cookies. One little fellow delighted in taking a banana and slowly squashing it in his hands until it was a pulpy mess, and then slowly eating it. We howled with laughter. But most memorable was Dicky Helm and his lunch. Dicky probably weighed in at 250 pounds, even in grade school. His lunch consisted in a package of lunch meat directly from the market, you know, in white wrapping paper with a string around it; then a loaf of bread, an entire package of cookies, and perhaps a bunch of bananas. It all soon disappeared before our eyes. There were moments of hilarious, stomach hurting laughter. A digression: I took a sack lunch for years to school and thought I was done with that until ASU teaching days when it all started over again. But I think those healthy sack lunches in retrospect were a tad better than the pizza and beer at ASU as of late.

II. ABILENE JUNIOR HIGH SCHOOL DAYS

SEVENTH GRADE. 1953. Age 12.

This was what we had all been looking forward to--a major step in growing up--the big move from grade school and the "little guys" to the Jr. High next door. We were fortunate in about 1953 to still be able to attend the "old" junior high, which was the same building as the "old high school" in Ike Eisenhower's days. There is a picture of Eisenhower and the AHS baseball team in uniform in front of the school; it must have been taken about 1915.

These memories are all helter-skelter, whatever comes to mind. But my first entry on the notes was "PUBERTY." And not an understatement was this! You really began to pay attention to the girls, mainly the 8th graders, but also a few select in my 7th grade class--we came to admire boobs! There were some cute, well and early endowed gals we kept an eye on.

But on the male side; it was the shower room after sports. Guys were growing pubic hair down there where there had been none before. The juices were beginning to flow. I don't know when I shaved for the first time, but I guess it had to be around this time.

The Farm

SPORTS AND OTHER TIMES IN JUNIOR HIGH

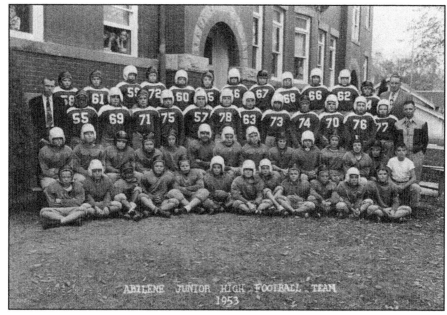

Team picture, 7th grade football

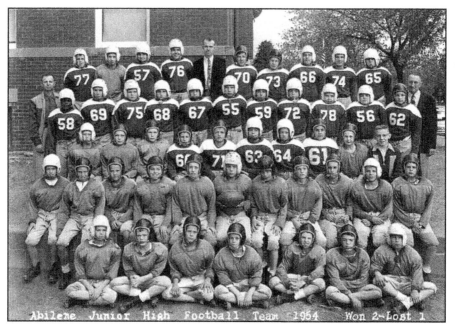

Team picture, 8th grade football

In 7th and 8th grade I played JHS football and probably weighed less than 100 pounds, and of course I wanted to play center, since that was what brother Tom played for the high school. He indeed was my role model in those days.

We practiced on the old athletic field north of the AHS field and stadium. I recall we suited up in the junior high building and then walked or ran to the practice field. Funny, but one of the memories is lining up opposite Ronnie Gardner, a big, big boy who would have great days ahead at AHS and then I think Fort Hayes State football and then a coaching career in high school at some major schools in the Kansas City area. I think Ron took it a bit easy on me in those practices. I believe Mike Kippenberger was the quarterback, Bob Hensley the half back, Kenny Klufa as well, and then the rest of us were the grunts. I remember Ronnie Garten, Gary Alford, Joe Fleagle, all us stalwart athletes. I'm sure I've left a bunch of hard nosed guys out.

The Junior High showed its age. It was a red brick building but with hard wood floors, lots of stairways up and down, all very creaky. Just fleeting images were math teacher Mr. Anderson's home room, the big room where we had "shop" under George Missimer, the big airy study hall with large windows facing the ball field, and the classroom of Mrs. Ewert, the fine English teacher and director of drama. I also recall Mr. Edberg of science class. My memory of "science" was when he stirred a glass of ice water, showed the condensation, and there was some lesson to be learned, somehow, out of that. Apparently not much stuck with me.

Like the rooms of the farmhouse, the rooms of Abilene Junior High all had memories for me.

Shop class was obligatory and we were expected to do projects. I somehow managed to make a lamp and an end table, both out of walnut. But I think future engineer and computer geek Rick Page must have helped me with the wiring; my less than rudimentary knowledge of electricity dates back to those days. Keah and Katie later on gave me a Father's Day present, a T-shirt with a Gary Larson cartoon: "School for the mechanically declined." It showed this geeky professor lecturing geeky folks and on the blackboard was a screwdriver on one side and a screw on the other; that day's lesson. That says it all. But shop was full of fun, lots of laughing, and the telling of dirty jokes. A curious memory comes to mind: the day the Polish immigrant boy arrived and we became somewhat aware that there were serious events going on outside of Abilene. It must have been 1953 or so. I think the immigrant family, Catholic of course, became tenant farmers east of our farm in Abilene. Every time I read Flannery O'Connor and her short story about immigrant farmers in the South, they come to mind.

Much of the time spent in shop class was spent heehawing when someone farted, the louder and the smellier, the greater our reaction. And too much carrying on or fooling around brought punishment--swats from the wooden board the teacher wielded so well, probably ironically made out of high grade walnut as well. I don't know if I got more than one or two, but the "regulars," Roy Palmer comes to mind, wore out that board.

Recess was big for us. There were games, but all according to season. We played tag football; you carried a strip of cloth in your rear pocket and were "tackled" when someone could grab it out of the pocket. The idea being: no roughness or tackling. Baseball was a great favorite, softball that is, a pretty democratic game because we played "work up," and everyone had a crack at each position and a chance to bat. Ole Mark was just "average," but the big boys, good athletes that is, spent a lot of time intentionally hitting the ball in foul territory and breaking windows in the study hall. Mike Kippenberger and Roy Palmer were the ones I recall most. I do not know where it all happened, but much of the time, or spare time, was spent telling dirty jokes, our "sex education" in Abilene.

It was in the study hall with the broken windows that I associated the coming of puberty, the interest in girls and in particular ogling the well-endowed girls. In effect big boobs! I won't mention names, but you know who you are! A tight white blouse or better yet, a cotton or woolen sweater brought moments of happiness to us all. As for studying, I suppose some work got done, but that's not what I remember. An aside: I did not begin to take academics seriously until about sophomore year in high school, more on that later. But I think native "smarts" kept me somewhat in the game without working too hard at it in Jr. High.

The 8th grade play, "Auggie Evans Private Eye"

An important memory was drama class, an extra-curricular activity in those days, with Mrs. Ewert. We did plays in both 7th and 8th grades, and I was fairly good at it. I can remember one play "Auggie Evans Private Eye" by title only. I can't remember a thing about the play, but I think I had the lead and was able to be around pretty young things like Linda Wright, Floy Little, and Sylvia Schwarz.

A related activity was to memorize "readings" and declaim them at contests like the declamation contest in Enterprise, a nearby town. One time I did a "shtick" as a sports announcer with several props: a microphone, a Walter Cronkite hat and maybe a pipe. The reading won a blue ribbon that day.

MORE ATHLETICS AND JUNIOR HIGH

Football I already talked about a little. The uniforms were funny, the helmets funnier yet; there was a hierarchy, the 7th graders getting the old-fashioned ones we can maybe associate now with Bronco Nagurski in 1919! The 8th graders wore "modern" helmets which we seventh graders would eventually inherit the following year. I remember bus trips to our two or three games, once to Concordia, Kansas, some 30-40 miles away, once to Hillsboro, Kansas to the South. We played in the afternoon before I imagine whatever students got out of class to see the game and a few adults. I have a picture that says our record was 2-1. Oh, the main activity on the bus ride to and from the game was all of us singing "99 bottles of beer on the wall," up to 99 and back down again. I surmise the bus driver and the coach needed a beer or two when they got home that night.

EIGHTH GRADE. 1954. Age 13.

Team picture, 8th grade basketball.

Basketball for me was a much bigger deal. As usual with my "average" only abilities, I would just barely make the squad, I think maybe 9th or 10th on a 10 man squad. But practices were held at the "old" high school, still in operation then, and at times in an old venerable place in Abilene, the old "city building," a drafty small gym just north of the city library. I'll get back to games later, but there is just one memory associated with that place which I need to recount. Back in grade school in the city basketball tournament, Garfield played McKinley school for the title, 6th grade it was. I was allowed in the game in the final minutes, a token substitution I think, and proceeded to ever so lightly tap the fingers of the crack McKinley guard, my introduction to J.D. Longbine, this while trying to guard him in a final desperation shot. Garfield must have had the lead at the time. Anyway, J.D. proceeded to make both foul shots and win the game for them. Among many low moments of my Abilene sports career, this was perhaps the lowest. Wracked with crying after the game, that's how I remember it. What I cannot remember however, is even one word of condemnation by teammates. I think there was much slapping on the shoulder and "that's all right, you did your best" sort of repartee. It is a lesson of life learned only years or decades later--we are our own worst enemy when it comes to punishing ourselves.

But there were greater, really happy moments associated with the old city auditorium gym. In those years even the high school varsity games were held in the auditorium. I think mainly on Friday nights. But I doubt I ever missed a game. We would actually sit on the "stage," with the regular audience facing us in the shape of a inverted "U." Memories are fading, but there was a terrific black athlete, Howard Wilkins who played center, a sharp shooting guard, Harry Shank (who dated my sister Jo Anne a bit in those years), and the excitement of it all. All this was prior to 1955, a watershed year for lots of reasons I'll get into later, when I was a freshman at AHS and we moved to the shiny, sparkling, "field house" in the new high school. The new gym had one major change--the new court has glass backboards! This was progress and a quantum leap in our lives as athletes!

THE COUNTY TOURNAMENT--BASKETBALL

This was a wonderful memory of growing up in Abilene. The games were held at the downtown old city building mentioned earlier. Teams were from local Abilene schools, but also all the tiny consolidated schools in the county plus other small county towns. It was a full two days I think, and you might be seeing Rural Consolidated school playing Woodbine or Enterprise. There were lots of country boys in those old style basketball shorts and jerseys. We all spent many hours watching, probably swilling down cokes and eating hot dogs and assorted junk.

4-H BASKETBALL

There's just one memory; the Abilene Aggies, my team, was playing a game out at Rural Center, a consolidated school about 10 miles south of Abilene. The memory was that Tom my brother was still around, and we actually played on the same team. And yours truly got hot for once in his life and made several long baskets. Only time in my life.

CHRISTMAS TIME, ALL THE CANDY AND SANTA CLAUS!

There were two separate events, the first sponsored by the Elks at, once again, the city auditorium. Faded memories, but there always was a short show, and I think it was an annual event for some local tap dancing school to bring in all the kids to perform. Tap dancing was not for me or anyone I knew. But I recall one older kid who hauled his marimba out on stage to perform. But we put up with it all because at the end, the Elks would hand out these great sacks of candy. I recall the peppermint sticks, chocolates with mint inside, lots of peanuts, and to make everything all right, an orange or apple. But the big event was the arrival of Santa Claus himself in his "sleigh." We attended this event for many years, and I daresay it contributed, along with Halloween trick or treat, and Easter eggs to a mouthful of cavities and silver fillings, the latter eventually hollowed out in Tempe, Arizona in 1969, my first year at ASU, by a certain Dr. Thomas who did gold crowns for me at about 35$ each! A college friend at the time called me and said, "Buy gold!" I think the price over night went to over $600. But any extra dough I had went to paying off loans from college.

But the Catholics were to not to be outdone. At about the same time as the Elks event, in the basement of old St. Andrew's church there were more bags of candy and Santa Claus as well. I recall my Dad was both a member of the Elks (his forte' the Sunday afternoon gin rummy games) and the Knights of Columbus, so he was working both events. Great times.

A "real" Santa Claus with red outfit, pillow under his shirt if needed, red cap with white fringe, black boots, and lots of "ha ha ha" was part of the deal.

THE FIRST DANCE.

There are these moments of growing up essential to all my generation. My first dance was a junior high school dance. Good buddy Mike Kippenberger went with Susan Neil and I with Kay Missimer (recall that her father was the junior high shop teacher). I think I talk of all this in "The Farm", but worthy to repeat here is the "mother conspiracy" or perhaps better termed, just plain ole' dance planning. Mom and Sarah Kippenberger put their heads together to outfit us youngsters for the dance. I am pretty sure we were decked out in purple corduroy sport jackets, grey slacks, and I think a pink shirt. And a tie. What the reader needs to know is that we were at the height of Elvis-Mania during those days, and those I think were colors in style from him. There were corsages and all. And of course, we were chauffeured to the dance--no car 'mon'--by I think Mike's dad. (There would be another chauffeured job by Joe Kipp after the home-from-college-for Christmas-vacation poker party at Jim Forren's house and escapade with Mike, me and Kenny Klufa, I think maybe during Christmas vacation, my first year in college. After several beers we were heading home to Mike's house and drove by the high school principal's house. Somehow or other we drove up off the curb and over his lawn. There was some discussion that no one was in sight, so take off! The blipping of the red and blue cop car lights came within a block or two; the policeman had seen the whole thing. Anyway I recall sitting in the police station, very worried about the mud on my shoes and peeling it off in little mud balls. Joe took us all home. Another encounter with the same principal at AHS comes later.)

Back to "the dance." I can't remember the dance; we probably stood around a lot. But hormones were raging, and those "close" dances put pepper in the pepper can. I had a bit of puppy love thing going for Kay in those days, that is, until high school when an upper classman snatched her away; I think he had a car.

About this same time we were going to dances at the Elks' club, I think maybe with Kay again, but who knows. But science and time march on. We eighth grade boys solved our "problem"--those close dances, cheek to cheek with those blooming young girls--or so we thought with a jock strap or athletic supporter under our shorts to ameliorate the problem. Curiously enough, the modern term "downsizing" did not exist in those days. Ah youth. Oh, there was an Abilene icon of those times present at those dances--the music was always by a local band with Linda Viola's dad on the drums!

About this time the Job's Daughters dance occurred; and prior to the dance there was a ceremony in the old Masonic hall. Susan Neil and Kay Missimer would sing perhaps "You'll never walk alone." We Catholics had to get special permission from the old Irish priest, Monsignor Roach, to attend. It was grudgingly granted, and we seemed to survive just fine. No epic battles between Masons or Catholics.

SUMMERTIME BASEBALL—JUNIOR HIGH DAYS

A saving moment for me, that is, saving me from work on the farm, was the fact my parents allowed me to participate fully in little league baseball. There are lots of wonderful memories growing up from all that.

You practiced in the morning (when you could; there was lots of rain and rainouts) and played games late afternoon; there were no lights so the games had to be over at sunset. My earliest memory was in "Pee Wees," the youngest group. One year I played for a team sponsored by Ehrsams, the company my brother worked for in nearby Enterprise, Kansas. We did not have uniforms, but did wear white team t-shirts with the Ehrsams name on them. It was important to have a nice glove, and I think mine was bought at the old RHV store on Buckeye Street in town. I think we wore tennis shoes, but I did have regular baseball cleats with metal spikes later on. Ehrsams was a loser, but it was still fun. My friend Joe Fleagle's dad coached the team. Arthur was known as a very fine player in his youth who was headed for bigger things until he "threw his arm out at some point." Anyway, I know I played most positions and even got to pitch one night. I walked every batter I faced.

But better times were ahead. A second team was sponsored by Dairy Queen and things improved, mainly because we had a young fireball pitcher named Ronnie Sheets who was a strikeout pitcher. We won the league, and after every win were treated to whatever we wanted at the Dairy Queen. Big thick strawberry malts were in order or big chocolate sundaes. But one memory stands out--I was playing third base and Sheets threw a pickoff ball or such to me. The force of the throw caused me to fall right on my butt on the third base. I don't recall if we got the out, but who cares. I'm just glad I did not have to bat against him. There was in past years a very fine pitcher for the Milwaukee Brewers with the last name of Sheets; I always wondered if it could be my friend's son or grand-son.

A memory at about the same time was facing my friend Mike Kippenberger who was a fair to middling pitcher, but I had Mike's number now and again and got a hit or two against him. Miracles never cease.

At some point, at a little older age, they instituted "T-ball" where instead of a live pitcher, you simply hit the ball off a T to start play. It was at this time that I made the "big catch." Johnny Anguiano hit a ball to left field, my position at the time, and it was a sure home run over the fence. But I happened to see the ball all the way, slowly backed up to the fence, stuck my glove over and made the catch, saving the homer. Whenever I would see Johnny in later years we had to reminisce over that one. "I wuz robbed," he said more than once.

I can recall early June when Mike Kippenberger and I would bicycle directly from Catholic Summer School with the nuns to baseball practice. These were the years when we were all buddies and just had a great time being together. I recall Eddie Jimenez at 3rd base, Bob Hensley at first with his new, shiny first baseman's mitt, Ronnie Gardner at catcher, and Jim Beavers as well. Jerry Hawks was around too. These are some of the guys I would only see again in 2009 at the 50 year high school reunion. Eddie was in to music and had the best 45 rpm collection amongst us.

In the final years when I played, I must have been a freshman or sophomore in high school, we "graduated" to play some games on the big diamond, where the Jr. Legion guys played. I was a catcher by now with a good arm for being such a skinny kid. My pitcher was Jim Switzer, an amazing high school and later college athlete. He threw the ball so hard I had to use a small sponge inside the catcher's mitt, and even them ended each game with a swollen hand. It was around this time that we had a big scare. Mike Kippenberger, playing shortstop, somehow misjudged a fly ball, a rare occasion, or maybe the wind caught it, and it came down square on his forehead. It actually made an indentation in the middle of the forehead, and he frankly was lucky he wasn't killed. But fortunately, he survived with I think a slight concussion. "Viver é muito perigoso," "living is very dangerous," says the Brazilian novelist João Guimarães Rosa, and so it was that evening.

Another memory was simply of practice, way out in the outfield on the big diamond catching or trying to catch amazingly long, high fly balls hit to us, "fungos" I think they were called. For me it was incredibly hard to judge the ball, and that was when my appreciation for the major leaguers like Mickey Mantle and especially Willy Mays grew exponentially. The fact I had trouble catching those fly balls, hitting a curve ball (or even throwing one, something we all tried to master as teenagers) came with the realization this would all end soon. In "The Farm," "games we played," I found the remedy to all this--a baseball made of hard Styrofoam that you could throw a curve with that broke two feet!

And summertime fun was all connected; we swam in the local public pool in Eisenhower park lots of times, but with the proviso TO NOT SWIM on the day of a game. And so it was. But your courage was tested by which diving board you could handle; there were three, but that high board was a doozy. About the only way I could handle that was to jump off rather than diving. And we had great fun playing "King on the Mountain" on huge rubber inner tubes of combine tires. As years passed, latter days were different when we also took time to ogle the blooming teen age girls. And there was a great snack shop on the top of the pool run by the junior high principal in a better role in summer days. But it was on top of that pool near the snack bar that I got another dose of sex education, flawed as it was, by listening to the dirty jokes swapped sometimes for an hour, remembering mainly Jerry Collins and Mike's cousin Jack Kippenberger telling the most.

There is a memory of the pool from much earlier years. I must have been about 10 years old; sister Jo Anne, brother Tom and I were all at the pool. My swimsuit gave way, split right down the middle of the crotch. Somehow or other I got Jo Anne's attention; a towel was tossed to me in the water, I covered my vital parts and departed to the dressing room. They used to talk of "most embarrassing moments' in those days--chalk one up for me.

There also was a time in those summer evenings when I would get the chance to keep score and even announce the baseball players on a tiny p.a. system at the big diamond. Those memories were associated with perhaps an earlier 4-H meeting at Sterling Hall, in front of the ball park, and terrific chocolate cake and homemade ice cream sold outside the stadium by the local 4-H clubs, maybe for 15 or 25 cents. And since hormones were coming on, we kept our eyes on the blooming girlies who attended the games, always in short shorts in that summer heat. Ah youth.

Back to memories of Junior High School. One of the memories about that time, while we were still in Jr. High, was the scene in front of the school while waiting for school to start. I just recall it was a big moment for socializing.

Transportation to school varied; I used to go over to the old high school to catch the school bus after school at Garfield and then Jr. High. But during high school I actually bicycled from the farm to high school, often on a hand me down bike from Tom. There may have been occasional days, rare they were, when I was allowed to take the family car to school. But I can remember getting rides from good buddy Gary Alford who always had a slick car. But there was a catch--Gary inevitably would say "Hey I'll buy you a hamburger." Okay for me, but Gary, called "Porky" by mean kids like all of us, mainly wanted company at the drive in.

At about the same time, there were the times when my buddy Jerry Hawks would proudly show off his "blue blood" pigeons in a pen kept in the back yard.

In those days we never missed AHS football games in the fall. There are vague memories of the CKL championship in 1951; Dick Whitehair was on the team. And there are memories of going to brother Tom's games. There were the black and gold uniforms, cheerleaders, and rickety wooden stands. It was about this time that my brother Jim took me to Enterprise to see an 8 man football game; only time ever!

I can recall one very cool fall night when Halloween corresponded to the high school game; there was trick or treating afterward and then ending up at a movie at the old Plaza theater with moments of bedlam on that Halloween. Such moments I'm sure will be recalled should any of my school chums read this book.

A BIG EVENT AT THE TIME—IKE FOR PRESIDENT!

It was 1952. General Dwight Eisenhower came to Abilene to launch his campaign for presidency of the United States; there was a big parade down Buckeye and then west on 3rd street to the city park where he would actually give the speech. Local 4-H clubs created floats for the parade. I played a young Eisenhower (this even before I shared Ike's semi-baldness). During the speech in today's Eisenhower Park the rain poured. Afterwards I jumped down from the stands, ran up to the Eisenhowers' black limousine, stuck my head in the window and said "Hi Mami, hi Ike." Try that today. I think I remember his smile.

ABOUT THE SAME TIME, THE DICKINSON COUNTRY FREE FAIR AND RODEO

On several occasions I drove a tractor from one of the local dealerships in the fair-rodeo parade and got comps or free tickets for the rodeo. Another way to get a ticket was to volunteer to lead an animal in the livestock parade before the rodeo. Imagine a leather halter, a huge heifer or steer a few hundred pounds bigger than you are, trying to avoid putting your foot in cow pies, and you've got the picture. But I did garner several tickets to the rodeo that way.

The "comps" or coupons were issued in varied colors, each color designated for a specific night of the rodeo. On the nights we did not have a "legitimate" ticket, we would sneak through a hole in the old outfield fence and hopefully show the ticket taker the right colored coupon and we were in! I think all this took place during the National Anthem.

There were great memories of the rodeo itself--the "grand entry" with all the cowboys, cowgirls, and the judges on their horses, riding at top speed around the arena. It all was very exciting. We intently watched and kept score of all the events--bareback bronco riding, calf roping, saddle back bronco riding, and my favorite, brahma bull riding. I yet today remember one behemoth all grey in color, the bull "Joe Lewis." Then there were the brave clowns who would protect the riders after they either jumped off or were thrown by the bull. The clowns would hide in a barrel right in front of the bull. And they would swap ribald commentary with the rodeo announcer, all I guess "arranged" ahead of time. But once again, it was great fun. I can remember the specialty acts in between events--the pretty girls in sequins doing "Roman Riding," that is, riding, standing with one leg on each of two horses. It was this memory that made me so happy years later to learn the country song "Everything that glitters is not gold" which deals with rodeo out in Phoenix. An event added much later, barrel racing for the girls, in my view never did cut it.

OTHER EVENTS AT THE RODEO GROUNDS

There was "The Joey Chitwood Auto Daredevil Show" and a night of smashing up cars in the local demolition derbies.

On one occasion the rodeo merited the Grand Ole' Opry show with no less than Roy Acuff! This was BIG TIME for Abilene. See the movie "Nashville" some time to see the behind the scenes role Acuff actually played in "country music USA."

THE FAIR ALONGSIDE THE RODEO

In the "good old days" both events, the Dickinson County Free Fair and Rodeo, were held the same week and complemented each other. I've written at great length about this in "the Farm." Some of the events and moments were:

-- Throwing water balloons from the top of the old CCC stadium

-- The watermelons we tossed from the top of the stadium

-- The great hamburgers cooked at the outdoor food stands

-- The gypsies who stole eggs from the 4-H poultry exhibit

-- The "carnies" and the great times we had at the carnival, flirting with girls upon occasion. There were the rides including the ferris wheel, bumper cars and the like. There was a "freak" show with all kinds of aberrations, and the "girlie show" for the older folks. And you could easily spend and lose your hard earned money from farm chores with the crooked or nigh impossible games at the carnival. I recall one in particular—a sort of mechanical crane with a tiny bucket; you cranked the crane to try to "fish out" silver dollars. And there was the ring toss where you would toss amazingly tiny rings to try to land on the tops of coke bottles.

-- Sterl Hall and all the inside 4-H exhibits: cooking, pies, cakes, and sewing

-- The stock barns and the animal exhibits--cattle, hogs, chickens, geese, or sheep. I recall the "herding board" I used to show Wilhemina my Sears' Gilt, this after washing, and brushing the animal. And of course the day came to part with her as a result of the 4-H livestock sale. And there was my disastrous participation in the animal poultry judging contest.

-- Ducks, chicken and geese. My 4-H project, the Grey Toulouse Gus Goose, became county grand champion. There is much more about this character in "The Farm."

-- The weather at the fair/rodeo brought a noticeable coolness, a sign that SCHOOL WAS ABOUT TO START! So that meant school clothes, and for the Curran's that meant for the most part J.C. Penney's and maybe Howard Keel's on a very, very special occasion. I think the main item was blue jeans, and Penney's brand was Dickies if I'm not mistaken. I was so skinny a kid that they hung on me anyway, and I can remember a photo with my belt tightened to hold them up and the jeans wrinkled around it. T-shirts were also acceptable, white as I recall, but I know I had colored shirts as well. I can't recall, but I guess tennis shoes were the norm. All this would change in junior high and especially high school. Shirts became a bit dressier, shoes were brown or black loafers, and I think some kind of dress slacks were worn to school, especially on the occasions when I had to speak to introduce lyceums, etc. as president of student council senior year. When we did wear tennis shoes they were high top. A related matter were school books. I can't recall where we got schoolbooks but I think at a downtown music store, the same place I would buy my first guitar at about age 14, a Stella steel string.

III. ABILENE PUBLIC HIGH SCHOOL 1955-1959

Ours was the first class to go all four years in the "new" high school located on 14th. St. in north Abilene. There was a then upscale housing development just east of the school; 14th street is on the north boundary, and a little west were Reitz's nursery and the Protestant cemetery. The parking lot of the high school was due west of the west entrance and athletic fields a bit to the south; a lot of sports were played there in required phys-ed. classes.

What was most impressive to me of the new AHS was the gymnasium, a first-class high school basketball venue for the times. How do I know? GLASS BACKBOARDS! I would spend hours in that gymnasium, more on that later.

HIGH SCHOOL FOOTBALL.

My hero and role model at that time was my older brother Tom who had excelled at football, music, mathematics, and the girls. Tom would go on to earn a Navy ROTC scholarship to Marquette U. in Milwaukee, but that's another story. Tom probably weighed in at 160 in high school and played starting guard. So that's what I wanted to do, but with a small problem--I weighed in at 114 freshman year. I recall the practices with all the calisthenics and the running of plays. I don't recall the games so well, because a brain concussion interfered with that bit of clarity. I of course don't remember it, but I do remember lying on this cool, clean, white, antiseptic bed in Abilene Memorial Hospital for observation. Gary Alford later told me about it, how funny it was, like the broken arm from pole vaulting to be mentioned later. I lined up to play center which I had played in junior high. They soon discovered that my bell had been rung. After a couple of weeks of rest, I returned to practice and this time I remember it well; we were running a play and then I experienced a splitting headache. I went to the sideline, sat on the bench, and everyone, all the coaches included, Shirk, Schaake, etc. decided my playing days were over.

Looking back, I don't think there was great disappointment; after all, it wasn't like I was going to be all Central Kansas League or even start. But I do think it was the "push" to excel at something else. How about basketball?

HIGH SCHOOL BASKETBALL.

Mark J. Curran

Team picture, freshman basketball

As in junior high, if there were ten boys on the team (by the way, read Pat Conroy's stories of sports growing up in Charleston, South Carolina, and the great way he has of telling about what we all experienced as schoolboys in the 1950s), I probably was number 10. Unlike Garrison Keeler and Lake Wobegon ("Where all the children are above average"), I was average, and maybe a tad below that. I've already talked about 4-H basketball and the memorable night at Rural School when I actually scored quite a few points. At AHS, this was not to be the case. Practices were long, tiring and fun. And I enjoyed the games, mainly watching Mike Kippenberger, Bob Hensley, Jim Nuss, Ron Gardner, J.D. Longbine, Roy Palmer, and who am I forgetting, do good things. Once again, there was the single happy memory--they put me in and I threw up a long shot, perhaps beyond today's 3 point line, and "zing go the strings." Mike Kippenberger let out a heehaw and big smile. Unusual things can happen.

A singular memory: I was sitting beside Bud Habacker after practice one day. He was under the weather with an immense hangover and told of the previous night of being up until three a.m. and some beer drinking going on. In our day, 3:00 a.m. was unheard of!

This could bring me to academics, but rather it leads me to a discussion of Coors beer and AHS. I can honestly say that I rarely drank alcohol in high school and mainly on "special" occasions. That all changed with college and vacations home and summers in Abilene after that. I can't recall, but

I am sure the legal drinking age had a lot to do with it, 18 years to drink in Kansas then if I'm not mistaken.

But here the farm and school merge. Brother Jim owned one of the pool halls downtown in Abilene. When we decided to have a party for the freshman football team, Curran's pond was the place to do it. There was a case of beer provided by the pool hall. We had a big bonfire, hotdogs and all included. There was lots of standing around, telling of dirty jokes, kidding around. I did not drink much, but can remember my hat going in the fire. I left and walked home through the pasture to the farm house.

The pond did provide a lot of other social occasions, some sleep outs or "camping" with Jerry Hawks and Phil Combs. It was all pretty innocent, the main factor I recall, being the plague of mosquitoes. And I recall how damp, wet, humid and miserable it all felt. I don't think we used sleeping bags, but maybe a couple of old blankets. Years later, after spending most of my adult life in Arizona and SW Colorado, the humidity of Kansas on visits to Abilene is always a bit of a shock. We were used to it then.

But there were other escapades during these football and basketball seasons. Those of us who were not good enough to make the varsity team still supported our buddies and our school by attending all the games, including away games. That is what brings me to recall two hair-raising experiences. The first was driving to a game at Junction City with a car load of buddies, the driver this time Buddy Habacker. I don't know who all was in the car, but I imagine Jerry Hawks, Phil Combs, and maybe others. Bud got his 1952 Ford to over one hundred miles per hour on old U.S. 24 on the way to the game. It turned out there was no harm done, and as I recall no alcohol involved. Just "guys having fun."

A second episode, like the first, was to a game in Macpherson. This time Bill Erhsam was behind the wheel in his shiny two-toned 1956 Chevy. Once again we reached speeds over one hundred miles per hour down the highway between Salina and Macpherson. But once again, there was no harm done since there was not any accident, and we all enjoyed the game. And perhaps best of all, Bill did not get a traffic ticket. Who won the game? I do not know. We were just again "Guys having fun." But there were occasional articles in the Kansas papers in those days of horrendous car accidents; I guess we were lucky, if not stupid.

Another episode, perhaps during senior year was the bright idea to paint the water tower, a tradition in Abilene for the senior class. This time I think Jerry Collins instigated the affair. I believe Jerry Hawks, Ron Gardner and I don't know who else was along. The water tower is like an upside-down cupcake, and to reach the outer walls you had to climb straight up a steel ladder, then climb, angling out to reach the paintable edge. I think the police came, but yours truly was on the ground. I was afraid to climb a step ladder, much less the water tower. Fear of heights can be a good thing.

RUNNING TRACK IN HIGH SCHOOL.

I was on the track team I believe through junior year. I remember coach Bill Schaake and running continuous quarter miles, then walking the end zone and running the straights. I was a skinny guy, so the running came fairly easily. I believe I ran a 63 second quarter mile once. But they settled me into the half mile. The culmination was a cold, rainy spring day at the state track meet perhaps in Wichita or Hutchinson. I did not place but ran my fastest half ever, I think maybe 2:28 or something. But the good guys flew past like the wind.

Once, out of sheer boredom, I was killing time during track practice over at the pole vault area. At this time they still used old, thick, heavy bamboo poles. I tried my luck, my hands slipped on the pole, and I fell across the hole it was supposed to go in for the vault. Result: another broken arm, but this time above the wrist at a 45 degree angle. Buddies heehawed at the sight of it. I think I was close to tears.

Another moment at track: One of the Wilson boys, a tackle on the football team, was forced to go out for track as were all football players, the idea to stay in shape. He was running the mile in a meet, was so far behind that he ran the last lap backward. Coach was furious and Wilson stayed after the meet to run endless laps around the track. But it was a hoot.

There is a wonderful memory related to track, I think not described elsewhere. The sport was big in the Big 8, the Big 10, etc. and there were many large sprint meets with titles like "The Texas Relays, the Kansas Relays, the Drake Relays, the Penn Relays," and such. The Kansas meet was one of the big ones, and the real stars of college track and field were present. So in junior and senior years, a bunch of my AHS buddies naturally drove down to Lawrence, Kansas, to the beautiful campus of Kansas University. The weekend was vaguely tied into fraternity recruiting, and I recall at least seeing some of the frat houses. They were indeed spectacular for the most part on the K.U. campus.

But we hung out as well, in this case in the student union and at the pool tables. Then came the surprise--no less than 7 foot plus Wilt Chamberlain of K.U. and national basketball fame came in and proceeded to play a few games with buddies, a couple of them about 5 foot 5 I guess. Wilt kind of leaned over the table just a bit to take his shots.

A bigger surprise was actually at the meet. As races proceeded, Wilt calmly walked out to the high jump pit, in K.U. track attire but with one of those sports-car hats jauntily placed on his head. Memories are foggy, but I think he high jumped the old fashioned way, like hurdling sideways. But I remember he did six foot six!

The Farm

The best memories at the relays, in spite of Wilt, were the quarter-mile, half-mile and mile races and respective relays. I thought I had arrived at track "heaven" with these incredible, gazelle-like distance runners. Texas stands out, but there were many others.

And I think Jim Ryan was still running the mile for K.U. The school and Kansas have had a major role in that distance in U.S. track history. The great Glen Cunningham made a visit to AHS at some time in our school days. But this was the time of the effort to fun a four minute mile, extremely uncommon in those days. A Brit, Roger Bannister, had accomplished the feat just a few years earlier, and I think Jim Ryan did eventually. I have a vague memory of Ryan taking a fall in the mile run in the Olympics.

A CHANGE IN DIRECTION

So with the concussion and its follow-up scare, that was the end of emulating brother Tom at age 14 and 114 pounds on the football field. But that was just in sports. Tom was still a model in other ways; he had been president of the student council in his years, and I guess in retrospect, I was on track. Having been elected class representative, I think, my first three years, it all culminated in being elected to the post of Student Council President for senior year.

I had not quite turned the academic corner as a freshman. Evidence was Latin Class with the schoolmarm Miss Edna Edberg. A more dedicated, hard-working and successful language teacher was hard to come by on the Kansas plains in those days. Her students were the "college bound," or so it was supposed, so most of those kids were in her classes, boys and girls. But among Linda Viola, Susan Neil, Carolyn Lehman, Kathy Wise, Janice Gary and other girls I am forgetting, it was my group of buddies that I remember best. We all talked in class, giggled and when someone farted exceptionally loud, it broke up the whole class. Jerry Hawks comes to mind.

How well I understand today the discipline of learning another language not to mention Latin! In the beginning I did the work, diligently filling out the work sheets the teacher patiently provided each day, but as the class progressed and became more complex, I studied less and actually began to fall behind. Should this be a surprise? But somehow I and my buddies struggled through the two years offered at the high school, and I confess, remember very, very little. An aside: years later when I had won a National Defense Education Act Fellowship to study for the Ph.D. in Spanish and Latin American Studies at a highly respected Jesuit university, St. Louis U., in my first interview with the program director, one Father Mazza, of Trinidad, Colorado, told me to "brush up" on my Latin and handed me the Ph.D. reading list which included many of the classics from Roman literature. Gasp. Gasp. I did read some of the works in translation, but no way could I handle the Latin!

Mark, "Mercury," and others at the Latin banquet

But a highlight of the years of high school Latin was the Latin Banquets. I have an old photo showing Mike Kippenberger and myself carrying in a ham to be devoured by all. And there is the photo of me dressed as Mercury, little hat with aluminum wings, and silver aluminum wings on purple house slippers, dashing in to deliver I don't know what. A hoot!

But, wait, redemption was in store. AHS followed the Latin sequence with two years of study in Spanish, and somehow, I caught on. There was little oral practice of the language, but the structure, the grammar, and the fundamentals were all provided once again by good ole' Miss Edberg. But this was a different story from Latin. It all fascinated me, was quite easy after Latin since the structure and grammar were related, after all Spanish being a Romance language. So I thrived and became really interested in both the language and the culture. I did well, but there were others who excelled, one I recall, Armond Belleau, a boy who really had the "gift." I heard that he went on to advanced study, but never saw him after high school. One of the girls, however, Linda Viola (Bankes) was talented, intelligent and motivated. She would go on to major in Spanish at Kansas University and come back to take Edna's place in the classroom for I think a few decades! A final memory: once I had achieved the Ph.D., traveled extensively and published well during the years at Arizona State, I kept in touch with Edna and did write a long letter of thanks and appreciation, which I understand through my sister Jo Anne, was emotionally and gratefully received.

But I never forgot the textbook for Spanish, "El Camino Real," "The Royal Road," and maybe forty years later would be reminded of it at the "Camino Real" museum south of Albuquerque, NM. This was the "royal road" of Spanish conquest and colonization from old Mexico City to Santa Fe.

The Farm

Mark playing "Malagueña" at the Spanish Banquet

And I forgot the Spanish Banquet. I played an "ersatz" "Malagueña" on the guitar and we were all impressed by farm boys, International Farm Youth Exchange guys who had been to Argentina and were guest speakers at the banquet. That kindled in me a desire to go to Argentina. After all these years and travels, I have not made it yet.

Another aside: I read voraciously in those days, and my favorite topic was science fiction, but I liked best simple stuff like trips to the moon, thus …

A MOMENT OF THE TIMES--CAPTAIN VIDEO TO SPUTNIK TO WERNER VON BRAUN AND THE MAN ON THE MOON

Just an aside, from my fantasy with the incredibly bad, by today's standards, old black and white Captain Video show on TV which Gary Alford and I particularly shared during junior high school, I would be fascinated during the high school years, now with color TV at home on the farm, and the Disney programs featuring the German Scientist Werner Von Braun who would become the brains and brawn for the United States' future voyages to the moon. I recall few details, but know that the way we finally did it was what he outlined on the TV in about 1959. (See the movie "The Right Stuff" which speaks of the controversy of Von Braun's theories of those times.) What goes around comes around--this would all culminate on a street corner in northeastern Brazil in 1969 when I watched on black and white TV the first landing on the moon and would be congratulated by the Brazilians for the mere fact of being an American! Good days were those! I would write of that moment in later books on Brazilian culture.

SPEECH AND DEBATE AT ABILENE HIGH SCHOOL

Another sign of a bit of maturation in academics was my wonderful experience with the teacher Mr. Rock in AHS English, Speech and Debate classes. We all imitated and parodied Mr. Rock's slow, calm, and mellow voice. There was a family connection and model for Mr. Rock's classes as well; my oldest brother Jim had done very well in drama and debate at the same AHS.

Speech was during freshman year and I excelled; since I can't plug in a lamp or do math beyond arithmetic, something had to come upon the scene. Speech was fun; I've already talked of the speech contests in junior high and the junior high plays. Good diction, pronunciation, and delivery were asked for and expected.

Standing: Mark Curran, Sponsor, Mr. Kenneth Rock. Sitting, First Row: Allen Mark, Frank Jordan, Mike Roberson, Rick Vancil. Second Row: Joyce Viola, Sarabeth Gugler, Barbara McCall, Pat Dawe. Third Row: Reuben McCornack.

Mark at the podium, debate class at Abilene High School

It was sophomore year when I "tried out" for debate and made the team. Junior year was even better. Memories are vague, but we did well, my partner being one Mike Roberson, one year ahead of me. The team went to state and did well, but it was senior year that culminated in my best achievement at AHS.

The Farm

State champs in debate, 1959.

    There are four members on the team, two for the negative against that year's proposition and two on the affirmative. We were trained to debate either side, and I think did so in diverse local tournaments. But I think by the end of the year, you specialized in one side or another. The topics were the same throughout the nation--one year we debated the merits of "foreign aid," you know, the folly of giving refrigerators to Eskimos and heaters to the Saudi Arabians. Another year was the debate as to farm subsidies and the federal agricultural support program, but I think it was senior year that the topic was debating the pros and cons of "merit ratings" or the British versus the U.S. forms of education. In England and most of Europe there were exams early in the grades that determined your future track--tech school, business or secretarial work, or a college future. The Abilene team was replete with intelligent kids--Reuben McCornack (older brother of my puppy love Mary Ann, who incidentally broke my young, tender heart), Trudy Meserve, a classy smart young lady, and my partner in crime, John McCullogh. I was the only senior on the team that year. From local tournaments at Russell, a big one at Topeka, and others, we moved on to the state in Wichita I think, and we won the darned thing! I can remember the announcement, all of us standing up, rushing up to get the trophy, and happiness all around! But it was the culmination of excellent training and many hours of hard work of reading and compiling note cards with research data.

I never did meet any of those kids again or have not up to this point. But a funny thing happened; perhaps thirty years after graduation, in 1959, AHS had won so many trophies in sports and academics that the trophy cases were full. They pitched all the trophies, and it was only by chance that my sister Jo Anne, who worked part-time at AHS, was rummaging through the boxes containing the trophies to be thrown out and saw the 1959 State Championship trophy, dug it out of the box and saved it for me. It sits on a mantle in our cabin in Colorado yet today!

And a final aside: I would try debate at Rockhurst College in Kansas City, Missouri in 1960. I made the team and participated in one or two tournaments. But this time the demands of preparing for debate clashed with studying and trying to pass college classes, so that ended, but not before a memorable bout with Harvard University in which we were trounced. It wasn't quite "The Great Debaters" film, and besides, we lost. These easterners with slick suits and ties came into the room trundling huge briefcases of "proofs," and that was that.

There is not much more to say about academics. I nearly flunked geometry (Mr. Tice), chemistry (Mr. …), but did well in history with Ms. Weisgerber, famous in those parts. Grades improved and I think I was second in the class to Linda Viola (Bankes) who was class valedictorian, but I better check on that. I flunked the entrance exam at Creighton University in Omaha, a Jesuit school my oldest brother Jim had attended for two years, mainly because I had no idea of advanced math or science. But I was accepted into smaller Rockhurst College in Kansas City, Missouri, another Jesuit school, based on my grades and I guess SATS. Things improved after that.

An important digression. One thing I have learned over all these years in academia, plus life experience, is that "book learning" or even a certain aspect of book learning, for example, being highly skilled in higher math, science, languages, or any other specific area, does not determine ultimate success in life. I always think of Don Campbell, the good friend who worked at Gambles with me; Don was not an excellent student in school, but he possessed incredible knowledge, understanding and skills elsewhere, i.e. mechanics, machines, construction. But on a much more personal note--if I had not been allowed to enter Rockhurst College based on my grades in the subjects I was good in, none of the good things that happened later would have taken place. This is why I have great empathy for the "non-language" people who end up in my Spanish classes at ASU or even now in adult classes for Spanish in Bayfield. One of the adults from the latter just the other days saved and fixed my car battery when I was clueless! Point made.

MUSIC, EVERETT SMITH AND SEEDS FOR THE FUTURE.

I wrote of this in "The Farm," but since it was an important part of high school for me, I've got to at least repeat part of it here. It all started I think junior year. I had begun the guitar at age 14, progressed from a steel string Stella for $15 at the music store to an electric Kay with small amplifier, the Kay a glitzy copper color. Eddy had an electric guitar and amplifier as well. We convinced the librarian during a joint study hall to allow us to go to the empty band room and play. As time passed we could do a lot of songs, like those by the Everly Brothers, Elvis and Ricky Nelson. The culmination was when we traveled to Salina, Kansas, and played in the school cafeteria for Jo Anne's class at Mary Mount College. However, Eddy, Janice Gary and other black kids had their own group, needless to say, playing music a little different from Eddy's and mine. They played all the black hits, a real rhythm and blues gig. Eddy was born with music and rhythm (pardon the cliché). He was, by the way, trained in classical trumpet, the guitar being a fun sideline. But ours evolved into a wonderful friendship and one of my best memories.

I had begun to learn the rudiments of classic technique on the guitar, this by virtue of an instruction book my brother Jim brought home from a business trip to Kansas City. The classic technique, using thumb and all four fingers on the right hand to "pick" suited me well. I learned several classical ditties and an ersatz of version of "Malagueña" which I played at the Spanish Banquet. Incidentally it was that banquet, with guest speakers being two young fellows who had to gone to Argentina on the International Farm Youth Exchange Program that instilled even more desire in me to learn Spanish and go to Latin America. Of course, Argentina briefly became the goal. Ironically, after 45 years I have not made it there yet.

BOYS' AND GIRLS' STATE.

Boys and Girls State Students, AHS, 1959

It was an honor for the top students in the junior class to attend Boys' or Girls' State, an event held generally in Wichita, a big city for us. Boys' or Girls' State was designed as a practice political convention with candidates for all offices of the state government, culminating in the election of the "governor." But I remember better the dance when we were hosted by local girls.

BUT I DIGRESS; TO LOVE, LAUGHTER AND DISAPPOINTMENT

A funny memory comes to mind; one of the major ways the hormones were locked in during high school was so simple yet seemed so important--the commotion of passing everyone in the hallways between classes, and spotting her! A smile or a wink seemed to make my day. But it was important to wave and smile at everyone or else you would get THE LABEL: Stuck up! I still don't think anyone ever was intentionally "stuck up," for all we know incredible shyness could lay below the surface of that particular student. But the aforementioned smiling or waving in the hallway, this little social deal was particularly important when you dated someone not in your class, as was my date for awhile junior and senior years. This was because your classes tended to be folks just from your own junior or senior class. And as I explained, the guys in my class in turn ended up dating girls a class level or two down, juniors, sophomores etc. while we were seniors.

One of the "big" activities for the boys and girls was sponsored by Student Council: the noon-time dance held in the corridor outside the entrance to the gym. We had an old stereo with a couple of speakers and all the 45 rpm pop hits of the day. As president of the council in 1958-1959 I inherited the duty of organizing the dance. But more of my memories of the noon time dance were from watching the "cool" upperclassmen a couple of years earlier on, like Eddie Corwin, or later Frank Jordan who would dance away with the chicks to the top hits. Elvis Presley, the Platters, Sam Cook, and Bill Hailey and the Comets were performers I remember. Of interest today perhaps is that fact, maybe mentioned elsewhere, that at that time in Abilene "country music" was not of interest to us. Some folks probably listened to the Grand Ole Opry, but it was pop and early rock that ruled our days. At the noon time dance, however, I think I mainly either ran the record player or just stood around.

The dance took place after you supposedly wolfed down lunch in the cafeteria, and that was preceded by a bunch of us guys who would drive downtown, eat 10 cent hamburgers or donuts from the bakery and then go back to school for the 35 cent lunch. So maybe we needed the dance to work off all the junk we ate. It is a vague memory, but I think the girls wore those big skirts, bobby sox, and maybe a white blouse, or sweaters in winter. The guys were almost always in blue jeans and a shirt and penny loafers.

DATING IN HIGH SCHOOL–AN INNOCENT AND PERHAPS TYPICAL STORY

Memories are vague, but I think there was no serious dating for me until junior year when I could drive, borrowing the family car, now being age 16 or 17 with a legal drivers' license. I've told of our modest cars, but I would still wash and wax the ole' buggy on a date night. I went out fairly often junior and senior years and recall driving many miles in the country to take out Janet R. from up north or another girl from south of town. But my first real puppy love, and I fell hard, was Mary Ann during senior year. She was a cutie, very intelligent and her brother was on the debate team.

The family prior to moving to Abilene lived in Phillipsburg, Oklahoma, if I am not mistaken. But they did open Abilene's first big time bowling alley up north on Buckeye. So I spent some time up there waiting to see miss Mary Ann.

It is interesting that religion might have been a factor later on, me being Irish Catholic and her family Presbyterian. But maybe not because most of the girls I dated were Protestants. Oh, an aside: there was a CYO group down at St. Andrew's Catholic Church, and there were funny dances in the church hall, so I dated a couple of the girls, but nothing too serious, one case being Kitty Callahan, bright red hair and Irish! Her older sister had dated brother Tom years before. But we also ventured down to the Chapman, Kansas, for CYO dances, and once again there was a younger sister of someone Tom had dated years earlier. But Chapman posed a problem--the Irish kids there really had a reputation for being tough brawlers, and beer drinking was pretty common. I think the girl was Katie Gorman. I was not a big fellow and getting a licking by the local Irish guys was not a good idea, so venturing down to Chapman never came to be a big deal either.

Back to Mary Ann. We dated fast and furious, I guess that means once a week, movies at the local Plaza Theater, school dances. But I met my comeuppance when J.D., one of the starters on the AHS basketball team caught her attention. I did take that one hard. I worked with his father at the local ice plant in the first two or three years after high school graduation.

The only other memory coming to mind at the present was the junior-senior prom senior year when I actually went with one of the cutest, most popular girls in our class, Linda W. Why did this fortuitous date take place, you may ask? Because all the girls in our senior class had dated upperclassmen who had graduated, and you could not go to the dance except with someone in school, that left, well, me and my buddies as possible escorts. That was what it felt like, an escort. So we did the formality, the dinner, the dance, the corsage, and I took Linda home immediately after the dance. The guys bought beer and went out to some fishing hole-camp outside of town; the girls had their own slumber party.

As I may have said in "The Farm," there was a far more serious consequence to that prom. Being more interested in girls than my baseball cards, on the occasion of decorating for the prom, I made the fateful decision (as did Mike K. and others) to GIVE Richard S. our entire card collections. Richard told me fifty years later that he sold them for over one hundred thousand dollars (if I am not mistaken) but would have gotten a lot more if he had sold a year either earlier or later. It turns out I kept some of my cards, duplicates I had marked with a big, blue X, thus ruining them for any value; but these were not the "top" stars. For buddies reading this, I got an evaluation of my cards a few years ago from a neighbor from Pennsylvania who is a major collector. He not only has one Honus Wager, the most valuable of all baseball cards, but two or three. I think each was valued at $80,000 apiece a few years back! Oh, there was perhaps one more consequence of the card collecting years, cavities from chewing all that rotten, sweet bubble gum.

I digress: there was a back to school party before my senior year. Instigated by Jerry C., we went to the drive-in movie with a bottle of Peppermint Schnapps, drank it warm, maybe with 7-up, passing the bottle around. I ended the evening under the car wash trying to sober up. My "good" buddies dropped me off in the yard in front of the farm house and later the report was something like this: I turned on all the lights in the house, stumbled up the stairway to my room on the second floor, and the entire thing was witnessed by brother Jim, and maybe Jo Anne.

Worse yet was that the next day was the Hi-Y book exchange, a time to get your text books for the school year. After rummaging around in the book room, I was leaving, and Mr. ... the school principal, saw me and called me into is office to talk about the new school year with his young student council president. Problem was – I was still reeking of Peppermint Schnapps and was in fact, still incredibly hung over. A good start to the year huh?

STUDENT COUNCIL AND THE FINAL DAYS

I've talked of the student council previously, but the memories keep coming. One duty of the year's student council president was to give the school announcements each morning over the PA system, which I handled quite well. Another was to introduce all assemblies. When you take into account all this experience, plus speech class, and particularly the debate team, it gave me a true sense of self-confidence for later in life for public speaking. And I've always maintained that from day one I was entirely comfortable in the classroom as a college professor, and without the Education courses made mandatory for grade, junior high and high school teachers. I think the speaking experience, some god-given native talent and of course solid preparation paved the way. Indeed.

The Farm

Mark's graduation picture, 1959

Well, time took its course; we had the customary graduation in the high school gym with "Pomp and Circumstance" and cap and gown. I spent the next two or three summers working at the ice plant in Abilene for summer income for college, but that is also another story. In the fall of 1959 I headed off to Rockhurst College in Kansas City, Missouri, and later to St. Louis University for graduate work.

The class of 1959, 50th year reunion picture, 2009

I attended the first high school reunion but not another until the 50th in the summer of 2009. It was terrific as they are supposed to be, and anyone who attended and who may read these notes has their own memories and pictures of that moment.

So, I think there is little more to say; for sure, my memories end here. It was an age of innocence, at least in my case, and a traditional Irish Catholic morality held sway, perhaps saving me from getting in a few more scrapes than I did. But Abilene and its public schools were indeed outstanding for their place and time. And in those innocent 1940s and 1950s we may have been more typical of our generation than one would think today. So, that is it for now. I hope you enjoyed the memories.

ABOUT THE AUTHOR

Mark Curran is a retired professor from Arizona State University where he taught full time from 1968 to 2002 and continues part-time to the present. He taught Spanish and Brazilian Portuguese languages and their respective cultures. He researched Brazil's folk-popular literature, "A Literatura de Cordel," and has published twenty-five scholarly articles and nine books in Brazil, Spain, and the United States on the subject. "The Farm" is a change of pace to the auto-biographical, recollections of growing up on a family farm in central Kansas in the 1940s and 1950.

Books published:

A Literatura de Cordel, Brazil, 1973
Jorge Amado e a Literatura de Cordel, Brazil, 1981
A Presença de Rodolfo Coelho Cavalcante na Moderna Literatura de Cordel, Brazil, 1987
La Literatura de Cordel-Antología Bilingüe – Español y Português, Spain, 1990
Cuíca de Santo Amaro – Poeta-Repórter da Bahia, Brazil, 1991
História do Brasil em Cordel, Brasil, 1998
Cuíca de Santo Amaro—Controvérsia no Cordel, Brazil 2000
Brazil's Folk-Popular Poetry—"A Literatura de Cordel" Bilingual Anthology in English and Portuguese, USA, 2010
Retrato do Brasil em Cordel, Brazil, 2010

Mark Curran makes his home in Mesa, Arizona, and spends part of the year in Colorado.
He is married to Keah (Runshang) Curran, and they have one daughter, Kathleen, who lives in Flagstaff, Arizona, and makes documentary films; most recently in 2010 her "Greening the Revolution" was shown at the Africa Diaspora Film Festival in New York City and the Milano Film Festival in Milan, Italy.

CPSIA information can be obtained at www.ICGtesting.com
Printed in the USA
BVOW09s0224310815

415502BV00009B/56/P